D1249267

Disorganizing China

DISORGANIZING CHINA

Counter-Bureaucracy
and the Decline of Socialism

EDDY U

Stanford University Press
Stanford, California

Stanford University Press
Stanford, California
© 2007 by the Board of Trustees of the
Leland Stanford Junior University

Library of Congress Cataloging-in-Publication Data

U, Eddy.
  Disorganizing China : counter-bureaucracy and the
decline of socialism / Eddy U.
      p. cm.
  Includes bibliographical references and index.
  ISBN 978-0-8047-5689-1 (cloth : alk. paper)
    1. Socialism—China. 2. Bureaucracy—China.
3. Organization—China. 4. Expertise. 5. Socialism and
education—China. I. Title.
HX418.5.U43 2007
335.43'45—dc22

                                    2007001252

Printed in the United States of America

Typeset at Stanford University Press in 10/13 Palatino

For my mother and late father

Contents

Tables

Preface and Acknowledgments

Between 1998 and 2003 I spent nearly two years in Shanghai reading newly declassified government documents and talking to secondary school teachers about their work in the Mao era. As I pieced the data together, four facets of faculty life loomed large. First, the profession contained a large number of people whom the state regarded as politically suspect or professionally unprepared to be educators. Second, a mixture of Communist Party members, most of them lacking teaching experience, occupied school management. Third, despite being banished from management, the prerevolutionary group of school principals and administrators received the best salaries in the schools. Fourth, a culture of distrust, disdain, and discontent pervaded the faculty. Because schoolteachers transmit political beliefs, technical knowledge, and moral values, they are critical to the reproduction of any political rule. As the Chinese Communist Party was deeply engaged in turning China into a modern socialist polity, China's schoolteachers seemed like an enemy rather than ally of the state.

The unpropitious conditions in the schools stir up old and new questions about China's transition to socialism: Why did the Communist state permit underqualified and questionable people to partake in the reproduction of its rule? Why did it reward individuals whom it regarded as untrustworthy with higher salaries? How common were these practices? How did the social friction or discontent that they generated affect Communist political rule? The fact that the teachers were alienated from one another and from the state raises questions about their involvement in the Chinese Cultural Revolution, if only because research and remembrance have largely portrayed them as victims of student violence and abuse.

More broadly, my findings stimulate questions on socialism and organizations. Two issues are particularly relevant: How did Marxism-Leninism as a transformative ideology shape the development of organizations in socialist societies? How did this development in turn influence the socialist project? For decades, research has depicted Soviet-type societies in political as well as organizational terms as archetypal cases of the "hyperexpansion" of bureaucracy. Since the decline of such societies some fifteen years ago, a dominant view has emerged that their demise confirmed the vulnerability of rule by bureaucracy. These understandings of Soviet-type societies have been traced to Max Weber's teaching that the ascent of socialism must lead to the growth of bureaucracy, an administration with the tendency to produce self-aggrandizing officeholders and to become unresponsive to public demand. Put simply, socialism apparently fostered the development of bureaucracy only to be buried by it.

There is a major problem of theoretical interpretation with these "Weberian" views on Soviet-type societies: Weber's teaching on socialism and bureaucracy was not aimed at such societies. It was a rejoinder to the reformist programs developed in Western Europe a century ago that espoused extensive official intervention in the market. In this context, he noted that socialism would advance the development of *modern bureaucracy*, a type of work organization that had already penetrated government and big businesses. Compared with traditional bureaucratic administrations, modern bureaucracy features a single hierarchy, competent staff, impersonal norms, and other rational characteristics. Weber never considered the Bolshevik revolution, which produced the original Soviet-type society, a genuine socialist uprising. In fact, he insisted that Bolshevik ideology and modern bureaucracy are incompatible, because class struggle against the bourgeoisie would reduce the types of specialized knowledge and skill necessary for developing rational administration. But Weber did not think that Bolshevik rule would therefore lead to an upsurge of traditional forms of administration. He noted before he passed away that Bolshevism would engender a form of administration different from modern bureaucracy as well as traditional types of bureaucratic administration. Many analyses of Soviet-type societies have misappropriated Weber's understanding of socialism and bureaucracy. Their critiques of bureaucracy in such societies resemble not his but the much less sophisticated thinking proffered by Lenin, Trotsky, and later Mao.

With the benefit of hindsight, this book expands on Weber's understanding of modern bureaucracy to suggest that the historical transition to socialism, indeed, produced a distinctive type of bureaucratic administration—an institution in many ways the structural opposite of modern bureaucracy. From a Weberian perspective, the institutionalization of Marxist-Leninist systems of rule in the last century engendered remarkably similar types of bureaucratic administration, with political appointment, shortages of expertise, arbitrary discipline, and other nonrational characteristics. I call this form of administration *counter-bureaucracy* not only because it represented the antithesis of the Weberian bureaucracy, but also because its operation was counterproductive to the welfare of Soviet-type societies. Counter-bureaucratic administrations imparted none of the benefits that modern bureaucracy can offer to organizations and governments, that is, technical efficiency, staff solidarity, and legitimate domination. Instead, they led to poor quality of work, social friction, and political resentment in the labor force. Their reproduction undermined the economic performance of such societies as well as the self-legitimating capacity of the ruling regimes. It was a principal reason behind the decline of Soviet-type societies.

To put this differently, as social revolutions based on Reason, the Marxist-Leninist projects of the last century were flawed from the beginning. Influenced by Bolshevik ideology, the bearers of the revolutions, the communist parties, created an administrative quagmire to achieve their rational objectives of promoting technical progress, social equality, and human freedom. Within government and other institutions that were supposed to establish ideas, values, and practices to maintain mass support for the transition to socialism, the regimes normalized a form of administration counterproductive to work efficiency, social solidarity, and regime legitimacy. The decline of Soviet-type societies was not caused by an excess of bureaucracy, as numerous commentators have indicated. Quite the contrary: Marxist-Leninist regimes were not bureaucratic enough. They failed to develop modern bureaucracy to support their political authority, let alone help transform socialism into a widely supported social system.

In the face of theoretical and practical developments after the decline of Soviet-type societies, which has been marked by a state-and-society dash for "free" trade, "open" market, privatization, deregulation, and their supporting ideologies, this reevaluation of what have been called "actually existing socialisms" is especially necessary. The demise of such societies—no doubt a cause for celebration—is dubious proof that the state's involvement in the economy must be kept to a minimum, or that capitalism is the only alternative for building a viable modern political economy. Despite the staggering resources Marxist-Leninist regimes expended on strengthening the state's role in society, they institutionalized not modern bureaucratic but counter-bureaucratic administrations that militated against the provision of public goods and the building of political consent. Actually existing socialisms were their own enemies. Their demise, which has reinforced capitalist exploitation globally, is not a moral, much less an analytical, reason for accepting that we have reached "the end of history."

In this book, I present an original case study of Shanghai secondary schools as workplaces during the Mao era (1949–76). The difference between how these schools were run by the local government and what Weber indicated to be modus operandi of modern bureaucracy is unmistakable. But my goal is not to merely illustrate the divergence. After all, Weber left no doubt that the rational bureaucracy he described is a theoretical construct. My argument is that the schools epitomized counter-bureaucracy, a particular form of administration specific to Marxist-Leninist systems of rule. To highlight the ubiquity, nuances, and consequences of counter-bureaucracy in Soviet-type societies, I have included in this book comparative data on workplace organization within Chinese officialdom and Soviet industry.

There are reasons for such research boundaries with regard to China and the Soviet Union besides the obvious ones of personal interest and practicality. First, China had an impoverished and mainly agrarian economy like other countries taken over by Marxist-Leninist regimes in the last century. Following the Bolsheviks in Russia, the Chinese Communist leadership aggressively pursued industrialization and ideological change, building and reorganizing governments, universities, newspapers, and so on. The Chinese experience thus serves as an excellent starting point for studying the development of bureaucratic administration within Marxist-Leninist systems of rule.

Second, the organization of the workplace is Weber's focus when he delineated the features of modern bureaucracy. The reconstruction of secondary schools as workplaces is central to any socialist project, because the faculty and staff occupy a critical position in the transmission of the knowledge and values needed to produce and reproduce socialism as a legitimate social system. Studying the organization of these schools should thus allow us to explore the composition and consequences of the everyday bureaucratic administration developed in socialist China.

Third, why Shanghai? Before the 1949 Communist revolution, Shanghai was China's preeminent urban center. It sheltered large numbers of capitalist establishments such as trading firms, factories, and banks, many of which had overseas sponsorship or influence. The city had a vibrant consumer culture that included a large market for illicit pleasures. It was a political base for the ruling Nationalist Party and housed governing bodies set up by foreign nationals. When the Chinese Communist Party remade Shanghai, it confronted politically and socially complicated situations that influenced the tactics of workplace reorganization it would deploy elsewhere.

Fourth, the discussion of Chinese officialdom and Soviet industry is intended to strengthen my contention that counter-bureaucracy was endemic in Soviet-type societies. It is well known that Marxist-Leninist regimes strengthened the role of the state and disproportionately invested in industry. By the late 1950s, serious ideological differences appeared between China and the Soviet Union. From the Chinese leaders' perspective, there was "continuous revolution" in their country and "revisionism" in the Soviet Union. Identifying the reproduction of counter-bureaucracy in the two privileged institutions of Chinese officialdom and Soviet industry before *as well as* after the two countries departed ideologically should lend support to my argument.

The empirical materials presented in the following chapters are drawn from four different sources: official documents of the Shanghai municipal government; firsthand interviews with former schoolteachers in Shanghai; Chinese-language scholarship, recollections of events, and newspapers; and English-language research and writing on China and the Soviet Union. The first two sources are particularly noteworthy. They provide the materials for my case study of Shanghai secondary schools.

In recent years, the Shanghai municipal government has been very receptive to overseas researchers using its official archives. I have therefore been able to visit the Shanghai Municipal Archives and read large volumes of heretofore inaccessible government documents that include laws and official regulations, state plans and instructions, and reports on people, compensation, political campaigns, and other issues related to the workplace. Written by party and state officials, the documents reflect the government's points of view. Their style, language, and level of detail are not always consistent. After all, they were compiled by a government whose leaders had not expected to take power as early as they did and whose ideology remained in flux afterward. Unlike official newspapers or materials for public consumption, however, these internal documents frequently contain in-depth and critical analyses of state policies, work establishments, and individual performance. Products of a state apparatus obsessed with surveillance, they contain a richness of data that cannot be found elsewhere. For my research, I studied selected documents of the Shanghai Education Bureau from the early 1950s to late 1960s. To understand general policy issues and workplace conditions, I also consulted documents of various Shanghai party and state agencies.

Besides archival research, I conducted over two hundred hours of interviews with sixty-two retired or retiring teachers in Shanghai about their work and lives before and after the 1949 revolution. I met the interviewees through formal introduction by academic institutions or snowball sampling. These interviewees joined the teaching profession at different times in different circumstances. They are almost equally divided between men and women. There were former school principals, school party secretaries, heads of instruction, and rank-and-file instructors. About one-third of them had been Communist Party members at some point during the period researched or throughout the entire period. The topics of discussion included their social backgrounds, occupational histories, political affiliations, and faculty experiences. Although these people worked in the same profession or even the same school or same kind of positions, they had different experiences that official documents captured in a broad sense but often not as detailed, effective, or poignant as their personal voices. Their unofficial perspectives not only provided further evidence on the counter-bureaucratic constitution of the campuses, but also helped me interrogate and corroborate apparent factual statements on official documents.

This book is based on the doctoral dissertation I completed at the sociology department of the University of California at Berkeley. I must first and foremost thank Peter B. Evans. He encouraged me to explore my own theoretical and intellectual interests and taught me the invaluable skills of social research, analytical thinking, and scholarly presentation. In the end, it is his pioneering Weberian analysis of the state in developing economies that led me to Weber in order to deepen my understanding of "actually existing socialisms." At Berkeley, I had the pleasure of working with Neil Fligstein, Thomas Gold, and Wen-hsin Yeh. They provided excellent instruction and encouragement and read and commented on many drafts of my thesis. I benefited from Michael Burawoy's and Jerome Karabel's teaching and the friendship of the staff in the sociology department.

Friends and colleagues have helped me turn my dissertation into a book. Linus Huang has been reading my work and offering criticism and encouragement for years. Helen Dunstan and Rana Mitter read the entire manuscript and provided innumerable valuable comments and advice. Robert Antonio shared his insights on Weber and taught me ways to improve my theoretical approach. Steve Lopez took apart my analytical framework many times and forced me to revise it. Timothy Cheek and Julia Strauss advised me on engagement with existing scholarship on China and state socialism. Ching Kwan Lee is a friend and a mentor. She asked challenging questions that helped me refine my analysis. Derrick Kwan provided assistance in the preparation of endnotes and the index.

My colleagues in the China dissertation group at Berkeley have been very supportive. They are David Fraser, Andrea Goldman, Shiao Ling, Mark McNicholas, Eugenio Menegon, Ruth Mostern, Allison Rottman, and Felicity Rufkin. I thank Robert Culp, Ka-ho Mok, Suzanne Pepper, Elizabeth Perry, David Priestland, S.A. Smith, Andrew Walder, and Martin Whyte for advice at different stages of my research. I am grateful to the participants in the China seminars at Oxford, SOAS, and Sydney University. I have received encouragement from many friends for many years. Shana Cohen, Rhonda Evans, Kim Lopez, Brian Powers, Lauren Rogers, Chris Watson, and Simona Yee immediately come to mind. My childhood friends, David Hon and David Yeung, have been particularly supportive.

This research was mainly funded by the University of California. A postdoctoral fellowship at the University of Oxford enabled me to concentrate on research and writing. A summer fellowship at the Peter Wall Institute of Advanced Studies of the University of British Columbia helped me sharpen the theoretical vision in this book. I thank the staff at the Center of Chinese Studies Libraries at Berkeley and at Oxford and at the Universities Research Center of the Chinese University of Hong Kong. In Shanghai, the Shanghai Academy of Social Sciences, East China Normal University, and Shanghai Municipal Archives provided research support. I am most grateful to Li Yihai, Luo Suwen, Tang Anguo, Wu Jue, Xie Anbang, Zhang Jishun, and Zhao Nianguo. I am most indebted to the retired teachers whom I interviewed and who will, however, remain anonymous. They kindly shared with me their personal experience as once young men or women coming to terms with a society that often seemed unfamiliar to themselves. Their insights on life under Mao were critical to the completion of this book.

At Stanford University Press, I would like to thank Muriel Bell for supporting this project. Muriel, John Feneron, and Kirsten Oster guided me through the publication process. I am grateful to Mary Ray Worley who copyedited the manuscript. Part of Chapter 2 appeared in "The Hiring of Rejects: Teacher Recruitment and the Crises of Socialism in the Early PRC Years," *Modern China* 30(1): 46–80 (2004). Part of Chapter 3 is based on my article "State Management of Careers, Workplace Conflict, and Regime Legitimacy in Socialist China," *The Sociology Quarterly* 46(2): 359–84 (2005). Part of Chapter 5 appears in "The Making of Chinese Intellectuals: Representations and Organization in the Thought Reform Campaign," *The China Quarterly* (forthcoming). I thank these journals for reprint permissions. *Comparative Studies of Society and History* allows me to use material from my article "Leninist Reforms, Workplace Cleavages, and Teachers in the Chinese Cultural Revolution," 47(1): 106–33 (2005).

My greatest gratitude goes to my mother and late father. They had difficulty understanding why I did not have a stable income for years and worried that I would never find a decent job. Nevertheless, they persevered in their support of my "reckless" pursuit, often financially. My brothers, Edwin and Edmond, and my sisters-in-law, Angela and Flora, are always there for me, even though I have seldom reciprocated. This book is dedicated to my family.

Disorganizing China

1

Socialism and Counter-Bureaucracy

Marxist-Leninist regimes are unique among modern political regimes: they have remade both the system of production and that of reproduction after taking power. Their goal was to marry industrial modernization and cultural domination based on three principles: Communist political rule, central planning, and working-class dictatorship. For decades, they seemed to be quite successful, ruling across Europe, Asia, and the Americas. They expanded the state and the public sector while turning private capital into a relic or subsidiary element of the economy. They provided previously disenfranchised populations with educational and career opportunities and reduced income and gender inequality. Notwithstanding periodic economic difficulties and political resistance, these regimes apparently established strong organizations and social stability in their own countries. To many, the sudden demise of the Soviet and Eastern European regimes during the 1989–91 revolutions therefore came as a surprise.[1]

This is a study of the workplace as an everyday administration under Marxist-Leninist political rule. What have been called actually existing socialisms were, after all, forms of organization that extended across state and society. Because the emergence of such socialist societies has invariably transformed the division of labor, workplace organization is a window on their nature and the problems they encountered in reproducing themselves. Like capitalist countries, such socialist societies differed among themselves, to the extent that their leaderships had condemned one another as traitors to socialist doctrines. Fortunately, this has not prevented research from building analytical models that stress the shared distinctiveness of actually existing socialisms or their departures from capitalist societies. An important fact is that the extended dominance of the former Soviet Union in the socialist world greatly influenced development in member countries, as their reconstruction of state and society was modeled partly after Soviet precedents.[2]

This book focuses on the workplace in China during the Mao era. The Chinese Communist Party (CCP) is still in power. But the socialist system it erected has disappeared. Like Russia before the Bolshevik revolution, China was an impoverished, politicized, and highly unequal country before the Communist revolution. The victorious CCP was determined to build a high-growth modern society with a socialist class formation. It adopted Soviet practices, nationalizing and expanding industry, education, and other institutions. It drew increasing numbers of people into nonagricultural work and reorganized the authority structure, compensation, and other aspects of the workplace. By the late 1950s, China's fallout with the Soviet Union prompted the CCP to further incorporate Chairman Mao's ideas of developing socialism, but by and large still within an institutional framework similar to that of the Soviet Union. A reconstitution of the workplace occurred gradually until the Cultural Revolution (1966–69) wreaked havoc upon state and society. By the time the CCP reestablished social order, the Chinese and the Soviet workplace had developed major differences. It was not until the Mao era ended that the two systems would show convergence again.

My main argument in this book is that the historical transition to socialism gave rise to a *modern* form of workplace administration that is the structural opposite of the modern bureaucracy described by Max Weber. According to Weber, modern bureaucracy features, inter alia, a single hierarchy, competent staff, rule-based management, and rational compensation. Whether the CCP followed the Soviet Union or struck out on its own, it established within the workplace multiple hierarchies of authority, status, and income, as well as a labor force of poor skills subject to intrusive and arbitrary discipline. There was hardly any modern bureaucracy in Mao's China. But the system of administration that emerged was also different from traditional types of organization. Like the Bolshevik revolution, the 1949 revolution ushered in a new form of workplace administration. I call the latter *counter-bureaucracy* to distinguish it from both traditional and modern bureaucracy.

My goal is not merely to debate the understanding, which has been stated in myriad ways, that actually existing socialisms represented the domination of bureaucracy. Weber's work contains nuanced insights that can help explain how workplace organization in Soviet-type societies damaged their sustainability. Because several dominant perspectives on bureaucratic administration in such societies have paid lip service to Weber, his thinking has not really been explored for such a purpose. Instead, research based on such perspectives suggests or implies that too much bureaucracy toppled actually existing socialisms, when, in fact, they had produced too little. This book seeks to bring Weber back to the center of the debate on the demise of Soviet-type societies.

In this opening chapter I use Weber's theory of bureaucracy to construct an analytical framework for studying workplace organization in Soviet-type societies. This framework will serve as a lens for understanding Shanghai secondary schools, Chinese officialdom, and Soviet industry as workplaces and their relations to the reproduction of such societies. Readers who wish to skip theoretical debates or to focus on workplace conditions under Chinese Communist rule can start with the next chapter. Here I begin with a critical interrogation of the mainstream view that actually existing socialisms were highly bureaucratized and compare it to Weber's work on bureaucracy, especially his understanding of the relation between socialism and bureaucracy. I then contrast Weber's thinking with Lenin's and Mao's theoretical and practical rejections of modern bureaucracy for socialist societies. My analyses culminate in an elaboration of the concept of counter-bureaucracy and how its features were traceable to Leninist and Maoist ideas. The final section of the chapter summarizes the themes of the rest of the book.

THE "BUREAUCRATIC" MODELS OF SOCIALISM

Even before the totalitarian theory of communism lost its intellectual dominance in the study of Soviet-type societies some forty years ago, the idea that such societies represent the domination of bureaucracy had entered mainstream academic thinking, often with explicit reference to Weber's work on modern bureaucracy.[3] It was used to explain the tenaciousness of Communist Party rule despite its intolerance for private property, liberal democracy, and individual freedom. With the more recent decline of such societies, the idea has been reinterpreted to demonstrate that too much bureaucracy created economic inefficiency, political resentment, and eventually systemic crises. The question we need to ask is, how much of this discussion of "socialist bureaucracy" reflects Weber's understanding of modern bureaucracy?

Sociologist Jan Pakulski was correct when he observed two decades ago that the concept of bureaucracy in research on Soviet-type societies tends to be vague and misleading, with different meanings that evoked Weber's teaching but never accurately.[4] His skepticism that such societies ever encountered an expansion of bureaucracy in the Weberian sense was shared by other scholars.[5] Their works constitute what can be described as a critical tradition of Weberian scholarship on bureaucratic administration in Soviet-type societies. However, this tradition of scholarship has been overshadowed by other "bureaucratic" perspectives on such societies. As a result, it is still a commonplace supposition that actually existing socialisms and bureaucracy were bedfellows to the end.

In part, this supposition reflects elite opinions inside the socialist world that repeatedly noted an undesirable presence of bureaucracy. Before his death, Lenin waged a famous struggle against what he referred to as bureaucracy and bureaucratism for threatening Russia's socialist reforms. A decade later, in the 1930s, Leon Trotsky took Lenin's argument to its logical conclusion by accusing the Soviet bureaucracy of betraying the Russian revolution. His indictment is repeated by the Yugoslav dissident Milovan Djilas in his now classic analysis that the political bureaucracy, rather than workers, formed the new ruling class in Communist Eastern Europe. In postrevolutionary China, Mao and other political leaders frequently spoke against the "evils of bureaucracy" plaguing the party and state and even the entire political economy.

What these and other political leaders or scholars called bureaucracy is not necessarily about how the workplace operated as an everyday administration. As we will see, Lenin and Mao had their own ideas of bureaucracy in this regard. Their thinking has important parallels to, but also basic departures from, Weber's understanding of modern bureaucracy. It would greatly influence workplace reorganization in Russia and China after the revolution. But Lenin's last struggle against bureaucracy was not about remaking the workplace as much as redistributing power at the elite level. He wanted to rein in the party and state apparatus, which he called bureaucracy.[6] Likewise, when Trotsky and Djilas took aim at the bureaucracy in Russia or Eastern Europe, they meant "the commanding stratum" or most powerful people in these societies, not any specific type of workplace organization.[7] By contrast,

Mao's attacks on bureaucracy expressed his dissatisfaction with the postrevolutionary setup of Chinese officialdom and, as I show later, his misconception that this institution was a variant of the Chinese state that had existed before the revolution or in capitalist societies. For Mao, what epitomized bureaucracy was a self-seeking, arrogant, unproductive, and incompetent official.[8]

Though differing among themselves, these views on bureaucracy in Soviet-type societies are at heart Marxist interpretations. Marx "identified bureaucracy with the state apparatus, a social stratum or caste [of officials] independent of the social classes defined by their position in the economic structure." Contrary to Hegel's belief that the state embodies "the image and reality of reason," he considered this institution indispensable for class rule and held that the bureaucratic personnel were mired in secrecy and their own interests, besides being incompetent.[9] The bourgeois state, he believed, would ultimately be destroyed during the socialist revolution, and the replacement socialist state would wither away as class struggle disappeared. Against this Marxist premise that they had once shared, Lenin, Trotsky, Mao, and others indicated in their own ways that the state had actually become an obstacle to socialist development after the Communist takeover. Their analyses of their own failings to anticipate or overcome this problem prepared the stage for later analysts to weave actually existing socialisms and the domination of bureaucracy together.

More important, the theoretical proposition that actually existing socialisms and bureaucracy were coextensive reflects a *questionable* borrowing of Weber's ideas on socialism and modern bureaucracy. Weber observed that modern capitalism has engendered the growth of rational bureaucracy. He also noted that socialism "would, in fact, require a still higher degree of formal bureaucratization than capitalism."[10] By this, he meant that a socialist state would need to further institutionalize technical and impersonal norms just to maintain a comparable level of economic efficiency previously achieved by the workings of private enterprises. In the 1950s, Barrington Moore noted that the Soviet Union could be seeing "creeping rationality" or the increased use of technical, rational, and legal criteria of behavior and organization.[11] Ten years later, Alfred Meyer did theoretically to Barrington Moore what Trotsky had done to Lenin, taking the argument further. He contended that the socialist and capitalist systems are not that different anymore, as both are based on complex modern bureaucratic organizations.

Like modern bureaucracy, Communist rule is essentially an attempt to impose *rational* management over social life by means of complex organization. This attempt leads to the emergence of structural forms, political processes, psychological adjustments, as well as malfunctionings which make Communist systems look remarkably similar to bureaucratic organizations in other parts of the world. An important difference which remains is that Communist systems are sovereign bureaucracies, whereas other bureaucracies exist and operate within larger societal frameworks, so that a Communist state becomes one single bureaucratic system extended over the entire society, or bureaucracy writ large.[12]

Other scholars of the Soviet Union and Eastern Europe did not explicitly compare those countries' organization with that of capitalist societies, but nevertheless they lent support to this thesis of bureaucratization under Communist political rule. To various extents, they borrowed from Weber the notion that bureaucratic administration tends to evolve toward centralized control, functional differentiation, technical specificity, as well as depersonalization and impersonality. As a result, numerous concepts, such as directed society, administered society, organizational society, mono-hierarchical society, and bureaucratic absolutism, were used to indicate that bureaucracy loomed large in Soviet-type societies.[13]

Research on socialist China has, too, borrowed from Weber and offered similar findings on organization. A common view is that after the revolution the CCP installed or harnessed elements of modern bureaucracy within state and society. As Harry Harding put it:

During the mid-1950's, the Chinese experimented with *rationalization:* rules and regulations were promulgated, a complex network of bureaucratic auditing and monitoring agencies was established, career lines were systematized, and specialized bureaucratic agencies were allowed to proliferate. Many later attempts to control the excesses of bureaucracy can also be understood as instances of rationalization: the reduction of staff implemented in 1955, the decentralization of measures of 1957–58, and the partial recentralization of the early 1960's all being cases in point. Even elements of the organizational reforms of the Cultural Revolution, particularly the simplification of bureaucratic structure and the decentralization of economic management, are best read as examples of a rationalizing approach to the bureaucratic dilemma.[14]

Although Franz Schurmann and other influential scholars offered a different interpretation of organization in socialist China, their views, too, supported the notion that extensive bureaucratization occurred after 1949. They noted that the CCP started to bureaucratize state and society after taking power, but the mass campaigns sponsored by the state, especially the Great Leap Forward and the Cultural Revolution, interrupted the bureaucratization. From this perspective, Chairman

Mao, who initiated both the Great Leap Forward and the Cultural Revolution, was the archenemy of bureaucratization, and President Liu Shaoqi, who was put in charge after the Leap famine and hounded to death during the Cultural Revolution, was a bureaucrat par excellence.[15] The fluctuation of bureaucratization within state and society is seen as a reflection of these men's competing leadership statuses.

Compared to Marxist formulations, these "Weberian" conceptions of bureaucratic development in Soviet-type societies focus more on how work was organized after the revolution. On the one hand, they indicate that the market was displaced by the state, which also penetrated into spheres of life such as religion, internal migration, and private consumption that had not been subjected to strict official control. On the other hand, they emphasize an increasing, though uneven, institutionalization of formal hierarchies, procedures, rules, and regulations in the political economy. Bureaucratization in this context means the emergence of a gigantic state machine and its drive toward regularization.

As Pakulski has convincingly argued, this adaptation of Weber's understanding of bureaucratic development during the transition to socialism is highly problematic. It ignores precisely his central thesis of modern bureaucracy—its embodiment of legal-rationality.[16] For Weber, what distinguishes modern bureaucracy is its single hierarchy of offices, meritocratic selection of personnel, and "*systematic* application of clearly defined impersonal legal norms in the form of abstract general rules regulating all procedures, as well as the rights and duties of officials." Pakulski has further shown that research on the Soviet Union and Eastern Europe (and I may add on China, too) contains plenty of evidence that the workplace possessed numerous deviations from the Weberian principle of legal-rationality, even during the post-Stalin years when state terror, violence, and radicalism had declined significantly. Examples are employment by political qualification, lack of job prescription, arbitrary exercise of power by party officials and management, widespread official corruption, proliferation of patron-client networks, and state interference in the private life of the labor force.[17] Pakulski concluded that "the *absence* of bureaucratic traits constitutes the distinctive feature of Soviet-type administration."[18]

As we shall see, the above "Weberian" perspectives on bureaucratic development in Soviet-type societies involve not only questionable departure from Weber's conception of modern bureaucracy but also contextual misreading of his view on Soviet society. Weber never claimed that Soviet Russia, which emerged shortly before he passed away, was properly socialist or would see a deepening of modern bureaucracy within state and society. To the contrary, he believed that the ascent of Bolshevism would hamper whatever rationalization was taking place in Russia before the revolution. I shall further note that the above "Weberian" views fail to take into account the Marxist-Leninist position on what to do with bureaucracy after the Communist takeover. Both Lenin and Mao explicitly opposed the use of modern bureaucracy. Consequently, China and the Soviet Union did not develop such administration but rather destroyed it during the transition to socialism.

Since the 1989–91 revolutions in the Soviet Union and Eastern Europe, research has pinpointed the bureaucratic coordination of the economy by the state as a major cause for the decline of Soviet-type societies. An oversimplified summary of this multidimensional argument, as exemplified by the works of János Kornai, goes something like this: unlike a capitalist economy, central planning places immense burdens on government to ascertain demand, manage supply, and satisfy need. It is therefore prone to simultaneously create shortages of goods and services and waste of resources. After early economic successes through forced growth or state decisions to invest disproportionately in targeted sectors, Soviet-type societies encountered perennial economic crises. Poor industrial efficiency, tight supply of consumer goods, poor-quality products, declining living standards, and other economic problems persisted. Popular resentment and elite diffidence followed and intensified, making socialist systems unsustainable.[19]

A powerful repudiation of Soviet-type societies, such an argument against bureaucratic coordination by the state shares the assumptions of the above Marxist and other interpretations of bureaucracy, which have little to do with Weber's model of rational bureaucracy. Kornai defines bureaucracy not as a legal-rational form of administration, but "the organization consisting of functionaries of the party, the state, the mass organizations, and also the managers of the state-owned sector collectively." He uses "centralized bureaucratic coordination" of the economy to mean that these people, or the Communist elite, had "the exclusive right" to dispose resources within "an undivided, totalitarian structure of power."[20] Bureaucracy is therefore regarded as the opposite of the market, too. Bureaucratization means that the state increasingly controls production, distribution, and consumption rather than the increasing deployment of formally rational rules and procedures in organizations, as in the Weberian sense. But when research on governmental coordination of the economy in Russia, Eastern Europe, or China probes into the workplace, its finding confirms that the latter's organization was fundamentally different from that of modern bureaucratic administration, as conspicuous stress on political ideology, personal loyalty, and coercion replaced the use of technical, legal, and impersonal norms.

In other words, such research obfuscates the roles played by state coordination of the economy and by modern bureaucracy in the decline of Soviet-type societies. It does not distinguish the damage caused by such coordination and by what its own research confirms to be an overall lack of rational administration. This analytical failure weakens the argument that official coordination of the economy was a major cause of the decline of such societies. The terminology of such research, or its use of "bureaucracy" and "bureaucratic coordination," however, trumpets the imprecise contention that too much bureaucracy precipitated the unraveling of actually existing socialisms. It reinforces the misunderstanding that these societies had been overbureaucratized.

From a Weberian perspective, what the above "bureaucratic" models demonstrate is not that modern bureaucratic administration loomed large in Soviet-type societies, but that it is questionable whether this administration had existed at all in those places. The corollary derived from such models that actually existing socialisms and bureaucracy have been inseparable to the end is therefore misleading. It is based on a misreading of Weber or conceptions of bureaucracy that have little to do with his understanding of rational administration. It trivializes the administrations developed under Marxist-Leninist rule by implying that they were variations of rational, bureaucratic organizations the world over.

A WEBERIAN ANALYTICAL FRAMEWORK

This book does not merely contend that Marxist-Leninist regimes did not establish modern bureaucratic administrations. Such an argument has already been made, even though its value for researching Soviet-type societies has not always been appreciated. I extend and revise Weber's understanding of modern bureaucracy to demonstrate two things: that the above regimes developed an administration that is the mirror image of the rational bureaucracy, and that the reproduction of this administration was a principal reason for the decline of Soviet-type societies. To understand what this alternative administration is and how it has affected actually existing socialisms, we must begin with Weber's theory of bureaucracy and then turn to Lenin and Mao to see what they thought of modern bureaucratic administration.

Weber indicated that for centuries in the West, patrimonialism, which has its origin in patriarchal authority, was the most common type of administration within the state, the church, and other hierarchical establishments. Those who exercised authority conducted their official business on the basis of personal discretion, whose limit was checked only by tradition and custom. They appointed the people they trusted and carried out supervision whenever they wanted. In general, staff had vaguely defined responsibilities and jurisdiction, because it was the masters' prerogative to dictate the content of their work. They were paid in kind, supported within the masters' household, or given the right to use their offices or the masters' properties to generate income. With patrimonialism, "practically everything depends explicitly upon personal considerations . . . upon purely personal connections, favors, promises and privileges."[21] The masters must see that the staff "are kept sweet" by material and other rewards; the staff in turn seek to limit the masters' demands within "the sanctity of tradition."[22]

According to Weber, the rise of capitalism and the rule of law engendered a new form of social administration—modern bureaucracy. In a world with increased economic uncertainties and competition, those who exercised authority had to pursue rational arrangements to minimize waste, delay, and failure in organizations in order to improve their chance of survival. The change to rational administration was most visible in businesses because they confronted the most ruthless competition. But it also penetrated governments, churches, and other establishments. In his ideal type that aims at capturing the distinctiveness of this administration, Weber laid out the characteristics of modern bureaucracy, which can be summarized as follows. There is a single hierarchy of offices occupied by individuals selected on the basis of technical qualification. They are hired on free contracts and paid by responsibility, performance, and qualification. Their official conduct is governed by impersonal rules, and they are promoted for job performance or seniority and subject to strict discipline. Official business is also carefully documented. For Weber, what modern bureaucracy represents is *formal rationality*, that is, the maximization of "the calculability of means through the standardization of action."[23] The growth of modern bureaucracy signifies the replacement of the rule of traditions and personal vagaries by the rule of law and impersonal norms.

Weber stated that the rise of modern bureaucracy has serious implications for the individual, work, and society. Compared to previous forms of administration, modern bureaucracy is much more efficient and reliable. The appointment of technically qualified staff constitutes a major source of advantage. It promotes speed, precision, and the uniformity and predictability of operation. The methodical calculation and execution of supervision, promotion, compensation, and punishment further benefit job performance by minimizing irregularities of effort and fluctuations of incentives.

Modern bureaucracy has a similarly profound impact on the office-holders. The presence of clearly defined systems of authority, discipline, and remuneration reduces these people's anxiety about responsibility, career, and livelihood. It nurtures a "highly standardized and impersonal type of obedience" that minimizes the intrusion of "love, hatred, and all purely personal, irrational, and emotional elements" into official business.[24] Modern bureaucratic organizations thus bind their staff more closely and stably to their work, colleagues, and the organization itself than did earlier kinds of administrations. As Weber put it:

The individual bureaucrat cannot squirm out of the apparatus into which he has been harnessed. In contrast to the "notable" performing administrative tasks as a honorific duty or subsidiary occupation (avocation), the professional bureaucrat is chained to his activity in his entire economic and ideological existence. . . . The individual bureaucrat is, above all, forged to the common interest of all the functionaries in the perpetuation of the apparatus and the persistence of its rationally organized domination.

He considered modern bureaucracy "the most rational known means of exercising authority over human beings."[25]

There are three common criticisms of Weber's ideas on modern bureaucracy and the ideal type he presents: he never demonstrates that deviations from the rational features actually cause work slowdown, staff friction, or waste of resources; he fails to explain how modern bureaucratic organizations with emphases on stability, uniformity, and predictability can adapt to the fast-changing environments typical of capitalist competition; and he assumes that nonbureaucratic elements, such as unofficial norms and informal staff relations, are not conducive to organizational efficiency and stability when such elements may be as important as the rational features in strengthening work performance.[26] These are valid criticisms of Weber's theory of modern bureaucracy. Nevertheless, research on organizations, especially on state agencies in developing societies, has repeatedly confirmed Weber's central argument on the rational bureaucracy. The presence of rational features within work establishments improves their performance by generating corporate coherence, esprit de corps, and usable knowledge and skills.[27]

On the flip side, Weber observed that the deployment of modern bureaucracy can exacerbate social inequalities. This administration is based on "domination through knowledge," which requires specialized training, sometimes for many years. Its growth has benefited those who can afford such training, namely, the economically privileged, and may therefore lead to "the universal domination of the 'class situation.'" The officeholders who possess valuable knowledge or skills are in "a position of extraordinary power" vis-à-vis the people they serve. They can further augment this power with work experience and access to "official secrets" and even exploit the requirement of "formalistic impersonality" in discharging their duties to protect themselves rather than provide goods or services.[28] If there are no mechanisms that check excesses and abuse, plutocracy, waste, and inefficiency inevitably follow the spread of modern bureaucracy.

In fact, Weber maintained that there is no necessary connection between modern bureaucracy as a tool for production and as a means of domination. At the extreme, this kind of administration can be captured by some interests *completely* for their own political or economic purposes. When this happens, the public face of the organization becomes a disguise for "the extraction, accumulation and control of [the coveted] resources." The everyday work of the organization "bears little relation to its official service goals, to the maintenance of social well-being or even to the long-term perpetuation of the bureaucracy itself."[29]

Above all, Weber feared that the rise of modern bureaucracy has proffered the political elite an unprecedented opportunity to establish "a monolithic power state" that has no meaningful check or balance of its power. Such a state had been impossible under patrimonialism because of its limited rationalization, but would now control every aspect of political, economic, and social life by means of a single bureaucracy spreading from the top into the deepest reaches of society. It would be staffed by large numbers of trained officials working according to state edicts and instructions. If this occurred, it would mean "a more complete and nightmarish bureaucratic domination."[30]

But what did Weber think of the relation between socialism and bureaucracy? Some studies of Soviet-type societies have noted that Weber believed that the development of socialism would further the bureaucratization or rationalization of the political economy. Such societies may therefore have invited, if not lived, the ultimate bureaucratic domination he feared most. Citing Weber, one observer hit this point home, arguing that the Soviet Union "established the most awesome bureaucratic system ever created." In an overview of organizations in socialist China, Martin Whyte argued that the CCP "created one of the most bureaucratized social systems known to man."[31] It is, however, absolutely critical to place Weber's ideas on socialism and bureaucracy within their own context, because they have nothing to do with the Soviet Union or any other Soviet-type society. Such studies of Soviet-type societies have misinterpreted Weber's comments.

In his discussion of socialism, Weber's focus was solely Western Europe, especially Germany. He dismissed the Marxian "pathetic prophecy" of a workers' revolution happening there, but debated his social-democratic contemporaries on the probable consequences of socialism.[32] The issue at stake was what would occur if, "by *a gradual process of evolution*, in other words by general cartelisation, standardisation, and bureaucratisation," the market were replaced by state planning in these capitalist, industrially advanced countries.[33] Weber contended that operations within the political economy would be increasingly informed by *substantive rationality*, that is, ultimate values of fairness and equity, rather than formal rationality. Rules and procedures would be altered or formulated on the basis of such values. Changes would appear in staff composition, compensation, and so on, and overall economic efficiency would decline because large sections of the workforce follow rules and regulations established at the expense of output optimization.

However, Weber never doubted that modern bureaucratic administrations would persist and even multiply in these industrialized societies, because as the state moves to control the economy, it still has to ensure efficiency in production, communication, and other operations previously performed by private enterprises. This is why he stated *in this context* that socialism "would, in fact, require a still higher degree of formal bureaucratization than capitalism."[34] What troubled him was that if an evolution toward socialism should occur in Western Europe, it would mean closer cooperation between the political and economic elite at the expense of the working class.

The unfortunate thing would be that, whereas at present the political bureaucracy of the state and the economic bureaucracy of private enterprise, of the cartels, the banks, and the large firms, exist alongside each other as separate bodies, so that, in spite of everything, economic power can be held in check by political, in the situation envisaged both sets of officials would form a single body with a solidarity of interests and would no longer be under control.[35]

The transition to socialism may thus result in social domination by one single, rational, and "unbreakable" bureaucracy that furthers the exploitation of workers rather than liberating them.[36]

Weber never considered postrevolutionary Russia a socialist society in the same manner as he pictured socialist evolution in Western Europe. Instead, he scornfully remarked that Bolshevik rule was just "a military revolt veiled in socialist drapery," not real socialism.[37] Furthermore, he noted that Bolshevik rule contained a virulent attack against the Russian bourgeoisie, the social class that possessed the expertise needed for developing modern bureaucratic administrations and, therefore, getting success in industrialization and other modernizing projects. By targeting the bourgeoisie, the Bolsheviks showed that they were "against formal rationalization."[38] The emerging Soviet system would thus feature not increasing bureaucratization but the opposite, the destruction of modern bureaucracy.

Put differently, Weber could not imagine how a modern society could be built in Russia, or anywhere else, without the use of modern bureaucracy. In his opinion, it would be impossible to have a debureaucratized and modernized Russia at the same time. He therefore did not think Bolshevik rule would last for long.[39] As Pakulski has pointed out, with the Bolshevik system of rule, what apparently interested Weber was how it might produce an administration of "a quite different type," something that would depart in basic terms from traditional forms of administration as well as from modern bureaucracy.[40] Unfortunately, he died before penning any definitive analysis of Soviet Communism.

At this point, there are four components that I draw from this Weberian framework to reexamine the relation between actually existing socialisms and bureaucracy. First, modern bureaucracy is a distinct type of administration that stresses a single hierarchy, technical competence, and other rational features. Second, like other forms of administration, it has specific implications for work, people, and society. Third, socialist development promotes bureaucratization or rationalization insofar as modern bureaucratic administrations are preserved. Fourth, the Bolshevik revolution did not engender the growth of modern bureaucracy but rather its destruction in Russia. In the conclusion of this book, I return to another important component of this Weberian framework, that is, Weber's concern that socialist development in industrialized societies may bolster the domination of modern bureaucracy *at the expense of the working class*. I shall argue that future theories of socialism must address this Weberian suspicion of socialism. But let us first turn to Lenin and Mao to see how they thought about bureaucracy and how their thinking affected organizational development in the Soviet Union and China.

AGAINST MODERN BUREAUCRACY: LENIN AND MAO

Marxist-Leninist regimes sought to modernize their countries on three principles oppositional to capitalist processes—central planning, working-class dictatorship, and Communist political rule. Both Lenin and Mao considered modern bureaucracy a product and means of capitalist domination that had to be replaced after the Communist takeover, a fact that much research on Soviet-type societies has overlooked. Like other political regimes, however, Marxist-Leninist regimes needed financial capital, technical expertise, and public support to pursue the modernization of the societies in which they ruled. As I shall indicate, Lenin provided a unique blueprint for harnessing such resources. His ideas greatly altered workplace organization in Russia and later in other countries. After the 1949 revolution, the CCP adopted the Leninist blueprint, but with Mao gradually asserting his own strategies of developing socialism. The Cultural Revolution led to the normalization of Maoism in the Chinese political economy. From a Weberian perspective, the transitions to Leninism and Maoism shared one thing in common: they engendered an administration that differed fundamentally from the rational bureaucracy.

Nowhere is Lenin's repudiation of modern bureaucracy so clear as in his famous tract *The State and Revolution*, written before the Bolshevik revolution. Like Weber, Lenin noted that capitalism has nurtured the rise of the modern state with features such as technically based recruitment, long-term career security, and graded remuneration. But he disdained Weber's "professorial wisdom of the cowardly bourgeoisie."[41] Following Marx and Engels, he considered the modern state an instrument of capitalist political domination. The use of career officials makes popular control of the state impossible; recruitment by technical qualification ensures the selection of the bourgeoisie to top offices; and graded compensation serves to align the interests of state officials to the interest of the capitalist class.[42] The modern state must therefore be destroyed after the revolution, along with the parliaments or "talking shops" that disguise capitalist political rule. Lenin regarded modern bureaucratic administration as entirely unnecessary. "As far as the supposedly necessary 'bureaucratic' organization is concerned," he wrote, "there is no difference whatever between a railway and any other enterprise in large-scale machine industry, any factory, large shop, or large-scale capitalist agricultural enterprise. . . . The workers, after winning political power, will smash the old bureaucratic apparatus, shatter it to its very foundation, and raze it to the ground."[43]

The State and Revolution contains the oft-quoted political structure that Lenin deemed to be appropriate during the transition to socialism. Modeled after the 1871 Paris Commune and ideas of Marx and Engels, "the dictatorship of the proletariat" has the following main characteristics: anyone except those designated for political suppression may take part in government; there is no separation between legislative and administrative functions; officials are popularly elected and subject to rotation and recall; and their pay may not exceed "ordinary workmen's wages." Behind this commune model of organization lies Lenin's belief that production and administration in modern societies are quite different matters.[44] He agreed with Weber that capitalist development has made technical expertise indispensable to production. Unlike Weber, however, he believed that such development has not made administrative tasks more complicated, but rather greatly simplified them to "simple operations of registration, filing, and accounting." He thus considered the elaborate modern state dominated by well-paid officials from the upper classes redundant. It is a "parasite" that perpetuates capitalist rule. The working class can run not only the socialist state, but also the entire political economy. It would hire its own "technicians, foremen and accountants, and pay them *all*, and indeed *all* 'state' officials in general, workmen's wages."[45]

Events after the Bolshevik revolution, that is, massive workers' casualties in the civil war, ideological resistance within the Bolshevik ranks, the failure of revolutions in Western Europe, and dire needs to revive the Russian economy, forced Lenin to modify his political ideas: ideas that would have promoted, especially in government, an egalitarian, antibureaucratic form of administration.[46] His new thinking on the role of hierarchy, expertise, discipline, and remuneration during the transition to socialism would become a paradigm of organization in Soviet-type societies. But, once again, he rejected modern bureaucracy.

To strengthen the Russian economy and quicken its modernization, Lenin insisted on thoroughly utilizing the prerevolutionary elite. As he put it, the working class had "no other bricks" with which to develop industry or other sectors apart from "bourgeois experts" and "petty-bourgeois intellectuals." It must take from capitalism "all its science, technology and art," set "definite tasks" for those with knowledge and skills, and "put every one of them to work." Lenin adamantly believed in this tactics of developing socialism. As long as "cultured capitalists" were cooperative, he told the Bolsheviks, they should assume "executive functions" to help improve the economy. Even those "old military experts, czarist generals and officers" who had been guilty of "bloody acts of repression against workers and peasants" should be absorbed into the Red Army.[47]

Aware that the former elite might exploit their entrusted responsibilities to sabotage rather than support Bolshevik rule, Lenin called for tight political control in the workplace. He no longer stressed the election, rotation, or recall of officials within or outside of government. Rather, the regime should appoint "workers' representatives" to the workplace to impose "a proletarian discipline" on bourgeois experts and intellectuals and compel them to work hard.[48] Having seen firsthand the complexity of managing an economy, he no longer believed that workers should instantly take on administrative work, but expected their representatives to learn from the former elite on the job, at the same time as they would keep these people under surveillance. This division of labor between the working class and bourgeoisie should last until the Bolsheviks produced an abundance of politically and technically qualified individuals, or what Antonio Gramsci later called organic intellectuals, to run the political economy. As Lenin told the Bolsheviks: "Our job is to attract, by way of experiment, large numbers of specialists, then replace them by training a new officers' corps, a new body of specialists who will have to learn the extremely difficult, new and complicated business of administration."[49]

Another component in Lenin's revised thinking deals with remuneration. He proposed that the Bolsheviks should pay bourgeois experts, especially "stars of the first magnitude," better than others to encourage their cooperation. That is, the party should "give them an incentive to work no worse, and even better, than they have worked before." Lenin considered this "tribute" to the experts "necessary and theoretically indispensable" for socialist development in Russia. But he still believed that professional workers in general should receive "ordinary workmen's wages" because excessive professional income had been a symptom of class exploitation that must be abolished.[50] Put simply, Lenin observed that until the party had enough organic intellectuals to control production and administration, it should exploit the former elite technically, suppress them politically, but reward them financially.

With this approach to organization, Lenin turned Weber on his head. In effect, he suggested an administration that is in key respects the opposite of modern bureaucracy. First, political rather than technical qualification becomes the criterion for administrative authority. Second, technical competence is not the only requirement for other offices because the latter have to be filled for the objective of modernization. Third, job assignment by the state becomes an important feature in place of free labor contracts between employers and employees. Fourth, strict political surveillance rather than rational discipline of job performance is preferred in the workplace. Fifth, a small group is selected for high salaries while others have their earnings suppressed. In short, Leninism promotes the use of political authority, state appointment, tight surveillance, and inequitable compensation in the workplace with partial consideration for individual competence.

After the 1949 revolution, the CCP adopted these Leninist measures as part of its so-called united-front (*tongyi zhanxian*) approach to governance. Mao virtually repeated Lenin's view on utilizing the former elite to help build a socialist society:

The national bourgeoisie will eventually cease to exist, but at this stage we should rally them around us and not push them away. We should struggle against them on the one hand and unite them on the other. We should make this clear to the cadres and show by facts that it is right and necessary to unite with the national bourgeoisie, the democratic parties, democratic personages and intellectuals. Many of them were our enemies before, but now that they have broken with the enemy camp and come over to our side, we should unite with all these people, who can be more or less united with.[51]

Unlike the Bolsheviks, the CCP stressed the "mass line" (*qunzhong luxian*) that it had developed before the revolution by encouraging popular participation in the political process controlled by the regime. The party frequently organized mass campaigns to discredit the former elite and strengthen local controls by party cadres. At the same time, however, Mao indicated that bourgeois experts and intellectuals were indispensable to the regime, because it would not be able to modernize China by "relying only on uneducated people like ourselves."[52] At this stage, the mass line did not engender workplace features that diverged greatly from the Leninist vision. Instead, it reinforced the use of political authority, strict surveillance, inequitable compensation, and state appointment and neglect of technical competence. By early 1957, Mao was apparently still committed to Leninism. "On the whole, the capitalists plus the democrats and intellectuals associated with them have a higher level of cultural and technical knowledge. By buying over this class, we have deprived them of their political capital and kept their mouths shut. The way to deprive them is to buy them over and make arrangements to give them jobs."[53]

In the late 1950s, however, Mao began to turn against Leninist organizational practices. What precipitated this change were intellectuals' attack on the Chinese Communist regime in the "great blooming and contending" of the 1957 Hundred Flowers Campaign and the deteriorating relations between China and the Soviet Union. Mao claimed that the role of the technical and cultural elite in building a socialist society had been overstated, as "the people who founded new schools of thought [in the past] were all young people without much learning." He emphasized "creativity of the masses" in enhancing production and began to see the mistakes and abuses committed by CCP members in a different light: as indicative of corruption in the party's working-class character and mission of realizing a genuinely socialist society.[54]

By the early 1960s, Mao's reflection on the Communist political system shared important parallels with Trotsky's earlier charges against Soviet officialdom. He observed that the appointment of career officials and management personnel with progressive remuneration had been reproducing a privileged bureaucratic class and that the CCP had been lax in party member recruitment. The party had taken in "sons and daughters of landlords and rich peasants," "petty-bourgeois elements," and intellectuals with dubious political consciousness. In addition, "some bad people have wormed their way" into the party membership.[55] For Mao, it seemed increasingly clear that the Soviet paradigm of developing socialism, with tight party control of the political economy and strong participation from the former elite, would not liberate the Chinese working class but continue its enslavement.

With Mao the primary sponsor, the Chinese Cultural Revolution (1966–69) led to dramatic changes in workplace organization. He endorsed the demotion, dismissal, and persecution of party officials, management personnel, and intellectuals. Once regarded as key to a modernized socialist China, these people were now considered liabilities. But Mao also blocked elite and popular efforts to set up workers' direct rule modeled after the Paris Commune. Instead, he summoned soldiers, workers, and peasants to the workplace and ordered the formation of "revolutionary committees." In his blueprint, these committees, except those within the military or highly sensitive government offices, should consist of some soldiers, workers, peasants, or students as well as some original staff and management personnel. Collectively, they would replace party domination of the political economy by popular participation in decision making. Mao furthered his attack on the role of expertise and stressed political study and physical labor for intellectuals so that they would return to the fold of the working class.

In organizational terms, Maoism was a departure from Leninism. Although political qualification remained as the fount of workplace authority, its requirement had changed. As the authority of former party officials and management personnel was curbed, expressed loyalty to Mao's political ideas became most important. Inside the workplace, the status of experts and expertise declined precipitously due to Mao's attack on intellectuals. But Maoism upheld the Leninist practices of strict surveillance and state appointment. As Chapter 6 shows, amid the political and social upheavals that marked the last ten years of Mao rule (1966–76), some "bourgeois experts" continued to receive disproportionately high salaries. Like Lenin, Mao never had sympathy for the rational bureaucracy. His political ideas, too, produced organizations sharply different from modern bureaucratic administrations.

COUNTER-BUREAUCRACY AS A
MODERN FORM OF ADMINISTRATION

The central contention of this book is that actually existing socialisms engendered not modern bureaucracy in the Weberian sense but a different type of administration. This book is devoted to developing an analysis of this administration. To be sure, this alternative administration had many features similar to those of modern bureaucracy: distinct offices, long-term careers, stable compensation, regular supervision, meticulous documentation, and the separation of work from ownership of the means of production or administration.[56] In other critical respects, however, it was the antithesis of modern bureaucracy. I call this administration "counter-bureaucracy" to indicate that it had the shell but not the content of modern bureaucracy and that it was also counterproductive to the survival of Soviet-type societies.

For Weber, modern bureaucracy appeared with the rise of capitalism and rule of law. It has a rational constitution that matches its purpose: the efficient completion of official tasks. Besides the elements listed above, single hierarchy, technical competence, rule-based management, rational remuneration, and free employment contract are basic features of modern bureaucracy. In comparison, counter-bureaucracy has an opposite set of attributes on these dimensions: a divisive system of political and technical authority, a general shortage of professional competence, intrusive discipline, contentious remuneration schemes, and job assignment by government. The origin of this administration is traceable to Lenin's postrevolutionary thinking on developing socialism; the reproduction of counter-bureaucracy in China was furthered by the ascent of Maoism.

The distribution of official authority within counter-bureaucratic administrations was based on political qualification. But a secondary hierarchy of technical qualification existed, due to various degrees of official recognition of the role of expertise in the process of state-led modernization. Promotion was thus based on political merit but tended to involve technical calculation, too. Because of the valorization of political qualification, technical competence among officeholders was generally not a dominant feature of such administrations. Indeed, it tended to be a serious problem especially when Marxist-Leninist regimes forcibly expanded the system of production or reproduction. Furthermore, the shortages of competent officeholders meant that significant variations in technical qualification existed among those holding the same type of office.

Intrusive and arbitrary discipline was another main element of counter-bureaucracy. Within Soviet-type societies, the workplace was a primary site through which the ruling regimes exercised political control.

As a result, it was penetrated by various mechanisms of state surveillance, the extent of which varied with the political climate but reached into private life. The definition of offense and level of punishment were not strictly controlled by laws and regulations so much as being prerogatives of government and officials. Moreover, because work within such societies had one single purpose from the official perspective, namely, building socialism, one's job performance was a proxy for individual political loyalty or compliance toward the state. Insubordination or unsatisfactory work was thus punishable as a political infraction.

Another feature of counter-bureaucracy was the lack of free labor contracts. The government controlled job assignment and termination and change of employment. This official privilege covered every organizational level. When exercised, it superseded the discretion of management and individuals. In other words, management had limited freedom in hiring, firing, promoting, and demoting staff, as the government often intervened in decision making through policies or action. Like their subordinates, management personnel's choice of work was limited. Their assignment and advancement, too, were subject to tight government control. Job appointment in counter-bureaucracy was therefore quasi-coercive.

Nonrational remuneration was another characteristic of counter-bureaucracy. Leninism dictates high salaries for "bourgeois experts" but "workmen's wages" for other professional workers. An earnings gap hence existed in establishments using these types of people. As a recurring process, remuneration within counter-bureaucratic administrations was not based on individual responsibility, qualification, performance, or seniority. Rather, the determination of salaries, pay raises, and benefits blended these rational criteria with official stress on political loyalty. In effect, compensation was heavily influenced by nonrational considerations.

In short, multiple hierarchies of authority, income, and status as well as a shortage of expertise, tight surveillance, and quasi-coercive appointment were core features of counter-bureaucracy. To be sure, the latter is proposed in this book as a Weberian-style ideal type, a theoretical construct that emphasizes those features within Soviet-type organizations with distinctive impact on the individual, state, and society. The constitutions of governments, factories, and other workplaces differed within any Soviet-type society and surely across such societies due to variations in local conditions, central policies, and historical circumstances. One should not expect the use of political appointment, state assignment and surveillance, and nonrational compensation, as well as the shortage of expertise, to be uniform across time, countries, or organizations, just one would not imagine that modern bureaucratic administrations are identical within or between any capitalist societies. My main point is that because both Leninist and Maoist organizational strategies were based on a rejection of modern bureaucracy, their dominance in China and elsewhere engendered a different type of administration.

Some might object that workplaces in Soviet-type societies were not modern bureaucratic administrations, but rather that because of their nonrational features they would be more rightly viewed as contemporary instances of patrimonialism. Trust-based distribution of authority, arbitrary discipline, irregular compensation, and the lack of emphasis on technical competence are all central features of patrimonial administration. Indeed, research has compared actually existing socialisms to patrimonial societies.[57] In other words, is it necessary to theorize Soviet-type organizations as a new form of social administration? Were they not incarnations of an age-old type of organization? My answer is that we would miss how modern Soviet-type organizations were by considering them patrimonial, just as we have underestimated their difference from modern bureaucracy by seeing them as its variants.

For Weber, patrimonialism is a premodern form of administration in which official authority is legitimized and limited by traditions and customs. At the top, political rulers lack the resources to penetrate into local levels and grant privileges to trusted local groups in return for their performance of public duties. A high degree of local self-government and intermittent control are thus hallmarks of the patrimonial state.[58] Marxist-Leninist regimes seized power in relatively underdeveloped economies with large agrarian populations. Their rule reproduced aspects of patrimonialism. But important differences separate Soviet-type and patrimonial administrations. The former were not founded upon traditions or customs, but through their destruction by revolution. They were established on the basis of central planning, which seeks to minimize gaps in government control. In fact, their objective was constant regulation of social life. Through ideology and organization, they tried to limit rather than promote local self-government. That is, the political calculation, arbitrary discipline, irregular compensation, and shortage of expertise within Soviet-type and patrimonial administrations do not share comparable origins. In one case, they are sanctified by traditions and made necessary by the limited reach of the sovereign. In the other case, they are outcomes of modern revolutions in which the victors sought to control society according to a set of modern political ideals. The concept of counter-bureaucracy thus distinguishes Soviet-type administrations from both traditional and modern bureaucracy.

From a Weberian perspective, it seems obvious that the deployment of counter-bureaucracy had harmful consequences for actually existing socialisms. Weber considered modern bureaucratic administrations superior because they emphasize technical knowledge and their rational organization reproduces legitimate domination. In other words, the officeholders are not only competent but also generally accept their subordination. This has an extraordinary political implication: modern bureaucracy "is a power instrument of the first order," practically indestructible when fully established.[59] This is precisely why Weber feared that the growth of modern bureaucracy may intensify social domination, especially when this administration is used by political regimes to control social life.

In comparison, Marxist-Leninist systems of rule normalized counter-bureaucracy, or an antithesis of modern bureaucracy. As they tried to erect a modernized socialist polity, this institution brought forth a different set of technical, social, and political implications for Soviet-type societies. Perhaps the most obvious impact of counter-bureaucracy on such societies was damage to work productivity. The emphasis on the political qualifications of management personnel compromised the level of technical expertise available to workplaces. Many appointed at management or lower levels during rapid expansions of the system of production or reproduction were insufficiently knowledgeable or insufficiently skillful. Furthermore, management's lack of hiring or firing privilege did not benefit staff quality, while quasi-coercive appointment, inequitable compensation, and arbitrary discipline lowered individual productivity by causing resentment, acts of insubordination, and other disruptive behavior in the labor force.

It seems apparent that the normalization of counter-bureaucracy harmed social relations in the workplace, too. Governments, colleges, and other establishments whose operations required professional expertise all had two hierarchies (political and technical) that coexisted uneasily. Those who had management authority had acquired it primarily through their political credentials; those who were technically superior did not enjoy such authority unless they were politically qualified, too. This political-technical schism heightened tensions between management and staff. Due to nonrational means of recruitment, compensation, and discipline, workplace tensions also existed laterally among people with the same type of positions but of incompatible backgrounds, qualifications, or income. Ultimately, such tensions hurt motivation for everyday cooperation and therefore productivity.

The reproduction of counter-bureaucracy also damaged Marxist-Leninist regimes politically. In his discussion of a peaceful evolution to socialism in Western Europe, Weber noted that when central planning strengthens, the state "would have to share the burden of the workers' hatred, which at present is directed against the entrepreneurs."[60] That is to say, in the absence or relative insignificance of the private enterprise, even a state that deploys rational workplace measures to control production and reproduction would still become a target of workers, and presumably others as well, who are dissatisfied with their salaries, assignments, or other work-related issues. Having institutionalized an opposite of the rational bureaucracy, Marxist-Leninist regimes could not but encounter an abundance of complaints on appointments, salaries, colleagues, and just work in general. The reproduction of counter-bureaucracy thus went hand in hand with a reproduction of a disgruntled labor force that chipped away at the legitimacy of Marxist-Leninist regimes.

The workplace was on the frontline in the remaking of state and society during the historical transitions to socialism. But Leninism and Maoism as transformative ideologies engendered the growth of counter-bureaucratic administrations at this site. The resulting organizational arrangements led to shortages of skills as well as staff tension and dissatisfaction. They dampened rational interest in accepting subordination. Weber's work on authority and legitimacy suggests that under such circumstances individuals would comply with or act against their superiors based on their own *material* and *ideal* interests or, concisely, purposive calculation and moral reasoning respectively.[61] On one hand, these interests are functions of personal factors such as official position, social status and background, and political belief. On the other hand, they reflect social conditions that influence personal choices and opportunities. In other words, the patterns of conflict and cooperation within counter-bureaucratic administrations were mediated by what each of the officeholders considered right or profitable under the circumstances, or reactions that modern bureaucratic administrations precisely discourage through their rational constitution.

For quite some time, Marxist-Leninist regimes, by altering and realtering the distribution of authority, privileges, and material rewards in the workplace, were capable of capitalizing on the material and ideal interests engendered by counter-bureaucracy to maintain control over state and society. They had seemingly proved Weber wrong by building modern societies without modern bureaucracy. However, the reproduction of counter-bureaucracy left a debilitating legacy—poor economic productivity, lack of social trust, and political disaffection—that weighed heavily on governments, industry, and the system of production and reproduction in general. By the 1980s, these regimes were embroiled in deep social, economic, and political troubles. In the end, changes came one way or another, leaving Soviet-type societies as a historical object.

Before we go on, it must be noted that nothing in the history of socialism suggests an inevitable victory of Leninism or Maoism or a predestined appearance of counter-bureaucracy. The adoption of the Leninist or Maoist approach in Russia, China, and elsewhere coincided with widely documented events featuring nothing short of bitter debates, personal attacks, lies and falsehoods, secret maneuvers, open intimidation, and even murders of opponents.[62] Based on this understanding, what I suggest in this book is not that socialism as an alternative to capitalism was doomed to fail from the beginning, but that Leninism and Maoism produced self-defeating socialist systems. Despite its stress on organizations, Leninism proposes not formally rational, but counter-bureaucratic measures for achieving the substantively rational objectives of socialism. Maoism is even more irrational or counter-bureaucratic than Leninism. Both ideologies contain an illusion that socialism can be built without modern bureaucracy, a thought that Weber would have considered absurd.

ORGANIZATION OF THE BOOK

This book offers an alternative understanding of Soviet-type societies. It contends that the historical transition to socialism engendered counter-bureaucracy rather than modern bureaucracy as has been claimed. It thus addresses the *administrative* origins of the decline of actually existing socialisms. The following chapters contain a primary study of Shanghai secondary schools as workplaces in the Mao era as well as comparative studies of the organization of Chinese officialdom and Soviet industry. My goal is to articulate the elements of counter-bureaucracy and illustrate how they evolved in context under Leninist and Maoist types of political rule and extended across sectors and societies.

To demonstrate that the schools, which played a critical role in China's transition to socialism, were organized as counter-bureaucracy, I focus on five variables in relation to the faculty: (1) social composition, (2) authority relations, (3) compensation, (4) discipline, and (5) personal experience. As far as I know, no research has systematically examined all of these features together in a Chinese or Soviet establishment. Their content in relation to Shanghai secondary schools depended upon state policy, local interest, and personal action. But they were also independent variables that shaped faculty reactions to colleagues, work, and the government. Over a period of almost thirty years, these features changed significantly due to societal modernization and political change. When described together, they illustrate the transformation of the schools as concrete sites of administration. The result is a picture of formal structure, workplace culture, and political behavior. It shows how little the schools resembled the Weberian bureaucracy and how their organization harmed the development of socialism technically, socially, and politically.

Social composition refers to the class, education, occupational, and political backgrounds of the faculty. After taking power, the CCP recruited teachers from numerous and unconventional sources. Within the faculty, there were formerly jobless people, state employees, demobilized soldiers, college students, high school graduates, blue-collar workers, and housewives. The regime also transferred party and state officials into the schools. The pattern of recruitment kept changing during the Mao era. I analyze how the CCP's approaches to building a modern socialist polity and the changing political and social contexts shaped and reshaped faculty composition.

Authority relations refers to the distribution and practice of power in the faculty. The CCP's quest for modernization and control of the workplace created two sources of authority on campus: political and technical. The former was sanctioned by the state; the latter, by the state and traditions. Faculty members with politically based authority acquired it from their work in the revolutionary movement, their working-class or "good" class background, their experience in CCP officialdom, or a combination of these factors. Faculty members with technically based authority derived it from their education or professional training, often associated with prerevolutionary class privileges. I delineate how political changes shaped authority relations in the faculty.

Compensation refers to the salaries, benefits, and opportunities distributed to the faculty. The CCP offered high salaries to "bourgeois experts" and paid other professional workers "workmen's wages." This instantly created a faculty income divide. Over time, faculty compensation changed because of salary reforms, promotions, and distributions of state-controlled benefits. I describe the patterns of monthly earnings, promotion, and benefits on campus as well as how income divisions, gaps, and contradictions appeared, evolved, and affected teachers' livelihoods and relations.

Discipline refers to the official punishments received by faculty members. The CCP meted out a variety of punishments such as demotion, dismissal, and labor reeducation to teachers guilty of wrongdoing. To effect socialist development, however, the party deliberately kept many lawbreakers and wrongdoers in the faculty so that they could continue to work. The transition from Leninism to Maoism did not significantly cleanse the faculty of these people. I document how the state administered punishments to those guilty of political, economic, and sexual wrongdoing and how such state action harmed relations between management and staff.

Personal experience refers to the relations of the faculty to their colleagues, work, and the government. The all-encompassing Leninist and Maoist administrative practices shaped the professional as well as the personal lives of the faculty. Embedded within the social hierarchies, divisions, and inequalities enforced by the state, faculty members expressed themselves, as Weber would predict, according to their material and ideal interests. I examine how faculty from different political, cultural, and economic positions behaved in the schoolhouse.

Chapters 2 through 5 describe, respectively the social composition, authority relations, compensation, and discipline in the faculty and how these features affected the work performance, social relations, and political behavior of faculty members between the 1949 revolution and the onset of the Cultural Revolution. As a whole, these chapters lay out the reproduction of counter-bureaucracy in Shanghai secondary schools for nearly two decades of Chinese socialism. The topics of Chapter 6 are faculty behavior during the Cultural Revolution and faculty conditions in the remaining Mao years (1970–76). I show that the counter-bureaucratic constitution of the campuses had a direct impact on the student Red Guard movement. Moreover, I show that the ascent of Maoism intensified the reproduction of counter-bureaucratic administration in the schools.

Chapter 7 is divided into two parts. The first part examines the development of counter-bureaucracy in Soviet industry from Lenin's to Stalin's rule (1917–53). The other part traces the formation of counter-bureaucracy in Chinese officialdom and how the reproduction of this administration was linked to the catastrophic outcome of the Great Leap Forward (1958–60) and the Cultural Revolution. The two parts show that two of the most privileged institutions in Soviet-type societies were constituted as counter-bureaucracy and that the dominance of this administration in such societies led to widespread social misery.

In the conclusion I extend Weber's understanding of modern bureaucracy and arguments within the critical tradition of Weberian scholarship on Soviet-type societies to address two issues: What role did counter-bureaucracy play in the decline of Soviet-type societies in the late 1980s and 1990s? Why did major intellectual perspectives on such societies fail to anticipate their decline? Furthermore, I suggest that the failure of Soviet-type societies confirms Weber's argument that modern societies, indeed, need modern bureaucracy. Any future theory of socialism must therefore take this institution seriously rather than dismissing its relevance for the transition to socialism, as Lenin and Mao did in the last century.

2

Shortages of Expertise

Even the awfully unqualified and undeserved (*a mao a gou*)
could become schoolteachers in those days!
—A retired school party secretary on
teacher recruitment in the 1950s

In the fall of 1961, or more than a decade after the Chinese Communist
Party (CCP) takeover of China, the Shanghai Education Bureau issued
a bleak report on teachers' qualifications. Among nearly twenty thousand instructors in regular secondary schools, almost half had completed less than three years of service. An almost identical proportion "had
not reached the appropriate cultural level" for their assignment, which
means that they were insufficiently educated. Meanwhile, the majority
of those with higher specialized training did not teach subjects compat-
ible with their learning. Only 20 percent of all primary and secondary
school teachers were experienced and qualified in what they taught.
Three-quarters of the rest lacked "basic knowledge" or teaching experience in their subjects. The remainders exhibited "rather serious problems in instruction, a grave inadequacy in basic knowledge and classroom experience, or fairly bad or very bad teaching performance."[1]

With this chapter, I begin describing the production and reproduction
of counter-bureaucracy in Shanghai secondary schools. Before the 1949
revolution, these schools contained distinguishable elements of the Weberian bureaucracy. One of the most remarkable changes afterward was
a steep decline in the faculty's technical qualifications. A main reason
for this was the rapid expansion of education under Communist Party
rule. Pressured to find teachers, the Shanghai authorities recruited a
heterogeneous population into the profession. Another reason was the
official deployment of what Lenin referred to as "workers' representatives" on campus, which led to faculty appointment by political rather
than technical qualification. Many of the people who joined the faculty,

though educated by societal standards, were ill prepared to teach or to run the schools. They hardly looked like educators who could effectively transmit knowledge, skills, or values beneficial to socialist development. The lack of pedagogical and management expertise on campus was a key indication that the schools were counter-bureaucratic.

Specifically, this chapter focuses on the appointment of three kinds of people who had not normally been used as instructors: unemployed intellectuals, transferred cadres, and former workers. Their hiring by the state greatly impaired the quality of instruction as well as faculty relations. Besides laying out the professional and academic records of these people and their relations to other faculty members and among themselves, I also describe their social and political backgrounds, which had major implications for official control of the faculty. But how such backgrounds shaped faculty organization and faculty life will be discussed in the next chapter. For now, my goal is to show that the CCP normalized a shortage of pedagogical skills in the teaching ranks.

Before detailing the institutionalization of counter-bureaucracy in the schools, a brief discussion of their organization before the revolution is appropriate. It shows that they had been undergoing rationalization despite the social and political upheavals that engulfed China. The discussion helps us grasp the gravity of the changes in school organization after the revolution and why faculty members responded to their work, colleagues, and the political authorities in the ways described in the rest of the book.

A PREREVOLUTIONARY TREND OF BUREAUCRATIZATION

China suffered major military defeats during the nineteenth century that prompted the elite to call for political, industrial, and cultural modernization. When the Nationalist Party, or *Kuomintang* (KMT), began to rule the country in the late 1920s, modern industry, banking, communication, transportation, and Western-style professionals such as scientists and engineers were already part of the urban landscape. The KMT leadership believed that China could be remade by "planned application of international technology under the leadership of home-grown scientific and technical talent."[2] Meanwhile, professionals desired political backing to expand their social influence. This interdependence fostered "a negotiated mutual tolerance and cooperation."[3] The government promoted professional training and regulated professional qualifications and conduct. Elite professionals assumed high posts in the planning, executive, and technical branches of the state.[4] And lawyers, journalists, and others formed their own professional associations to foster official recognition, self-regulation, and formal training and certification.[5]

Within the state, such development engendered Weberian-style bureaucratic development, even though it was compromised by traditions and factionalism. The establishment of the Examination Council (*kaoshi yuan*) and the Ministry of Personnel was indicative of this.[6] Theoretically cornerstones of a modern Chinese state, these institutions were charged with setting up technically based exams to recruit officials and systematizing the authority, remuneration, and qualifications of those recruited. In practice, they were both ineffective. Long-standing reliance on patronage and nepotism, elite factional struggles, and the lack of administrative support for both institutions ensured that from central ministries to local governments, hiring through personal networks prevailed. Nonetheless, meritocratic appointment strengthened under KMT rule. Thanks to organizational location or leadership style, some state agencies virtually adopted the Weberian ideal, building "internal cohesiveness of personnel around bureaucratic, professional, depersonalized norms."[7]

The Japanese invasion of China, however, impeded the process of rationalization in government. As the invasion intensified in the mid-1930s, the KMT used its military personnel and party members to control the state and the public sector in order to muster resources and compliance for its defense strategy. These people even penetrated private establishments and professional associations.[8] Beset by fiscal problems and public disaffection toward the regime, the KMT never achieved comparable levels of control in the above areas. Whereas political appointment in the state sector was obvious, meritocratic hiring gained ground outside. The government intervened in professional work, to be sure, but professionals still had plenty of room to maneuver. What Shanghai secondary schools experienced was an excellent example of incipient rationalization in the context of traditions, professional interests, state intervention, political strife, and war.

A quick look at the academic degrees in the faculty reveals the significance of meritocratic appointment, which is the most important element of modern bureaucratic administration. In 1930 almost 40 percent of the faculty and staff in the public schools were university graduates.

By 1947 three-fifths of the entire secondary school faculty and staff were university graduates.[9] At the city center, 85 percent of the teachers had attended a postsecondary institution.[10] The instructors in a nearby rural county were less educated, but still more than two-thirds were post-secondary school graduates.[11] In the best schools, faculty qualifications rivaled those in industrialized countries. When the foreigner-controlled Shanghai Municipal Council opened a girls' school in 1931, the school principal was a Chinese woman with a master's degree from the United States who had done education research at the University of Chicago. Among the fifteen teachers she hired, five had a master's degree and nine had studied in the United States.[12] On the eve of the 1949 revolution, the school principal and the head of instruction (or head teacher) at City West Secondary School had a master's degree from Colorado Teachers College and the University of Chicago, respectively. Among forty teachers, three had a master's degree and thirty-one had a bachelor's degree. At the exclusive McTyeire School for girls, the school principal was a former PhD student of education at Columbia University. In a faculty of forty-four, six had a master's degree and twenty-seven had a bachelor's degree.[13]

Such faculty qualifications reflected state policy as well as campus control by professionals. The KMT did not promote mass secondary education. In 1936 Shanghai had roughly 4 million people, but only 120 nonvocational, mainly private secondary schools with a total of 32,000 students. By 1948 there were 5.2 million people, 232 such schools, and only 98,400 students.[14] At the top level, a small number of schools run by missionaries, foreigners, and veteran educators attracted students from well-to-do families with an exclusive education aimed at college enrollment. In the middle, private and public schools enrolled middle-class students to help them obtain white-collar jobs or higher education in the future. At the bottom, churches, local notables, and later the Communist underground operated a few secondary schools for poor children.[15]

The government regulated the schools through edicts and supervision. It promulgated elaborate rules on faculty qualifications, stressing college education and teaching experience. Junior high school teachers had to be college graduates; otherwise they had to enter teacher training, pass an official exam, or show proper experience. The standards for senior high school teachers, heads of instruction, and school principals were progressively elevated. To be a senior high school principal, one would need to have been a lecturer in a public university, a senior education official, or a junior high school principal for three years.[16] To increase compliance from schools, the government instituted a process to appraise faculty qualifications and sometimes closed campuses that violated the rules.

Such regulation facilitated campus control by professional educators. To be sure, these educators frequently followed tradition and appointed relatives, friends, or acquaintances to faculty posts. But due to state monitoring and lack of pressure to expand student enrollment, such informal (but still technically based) hiring promoted, precisely, a relatively homogeneous yet well-qualified faculty. As research on developing countries has shown repeatedly, this kind of informal but meritocratic recruitment is a major mechanism that leads to the buildup of expertise and esprit de corps in the workplace.[17]

By the mid-1930s, faculty qualifications in Shanghai began to decline as the number of ill-equipped "diploma mills" surged with rising demand for schooling. But the Japanese invasion curbed the fall. As schools struggled financially, class sizes expanded much more quickly than the number of teachers.[18] The influx of refugees into Shanghai also enlarged the pool of teacher candidates, giving the campuses the relative luxury of choosing the most qualified.[19] When the KMT regained control of the city in the mid-1940s, before the civil war began, it again publicized regulations on faculty qualifications and required teachers who did not meet official standards to pass an academic exam or prove their capabilities to keep their jobs.

Because of foreign, state, and local sponsorships, the schools paid their faculty according to different standards. One report states that faculty members received 100 to 200 yuan per month in the mid-1930s; another report, 50 to 140 yuan. Even the lower range represented middle-class income or close to it, for the reports indicate that manual and clerical workers earned 14 to 30 yuan per month, and a family of five needed 66 yuan per month to maintain a "middle" lifestyle.[20] The faculty in top missionary schools, renowned private schools, and schools sponsored by the foreign authorities were particularly well paid. But the faculty in the public schools saw their pensions, vacations, and other benefits written into official regulations. The government planned to pay teachers by academic qualification, teaching experience, and faculty post and to guarantee them a middle-class income.[21]

Spearheaded by the state, the effort to rationalize faculty compensation came to a halt in the late 1930s, as warfare and chaos engulfed Shanghai. Schoolteachers were forced to accept pay cuts and delays and payment-in-kind. Like others in the city, they became victims of wild inflation, and some fell into destitution. But the KMT still regarded the secondary school faculty as professionals who deserved comfortable incomes. When it revised salary schedules for the public school faculty in 1940 and 1946, the figures still represented middle-class earnings, even though they were quickly rendered meaningless by the chaos resulting from warfare.[22]

Although professional educators dominated the secondary school faculty, the campuses were never immune from KMT intervention. The government appointed KMT members to various offices in the public schools and pressured private schools to hire its approved people to teach mandatory classes on party doctrines and ideas. To control the students, it introduced military and Boy Scout training and required each campus to appoint a "head of instruction and training," who had to be a KMT member. Oftentimes, it simply assigned a person to the post. After the Japanese invaded Shanghai, the KMT established the Nationalist Youth Corps, or *Sanmin zhuyi qingniantuan*, to exert further control on schools and universities. It even used its intelligence agency, the Central Bureau of Statistics and Investigation, to monitor faculty and student behavior.[23]

KMT intervention in the schools escalated during the civil war. Additional party officials, retired soldiers, and undercover agents were sent to the campuses to attack political resistance.[24] When the CCP took over Shanghai in the spring of 1949, it noted that the powerful right-wing C.C. Clique within the KMT leadership controlled most of the nineteen public secondary schools, while "reactionary elements" dominated fifty-four private schools and had "close relations" with twenty-eight other campuses.[25] The renowned Yucai Secondary School, for example, had reportedly been run by a party official who had two Central Bureau agents placed on campus to "monitor, follow, eavesdrop, and report on" the faculty and students. He apparently had fired seven teachers and replaced them with people he knew.[26]

The KMT was not the only political force involved in faculty life. When Shanghai was under Japanese occupation, the occupiers trained their own teachers and used cooperative faculty members to control the schools. They imported native Japanese to teach language classes and paid them disproportionately high salaries.[27] The CCP was also involved among the faculty. Beginning in the mid-1930s, the party deployed an underground network of members in the schools.[28] Underground Communists organized teacher associations, cooperatives, financial assistance, seminars, and protests against the government. They set up student groups and activities to promote political resistance. They even ran a handful of campuses and used them to provide cover for party members fleeing persecution. Although such activities indicated that the secondary school was an important battleground in the Communist movement in Shanghai, the dominant relationship the CCP forged with the faculty was based on disdain and disregard. Uncomfortable with these people's middle-class backgrounds and outlooks, the party recruited only a very small number of them into the underground network.[29] The rest were considered too politically backward or unreliable to be at the forefront of the revolutionary movement.

Because none of the above political forces had sufficient personnel, public support, or organizational means to penetrate the schools, none acquired consistent dominance over the faculty. Throughout the 1930s and 1940s, Shanghai secondary school teachers had a great deal of room to decide appointments, curricula, salaries, and other work-related issues. Their professional training, social status, and daily involvement in the schools facilitated the latter's rationalization, which was both assisted and interrupted by KMT policies. The Japanese occupation and the civil war strained this rationalization by dividing the faculty and reversing gains in organization. Nonetheless, on the eve of the 1949 revolution, the schools were basically managed by well-educated people controlling their own work. Their bureaucratization, albeit immature, would influence the ways in which faculty members reacted to Leninist-based reforms of the campuses.

THE MASS HIRING OF "UNEMPLOYED INTELLECTUALS"

Faculty composition in Shanghai secondary schools underwent dramatic changes after the Communist revolution. Thousands of people whom the authorities referred to as "unemployed intellectuals" (*shiye zhishifenzi*) were hired as classroom instructors between 1949 and 1957. These were former KMT officials, military officers, and state employees; enterprise managers, bank employees, and shop owners; schoolteachers and white-collar workers; as well as members of landlord families, housewives, and students.[30] Although their recruitment facilitated an unprecedented expansion of schooling opportunities, it deflated the academic qualifications of the faculty and destroyed its relative social homogeneity.

TABLE 2.1

*Secondary School[a] Administrators, Teachers, Staff Members,
and Students in Shanghai, 1946–65*

Academic year	Teachers, administrators, and supporting staff			Students	Students per teacher
	Teachers	Administrators[b] and staff members[c]	Total		
1946	–	–	4,469	74, 415	–
1947	–	–	–	–	–
1948	–	–	5,474	83,388	–
1949	4,478	1,309	5,787	85,455	19.1
1950	3,912	1,679	5,591	92,319	23.6
1951	3,990	1,644	5,634	102,563	25.7
1952	4,699	1,787	6,486	147,060	31.3
1953	5,270	1,978	7,248	161,758	30.7
1954	6,881	2,412	9,293	198,936	28.9
1955	7,441	2,496	9,937	225,398	30.3
1956	10,581	3,376	13,957	291,338	27.5
1957	12,330	3,891	16,221	308,087	25.0
1958[d]	14,234	4,769	19,003	362,664	25.5
1959	14,467	5,110	19,577	339,141	23.4
1960	15,503	5,588	21,091	356,660	23.0
1961	17,051	5,968[e]	23,019[e]	358,407	21.0
1962	18,611	6,267	24,878	394,243	21.2
1963	21,276	6,969[e]	28,245[e]	442,726	20.8
1964	24,115	7,688[e]	31,783[e]	521,602	21.6
1965	26,688	8,354	35,042	576,185	21.6

SOURCES: Figures for 1946 come from *Zhonghua minguo sanshiwu nian Shanghaishi jiaoyu tongji* (1947, 3); figures for 1948 come from *Shanghaishi zhongdeng jiaoyu gaikuang* (1948, 18); figures for 1949–65 come from SMA B105-1-1502 (1956, 6), B105-1-1171 (1957, 2), B105-2-132 (1958–59, 12), B105-2-146 (1959, 1), B105-2-273 (1960, 4), B105-2-527 (1963, 6), B105-2-901 (1965), and B105-2-967 (1966, 7–11).

[a]The figures include Western-style schools in urban and rural areas but not technical schools, temporary schools, and schools run by local communities or work organizations.

[b]Administrators include school principals, heads of instruction, and heads of general affairs. Party branch secretaries and political counselors are also included in this category.

[c]Staff members include administrative and instruction assistants and medical, technical, and library staff.

[d]The growth in 1958 is partly due to the incorporation of ten Jiangsu counties into Shanghai.

[e]My estimate.

After the revolution, the CCP adopted a Leninist approach to building a high-growth socialist society. One of its main strategies was to expand education to meet personnel needs for industrialization and the quest for cultural hegemony. In Shanghai, the secondary school system expanded rapidly. After 1949 student enrollment increased threefold, reaching three hundred thousand by 1957. By 1965 it had soared to six hundred thousand (see Table 2.1). Because the labor market was rather quickly replaced by official job assignment, the Shanghai municipal government was increasingly responsible for finding teachers to cope with enrollment expansion. From the beginning, however, a list of factors complicated the official effort.

The higher education system that had provided Shanghai with most of its secondary school teachers had been quite small. Its postrevolutionary growth, although impressive, could not keep up with the schools' demand for instructors. Concurrent reforms of government, industry, and other institutions further diverted college graduates from teaching positions. Even senior high school graduates, who had commonly entered teaching directly before 1949, were in short supply; they were targeted by the state for college enrollment. Moreover, the CCP steered other educated people away from teaching with promises of official or military careers. It purged from the campuses faculty members whom the local authorities found to be incompetent or to have had close ties to the KMT regime, and reassigned others who had been underground Communist agents to nonteaching posts or to work outside Shanghai. Last but not least, some teachers left the profession or the city entirely because of the political changes.[31]

Without sufficient access to desired teacher candidates, the government turned to the so-called unemployed intellectuals (see Table 2.2). Its action reflected the Leninist-based belief within the political leadership in Beijing that people with knowledge and skills should be utilized in the building of a socialist political economy. The 1952 Five-Anti Campaign reinforced this official decision. As the party attacked malfeasance in the urban economic sector, unemployment skyrocketed.[32] According to government statistics, Shanghai's unemployment jumped from 75,000 to more than 350,000 people.[33] To defuse a looming urban crisis, Beijing resolved that state agencies as well as public and private organizations should "absorb various kinds of unemployed individuals extensively."[34]

In the summer of 1952, the Shanghai Education Bureau (SEB) recruited three thousand unemployed intellectuals for training to be primary and secondary school teachers. The first of many groups to be recruited, these people seemed well suited to be schoolteachers. Two-thirds of them were college, technical college, or senior high school graduates; half were former schoolteachers. Most were rather young, with ages between twenty-five and thirty-five. Politically, however, the authorities were far from impressed. From confessions (*tanbai*) required by the authorities, it was revealed that six hundred of the unemployed intellec-

TABLE 2.2

Supply of Secondary School Teachers in Shanghai, 1949–63

	1949–57 (%)	1958–63 (%)
JUNIOR HIGH SCHOOLS		
Unemployed intellectuals	53	15
Transferred cadres	20	17
Former primary school teachers	14	1
Teachers college graduates	13	67
TOTAL	100	100
SENIOR HIGH SCHOOLS		
Unemployed intellectuals	67	4
College or teachers college graduates	23	95
Former junior high school teachers	10	1
TOTAL	100	100

SOURCE: Lü Xingwei (1994, 294).

NOTE: The figures do not include part-time teachers and full-time administrators.

tuals had had ties to the KMT regime.[35] Forty-nine had held leadership positions in the Nationalist Party or its branch organizations, mostly as local party organizers or brigade heads in the KMT Youth Corps. Forty-eight had worked for one or more intelligence or paraintelligence agencies—half for the powerful Military Bureau of Statistics and Investigation or the Central Bureau of Statistics and Investigation. Another thirty-eight people had held powerful offices in the KMT government. One had been a vice minister in the central government; another, a former head of the SEB. There were former military and police officers, former landlords, drug traffickers, and convicts, as well as recently dismissed state employees.[36]

Given the situation in both urban and rural areas, it is hardly surprising that the SEB found many of the unemployed intellectuals it had recruited politically questionable. The CCP takeover of all levels of government and key areas of the public and private sectors displaced many KMT officials, military officers, and party or Youth Corps members. The expropriation of rural land in the early 1950s had forced landlords and their families to seek refuge in urban areas. The closure of unwanted or unprofitable establishments (for example, trading firms and dance halls) by the authorities or by their owners created a large group of unemployed managers, shop owners, and white-collar workers. Many of the displaced had signed up for official assistance as unemployed intellectuals.[37] When the government began to recruit schoolteachers among unemployed intellectuals, they automatically became teacher candidates.

Although the government was aware of the recruits' backgrounds, it still installed 99 percent of these people in teaching positions after six weeks of political and pedagogical training.[38] With the dire need to tackle climbing unemployment as well as teacher shortages, the government truly had no other solution as viable or convenient as letting these recruits teach. With policies that accelerated unemployment and education expansion at the same time, the Communist regime had, in effect, reinforced its own Leninist stance that it would have to exploit the former elite to pursue socialist development.

A close look at another teacher-training class further clarifies the backgrounds of the unemployed intellectuals who became secondary school instructors in Shanghai in the 1950s. This class that took place in 1955 was strictly designed to prepare secondary school teachers; the students were selected through an open academic exam. Nearly 4,000 unemployed intellectuals took the exam, and 801 were admitted. Thanks to the exam, the class was well educated, as 90 percent of the people had finished senior high school. Compared with the prerevolutionary faculty, however, they had far fewer college degrees. Their proportion of college graduates, 30 percent, was half that of the prerevolutionary faculty.[39]

According to their confessions, the class contained quite a few delinquent, disgruntled, and undisciplined individuals. Six percent had been dismissed from their previous jobs; another 6 percent were college graduates who had refused job assignments; almost 3 percent had been convicted of embezzlement, theft, or counterrevolutionary behavior; and an unspecified number were former government employees who had rejected reassignment or offers for relocation. Furthermore, many others stated that they had little professional experience: 20 percent reported chronic unemployment or poor health, 18 percent claimed to be college dropouts, and 4 percent identified themselves as housewives.

Because this class coincided with *Sufan* (the 1955 Campaign to Wipe Out Hidden Counterrevolutionaries), another—substantially worse—picture of the unemployed intellectuals emerged as the SEB suspended teacher training to investigate whether "counterrevolutionaries" were present in the class. Skeptical of the confessions, class officials contacted the work organizations, public associations, and people named by the unemployed intellectuals and sought assistance from the police. They discovered that many had "fabricated history, misrepresented age, concealed identity, and forged letterheads, official seals, and identification documents" to enroll in the class.[40] Former KMT personnel underreported their ages to hide their rank. Former landlords, capitalists, and their family members lied about their upbringing. Some people used counterfeit letters of appointment or teacher certificates to demonstrate work experience they did not have or conceal work they had done. After the investigation, the SEB indicated that roughly half of the class were "unproblematic," but the rest "more or less had some problems."

In particular, eighty people were said to have "key problems." They included individuals whom the government identified as former "special-service agents" (*tewu*) or "ranking officials" associated with the Nationalist regime, "suspects who had been sent [to the Mainland] by [enemies in] Taiwan and Hong Kong," and "members of the five-categories of counterrevolutionaries" who had so far evaded punishment by the CCP authorities. There were "fugitive despotic landlords," "class enemies," and "Trotskyite suspects," as well as "various types of bad elements, CCP traitors and defectors, degenerates, hoodlums, and law-breaking and criminal elements."[41]

In an intense political climate, the SEB probably exaggerated the political or criminal backgrounds of some of the people, especially those who had not been cooperative during the investigation or whose confessions seemed disingenuous. Some in the class may have confessed to fictitious wrongdoing or political activity to prove their "honesty" or commitment to the campaign. In Chapters 3 and 5, I probe further into the confessions and investigations imposed on Shanghai secondary school teachers by the government. Suffice it to mention here that the truth about the backgrounds of this or any class of unemployed intellectuals probably lies between what they "volunteered" in confessions and what the authorities claimed to have discovered later through further investigation. But, as we have seen, even the information collected through confessions proved troubling to the authorities.

In the end, the SEB expelled forty-four people from the class. Some were arrested, and others were simply sent home.[42] The number of expulsions, which may seem small in light of the authorities' insistence that half of the class had "problems," was not a tacit acknowledgment that class officials had overreacted toward the problematic candidates. To the contrary, it shows that as the authorities tried to alleviate both the teacher shortage and unemployment, they recruited as many un-employed intellectuals as possible into the teaching profession—even those known to have "dubious" political or criminal backgrounds. When the *Sufan* campaign ended, the SEB still maintained that the social composition of the class was "complicated." But it suggested that few of the unemployed intellectuals matched the definition of counterrevo-lutionaries or criminals, as "the *overwhelming majority* of the class were decent people with *severe problems*."[43] What this means is that when in-terrogated, most of the unemployed intellectuals confessed their class backgrounds, work history, criminal records, or political involvement to the authorities' satisfaction. They were thus permitted to continue their teacher training.

A brief look at two of the unemployed intellectuals targeted for spe-cial investigation suggests the extent to which the government toler-ated the use of former KMT officials and other "dubious" people as schoolteachers. The SEB reported that Wang Zhengfu had worked closely with the KMT regime, especially its military. He had been a secretary to second lieutenants in a paramilitary unit, an assistant to second lieutenants in the Chief Operation Headquarters of the Military Commission, and a secretary to lieutenant colonels in the Military Af-fairs Bureau. He had also been an editor of a KMT-sponsored newspa-per and had contributed to the blacklisting of CCP sympathizers. After the revolution, he fabricated attendance at a teachers' school to hide his political work. After his past was dug up by the SEB, he was permit-ted to stay in teacher training.[44] The SEB also allowed Hua Weilian to become a schoolteacher despite her background and wrongdoing. She had grown up in a landlord family, joined the KMT Youth Corps in the early 1940s, and developed "complicated social relations." During *Su-fan*, the authorities found out that she had lied about her age to conceal what she had done after the revolution; in fact, she had "wormed her way" into a government office in Guangdong. She had also "seduced" a district CCP secretary in an attempt to steal materials to forge proof of membership in the Communist Youth League. Dismissed from her job in Guangdong, Hua later came to Shanghai and signed up for teacher training.[45]

By the mid-1950s the SEB was encountering unemployed intellectu-als of "questionable" political background with increasing frequency. Because they feared or disdained the new regime, former KMT agents, business owners, rural landlords, and others had avoided state assistance in the early 1950s despite being unemployed. But as they depleted their savings, some began to need work. Teacher training offered such people an opportunity to earn a livelihood. By mid-decade, the population of unemployed intellectuals also contained white-collar workers who had been dismissed for wrongdoing after the revolution as well as the persistently unemployed—that is, people who had been rejected by multiple employers. These fired employees and unemployables also regarded teacher training as a way to return to work.

In a 1956 teacher-training class that contained twelve hundred people, the SEB discovered one hundred "counterrevolutionaries, moral degenerates, and total incompetents." It quickly dismissed fourteen, recommended forty for removal, and identified forty for further investigation. Some of those who were removed or about to be removed were guilty of sexual assault. Some reportedly had poor work ethics, and others were found to be politically, academically, or mentally unqualified to be teachers.[46] For good reasons, the SEB had tightened the recruitment of unemployed intellectuals because after two years of official intervention, Shanghai's unemployment had dropped below one hundred thousand from some three hundred thousand. The government was therefore less pressed to find jobs for the unemployed. Thanks to the growth of higher education, the SEB also had better access to college and teachers college graduates. In a word, unemployed intellectuals had become less indispensable as teacher candidates (see Table 2.2).

THE ARRIVAL OF TRANSFERRED CADRES

After the 1949 revolution, Shanghai secondary schools absorbed large numbers of what the government called transferred cadres (*zhuanye ganbu*) into the teaching ranks. These were originally staff members in government offices, mass organizations, or state-owned enterprises.[47] The authorities inserted a substantial number of Communist Party members into school management. Also called transferred cadres, these campus administrators are not included in the teacher statistics in Table 2.2. As the next chapter shows, their arrival entirely transformed the school authority structure. My focus now is on those transferred cadres who acted as ordinary instructors. Their recruitment surged after 1954 and reshaped faculty composition in academic and political terms that worried the authorities.

On paper, the transfer of these cadres to the schools provided "help and support" in classrooms as student enrollment climbed. In reality, it was part of an official plan to downsize a state and a banking system Beijing considered too unwieldy for the economy.[48] Some of the redundant staff would be used to alleviate teacher shortages. Under this circumstance, the Shanghai Education Bureau approached government offices and state-owned enterprises to outline its requirements for the transferees. These establishments would deliver selected personnel files (*dang'an*) to the SEB so that it could choose the people it wanted. In practice, the organizations that had been ordered by Beijing to reduce their labor force gained an opportunity to rid themselves of unwanted staff. Acting in their own best interests, they kept their most highly qualified employees and released the less desirable. At the other end, the schools received people whom management might have chosen to reject had it been given more authority over hiring. Sometimes, the transferees were offered teacher training by the SEB; at other times, they reported directly to schools.

In spring 1954, the SEB received the first batch of personnel files from twenty-four establishments within or near Shanghai. Out of 788 cadres, it selected 450 to be secondary school teachers and 119 to be primary school teachers. Those chosen were quite well educated, as 73 percent had gone to college, but they included 117 former Nationalist Party or Youth Corps members. Also among them were 14 Communist Youth Leaguers and 2 Communist Party members, but one of the Communists was suspected of being a former KMT special-service agent.[49] The SEB categorically rejected 158 people: 71 suffered from health problems such as tuberculosis and arthritis; 57 had "relatively serious problems in their history or complicated backgrounds"; and 30 did not meet the education requirement or "other conditions" to be a teacher.[50]

That so many of the cadres made available to the SEB were unsuitable was no accident. The SEB complained that some establishments "had not seriously screened their candidates for transfer; to some extent, they had the idea of pushing out unwanted staff members." Others did not forward to the SEB the performance evaluations or political reports of the candidates as requested by the agency. Even worse, some of the personnel files contained such remarks as "this staff member has a complicated history; deliver to the Shanghai Municipal Department of Education and Culture for handling" or, more bluntly, "cleanse and transfer to other kinds of work."[51]

Nevertheless, transferred cadres presented a lesser political challenge to the SEB than unemployed intellectuals. The CCP had already removed unwanted people from governments and state-owned enterprises during its political takeover and during the political campaigns conducted afterward. The fact that the above cadres still had jobs indicates that they had passed some kind of political screening. By contrast, unless the SEB carefully investigated an unemployed intellectual, it could not reliably understand his or her background.

If transferred cadres had better political records than unemployed intellectuals, they also had weaker professional qualifications to be teachers, because they were generally referred to the SEB rather than selected by open exams. In the 1955 class in the last section that solely enrolled unemployed intellectuals in teacher training, it was reported that they responded well to the training, and some actually felt that the instruction was too easy. By contrast, in a later class containing both transferred cadres and unemployed intellectuals referred by government offices and neighborhood resident committees, the SEB reported the following observation.

The teacher trainees have a fair cultural level, but they are quite old (usually around 40) and have difficulties remembering new things. They have been out of school a long time and have largely forgotten what they learned. In reality, their level of knowledge is far below the students who are currently studying in high school. In a test given to the trainees in biology, 37 out of 120 people did not have a junior-high-level understanding of the subject.[52]

Even those who had earned a college degree were found lacking.

Most of them have studied or graduated in finance, politics, law, etc. Only a few have their major matching the subject they are now studying. As for their level of professional knowledge, most of them are practically comparable to senior high school graduates. In addition, since what they learned in high school differs from what is taught now, and they have been out of school for a long time and forgotten much of what they learned, they may not even have the level of knowledge of a senior high school graduate.[53]

In the course of training, SEB officials realized that they had expected too much from the class, as many were overwhelmed by the instruction. They complained that the materials were "too much and too difficult," and the pace of the class was "too fast." The agency was forced to revise the curriculum to concentrate on junior high school texts, a change that made the class feel "much relieved." In another class, the SEB confronted the same problems. "Based on the experience" of the previous class, it decided to use only junior high materials and "eschew strict requirements and relatively high expectations" regarding the performance of the class.[54]

The People's Bank of China was the biggest supplier of transferred cadres to Shanghai's primary and secondary schools, shipping out more than two thousand people between 1954 and 1957. What occurred with the transfers illustrates another problem associated with teacher recruitment. From "plenty of letters and visitors," the SEB found out that the bank had released many of its least healthy employees. Some complaints went directly to the Central Ministries of Propaganda and Education or other higher authorities. They accused the SEB of "padding the number of teachers without regard to quality" and the bank of dumping unwanted employees on the schools. Questioned by Beijing, the bank admitted that "some individual branches had shipped out cadres of relatively poor health," including individuals with "physiological deficiencies" and "stuttering."[55] Those now employed in the schools were found to have a range of health problems, from tuberculosis, heart disease, and poor eyesight and hearing to nervous conditions. The SEB noted that one district government received sixty-three bank transferees but returned twenty of them.[56] Another district government complained to the Shanghai Municipal Committee that none of the ten it had received were fit to be primary school teachers:

One person had severe anemia and a weak heart, and could not stand up for an extended period. After teaching for a few days, he really could not hold the post and was returned [to the SEB]. Five other people had various illnesses, and they were gradually returned, too. Now, four of them are here, but some are on sick leave, and others have asked the school to report to the authorities their hardship in keeping the posts. . . . Our schools have a lot of complaints about the way cadres are transferred and assigned. They feel that it increases confusion and disturbs teaching. Parents complain, too. One of the parents even took the complaint to court.[57]

Some of the health problems were age-related. In 1956 nearly 40 percent of some twelve hundred bank transferees were above forty years of age; the bank had probably shed its older staff members because Beijing considered younger ones politically more reliable.[58] Other health problems were probably exacerbated by the stress of job reassignment. The bank transferees saw their careers totally, suddenly, or involuntarily transformed. Most suffered a loss in prestige; some had to travel greater distances to work. These changes caused some of them to overstate their health problems in the hopes of pressuring the SEB to return them to the bank. After receiving a deluge of complaints, the SEB approached the bank and reiterated the requirements (including good health) that transferees had to satisfy. To forestall further damage, it more carefully examined those transferred, rejecting the unhealthy or unqualified before putting the rest into teaching positions.

The Hundred Flowers Campaign of 1957 resulted in basic changes in the reassignment of cadres to schools. With official sanction, professionals, intellectuals, and students nationwide criticized the government. Intended by Beijing to be constructive and comradely—like "a gentle breeze or mild rainfall"—the criticisms intensified into scathing attacks against the ruling regime and local officials. Angry and embarrassed, the CCP leadership ended the campaign abruptly and launched the Anti-Rightist Campaign to reassert control over state and society. Having been hotbeds of dissent, schools and colleges saw a major change in their authority structures. The CCP initiated "the replacement of white flags with red flags" (*ba baiqi cha hongqi*) by assigning officials and military officers who were party members to occupy management and teaching posts. At the same time, it continued to use other cadres to fill teaching positions. In 1958 and 1959 alone, the schools received more than fifteen hundred cadres, most of whom had worked in the Shanghai municipal government or nearby provincial governments.[59]

The cadres who were given teaching positions during this period included former college students and graduates as well as people who had taught before. As a group, however, they were just as, if not more, ill qualified to teach than the transferred cadres who were already in the faculty. The only academic requirement for the transferees set by the SEB was that they have "the cultural level of a senior high school education" or "a cultural level comparable to that of a senior high school graduate."[60] This encouraged the transfer of such people to the schools. No wonder, then, that when the SEB surveyed the cadres it had received, it reported that they were "not familiar with educational work, and their cultural levels were not high."[61]

Thanks to the state objective of strengthening political control over the faculty, these cadres had better political backgrounds or records than the earlier arrivals. Before the start of the 1959 academic year, the SEB placed almost two thousand cadres in teaching positions in primary and secondary schools. It reported with satisfaction that 53 percent of these people were CCP members or "activists on the left," and

20 percent were from peasant or worker families.[62] But this does not mean that the transferees did not include cadres the authorities considered politically unreliable. Precisely because the transfers occurred during and after the Anti-Rightist Campaign, some organizations shipped away staff members deemed to be political liabilities. Although these people were not labeled or punished as "rightists," they were removed from their workplaces practically against their will.

Among the transferred cadres I met who became schoolteachers during this period, one was a CCP member who had been a section chief (*kezhang*) in a district department of propaganda in Shanghai. He recalls that his superiors had sought unsuccessfully to "catch his pigtail," that is, find evidence that he had attacked the CCP, during the Anti-Rightist Campaign. But they transferred him out of the department anyway when it had to send cadres to "support" the schools.[63] Another former cadre who had worked in the Shanghai Public Security Bureau insists that had she not been born to parents of "bourgeois background" she would have remained at her government post, untouched by the movement. She still believes that she was taken out of the bureau because of her class background.[64]

CHAN SHAZI: INSERTION OF WORKERS

Officially running a workers' state, the CCP both programmatically and strategically appointed industrial and manual workers as secondary school teachers to counterbalance a profession it considered too bourgeois in composition and influence. It called this use of workers *chan shazi*—literally, the insertion of sand particles. Borrowed from the construction industry, the metaphor means the mixing of sand into cement paste to produce firm concrete blocks, suggesting that the transferred workers could help turn the faculty into a stronger instrument for building socialism. In practice, their recruitment further depressed the technical qualifications of the faculty.

The appointment of workers to Shanghai secondary schools began in the late 1950s, as the CCP sought to "replace white flags with red flags." For example, in 1960 three hundred workers arrived at the schools.[65] Compared with unemployed intellectuals and transferred cadres, the number of such workers in the faculty was small, no more than three or four per school. Due to family hardship, these people had normally joined the workforce as workers, laborers, or apprentices when they were teenagers. By the time they were reassigned to the schools, most of them were Communist Party members and not strictly workers anymore. They held low- or midlevel administrative posts in state-owned or collective enterprises, often in the areas of organizing young workers or propaganda.

As a group, these former workers formed the most undereducated segment of the teaching staff. They usually had attended junior or senior high school, but intermittently and in less esteemed campuses due to inability to afford a regular or prestigious education. Even though they might be junior or even senior high school graduates, their academic training was inferior to that of other teachers with the same level of education. Because of their worker and party backgrounds and limited education, these worker cadres concentrated on teaching politics classes. After the revolution, the CCP changed the secondary school curriculum. Although most subjects were preserved, their content, especially in the case of history, literature, and geography, was reinterpreted and rewritten based on Marxist-Leninist principles. The regime added classes on socialist politics to help students gain a "correct" understanding of socialism, the Chinese Communist Party, the 1949 revolution, and recent events inside and outside China. These classes were originally taught by CCP members or activists within the faculty. With the outpouring of faculty and student disaffection during the Hundred Flowers Campaign, Beijing decided to strengthen political indoctrination in the school system. *Chan shazi* was a key strategy; political training of students by workers was an important tool.

Yan Lanfen, another retired teacher whom I met, was an excellent example of the workers appointed to the schools. Her parents were illiterate and only able to support her primary education. In 1953, when she was seventeen, she found a job in a small factory and began to enroll irregularly in an evening junior high school. She later took some senior high school classes and moved to a larger factory. In 1956 she joined the CCP and then the factory administration. Four years later, she was reassigned to teach politics at the secondary level. She also became a homeroom teacher (*banzhuren*) responsible for the academic, political, and moral development of fifty students.[66]

In the beginning, Yan was completely unfamiliar with her work. She had trouble writing and giving lectures as well as keeping classroom order. The fact that she taught politics, rather than a conventional subject such as mathematics or history, should have helped her performance.

In practice, it barely did. In an unstable political climate, she needed to constantly reinterpret old political texts and grapple with new political ideas. Yan remembers her difficulties vividly.

I was not used to the school at first. Life was very difficult. I taught classes and handled homeroom responsibilities immediately after I arrived. I was a party committee member organizing the school Communist Youth League. I also had two kids at home. On the first day of class, I greeted the class with "Comrade, how are you doing?" The whole class laughed at me [because no other teachers would do that]. I felt very embarrassed. . . . The school principal told me that I could do whatever I wanted in the class. There was no textbook for the class. I picked out newspaper and magazine articles and helped my students study them. . . . My classes were boisterous. The students did not listen to me. Still, I kept working, unlike some workers who left and returned to their factories.[67]

Despite difficulties like these, the ex-workers who stayed in the schools were generally more receptive toward the reassignment than the cadres from banks or governments. For one thing, the CCP valorized workers' participation in the faculty as a remedy for the ills exposed during the Hundred Flowers Campaign. It bestowed their work with extraordinary prestige. Furthermore, although official attacks on the "backward" politics or thinking of intellectuals intensified after the campaign, some workers still considered their reassignment a promotion. This had to do with the traditionally high status accorded to scholars and the learned in China. No doubt the CCP had challenged, quite successfully, this deep-rooted thinking, but it did not therefore eradicate such admiration even among workers who were the main beneficiaries of the party's anti-intellectualism. As Yan recalls, she had always wanted to become an intellectual (*zhishifenzi*), and therefore, she regarded her assignment as "an opportunity to make her wish come true."

In the early 1960s another group of former workers and laborers began to join the faculty. They were much more qualified to teach than the above workers, because they had come through the university rather than directly from the factory. Once they arrived, they taught a variety of subjects besides politics. Retired teacher Tian Yipeng was an example. Born to a poor family, he had started working as a teenager and was hired by the SEB before the revolution as a janitor-messenger. After the CCP takeover of the agency, he supported official policies, personnel, and activities and was recruited into the party in 1953. Recommended by his superior, he enrolled in a so-called worker-peasant intensive high school (*gongnong suzhong*). Four years later, he graduated from the school and passed the college entrance exam. He then studied Chinese at college level and interned as a secondary school instructor. In 1961 he graduated from college and became a secondary school teacher.[68]

After the government abolished worker-peasant intensive high schools in the mid-1950s, it trained former workers by other means to be secondary school teachers, especially politics instructors. In Shanghai, the East China Normal University offered a two-year academic program for such workers.[69] Although enrollment was based on recommendation by the local authorities, it was actually harder for workers to become schoolteachers than before. Most colleges were reluctant to invest in people without proven secondary education; they tended to screen the referred workers rigorously and reject most of them.[70] It is not known how many workers became secondary school teachers in Shanghai in the early 1960s through such college training. The number was probably in the low hundreds.

A DECLINE IN TEACHING PERFORMANCE

The recruitment of unemployed intellectuals, transferred cadres, and former workers as secondary school instructors contributed to a rapid decline in faculty academic qualifications. Before the revolution, 60 percent of the entire faculty and staff were university graduates. A decade later, the proportion was cut by half—30 percent of the faculty, including almost 30 percent of the teaching ranks, were university graduates. A similar proportion of the rank-and-file instructors did not have any college education (see Table 2.3). More important for our analysis, teaching performance dropped precipitously.

As early as 1955, the SEB reported that the new teachers—at that time mainly unemployed intellectuals and transferred cadres—made up 60 to 80 percent of the faculty in most campuses. It indicated that they had "poor basic knowledge and lacked teaching experience."[71] The following year it surveyed seven schools of different academic standing and noted that there were "many problems" with the new teachers. Some of them could not lecture smoothly, interestingly, or correctly even after they had worked hard to prepare for classes. The transferred cadres, former housewives, and others whose own schooling had ended long ago found writing lectures a very demanding task, and they had already received course reference materials during teacher training. In general, primary school teachers who had been promoted to the secondary level lacked "professional knowledge" (see Table 2.2). Their

TABLE 2.3

Levels of Education of the Shanghai Secondary School Faculty, 1959

	University graduation or above		Some college education		High school graduation or less		
	n	%	n	%	n	%	Total
Principals	148	31	129	27	206	43	483
Party secretaries	9	9	28	27	66	64	103
Heads of instruction	238	44	179	33	120	22	537
Teachers	4,532	29	6,838	45	4,145	27	15,515
TOTAL	4,927	30	7,174	44	4,537	27	16,638

SOURCE: SMA B105-2-138 (1959).

lectures were "not penetrating, encompassing, or effective for student learning."[72] They and other teachers needed seven or eight hours to prepare one lecture, which could still turn out "relatively dry."[73] Moreover, their unfamiliarity with the profession made it harder for them to do a good job. They had difficulty using the grading system, classroom diaries, student handbooks, and other standard teaching tools. They were not ready to manage the classroom, and they often became "passive and inactive" when their efforts at classroom discipline failed.[74]

In 1957 the SEB issued another gloomy report on teachers' capabilities. Its views might have been influenced by the faculty's political complaints and attacks during the Hundred Flowers Campaign. Still, they were consistent with other evaluations of teachers in the 1950s and even 1960s and represented genuine concerns about teaching performance. It was estimated that only 20 percent of all primary and secondary school teachers had "thorough knowledge" of the subjects they taught and the ability to learn to teach new material on their own. These instructors had usually been teaching for some time. Another 40 percent had "basic knowledge" of the subjects but did not understand them thoroughly and, without retraining, would have trouble teaching from a new syllabus. This group of people generally lacked teaching experience, and the quality of their instruction was only average. A discouraging 40 percent of the teachers could "barely manage" or "had grave difficulties" with the subjects they taught. Both their level of knowledge and teaching performance were quite poor. They needed to be retrained in these subjects before being allowed to teach anything new.[75]

Where new teachers predominated, the quality of instruction seemed to have suffered most. The teachers at Xinning Secondary School were mostly former unemployed intellectuals, state cadres, or primary school teachers, and 60 percent of them had no more than two years of teaching experience. The school principal there reported that 90 percent of the teachers were not familiar with teaching or pedagogical methods, and those who had been reluctant to come to the campus in the first place were "mentally and emotionally confused" after they arrived.[76]

To be sure, the new teachers' poor performance cannot be blamed solely on their lack of academic qualifications. Because student enrollment increased rapidly, most of them had received brief or even no training before their appointments. Many became teachers not by personal choice but by state order or as a last resort, and they had come to resent their job. The sudden expansion of secondary education inserted into the schools a large number of working-class youths from illiterate or poorly educated families who were unfamiliar with classroom conventions. Moreover, teachers were compelled to use new textbooks or to reinterpret familiar texts according to changing official thinking. In short, the state did not provide these teachers with a stable working or learning environment. Ultimately, however, the cause of the new teachers' failures made little difference to the socialist project, as the result was the same: harm to the academic performance of the schools and, therefore, to the development of a successful socialist system.

As the new instructors gained teaching experience and the schools obtained larger numbers of college and teachers college graduates to fill teaching vacancies, teaching performance improved, as the SEB had expected. However, it did not improve to the extent that teaching competence became the rule rather than the exception. In the early 1960s the SEB still expressed serious concerns about teaching performance while acknowledging improvements. Despite all the gains in size, Shanghai secondary education had hit an impasse in pedagogical development. "The group of teachers who are experienced and effective is rather small. Some teachers have poor knowledge and teaching performance. In general, the professional levels of the teachers in our schools, except large schools and key-point schools, are still not good enough to meet the demands of raising the quality of education."[77] In most campuses, the SEB stated, about 20 percent of the teachers were competent and effective; 55 to 65 percent lacked teaching experience or understanding of their subjects of instruction; and the rest were just poor teachers.[78]

What happened with the politics classes the government inserted into the curriculum was especially indicative of this failure, because they were intended to help students develop a firm commitment to socialism and Communist Party rule. Even here, however, the SEB detected that there were few effective instructors. Most teachers were cadres from government or the military or borrowed from other courses. They generally had no training in teaching Marxism-Leninism or political topics. As for the workers who had recently joined the faculty because of *chan shazi*, they had a "relatively low cultural and theoretical level"— too low for them to be effective instructors. Whether SEB officials were aware of this or not, they had contradicted Beijing's belief that these ex-workers would strengthen students' political instruction.[79]

To the Shanghai authorities, however, it seemed that these unfavorable conditions in the schools would end soon. After all, large numbers of college and teachers college graduates had begun to join the faculty annually (see Table 2.2), and teacher retraining programs had been established. With such recruitment and retraining, the SEB estimated that a breakthrough in the quality of education should occur in a few years. To quicken the process, it planned further training for the top performers, politically and professionally, among those new teachers who were recent graduates. The intention was to turn them into "leading members of the teaching staff" (*jiaoyu gugan*). By 1966, the SEB predicted, the schools would have three hundred of these young, energetic, and capable teachers to oversee academic instruction.[80] The breakthrough, of course, did not happen. Instead, the Cultural Revolution ravaged the entire institution of education, leading to a deepened crisis in the faculty.

CULTURAL CLEAVAGES IN THE FACULTY

Besides hurting academic instruction, the post-1949 methods of teacher recruitment engendered new types of faculty tensions. As the government compelled people who had been separated by class, education, or lifestyle to work together, individual values, expectations, and habits clashed, creating what can be called cultural tensions. Throughout this book, I will describe different types of faculty tensions that resulted from the production and reproduction of counter-bureaucracy in the schools. An integral part of the faculty culture, these tensions had political, cultural, economic, and ethical roots that reflected the material and ideal interests of faculty members. My aim is to demonstrate that Shanghai secondary schools became a severely divided workplace that harmed rather than benefited socialist development.

As unemployed intellectuals and transferred cadres joined the faculty on state orders, a schism developed immediately between these people and the prerevolutionary faculty. Well educated, middle class, and still quite well respected in the early years after the revolution, the senior teachers disliked having colleagues with inferior education and little professional experience, or who had been pushed out by their previous employers. They regarded the hiring of rejected employees, semiskilled wage earners, and irregular labor force participants as an affront to the teaching profession, a death knell to its prerevolutionary status and prestige. A minority of the new teachers received warmer welcomes. These individuals had taught in secondary schools, gone to college, held a respectable job, or passed a teacher-recruitment exam. Some of them had no teaching experience, but in the senior teachers' eyes, they were at least qualified to begin a teaching career, unlike the rest of the newcomers.

For fear of punishment by the authorities, the senior teachers seldom attacked their new colleagues openly. Instead, they avoided these people, providing them with little assistance even though that was what they needed most. Xu Ruhua, a housewife of working-class background who started teaching in the mid-1950s, had this to say about her initial experience as a teacher. Her testimony betrays at once her lack of training, her difficulties in the classroom, and her isolation from her colleagues.

Although I passed an entrance exam for a teacher-training class and received months of training, I felt uneasy to become a schoolteacher, especially, a senior high teacher. Other teachers had gone to college, but my cultural level was not adequate. At first, it was very difficult for me. Students did not listen to me. I did not get any help from other teachers. I did not want to ask them for help either. I felt that those teachers who had a better education looked down upon me. Some of the teachers had opinions about my teaching. I worked on my own, and I was very busy.[81]

During the Hundred Flowers Campaign, the senior faculty expressed their genuine, disparaging opinions of the newcomers. In a series of "airing view" (*mingfang*) meetings organized by the SEB, they attacked the official policy of teacher recruitment. One teacher succinctly captured their status-based dissatisfaction. "Anyone can become a schoolteacher—people expelled from government organs, housewives, and politically dubious people. They thrust into the profession. As a result, people do not respect schoolteachers. They look down on them."[82]

SEB officials heard a multitude of complaints about the new teachers from teacher-training classes: they were "of inferior quality"; some "had very low levels of education"; and some had forged academic certificates to enter the classes. They allegedly put wrong characters on the blackboard and did not know how to control the classroom. Some senior teachers complained that the newcomers did not lecture but instead recited notes from teacher-training classes. There were complaints that chemistry teachers did not remember chemical formulas; one math teacher dared to write $41 \times 1 = 1$; another math teacher had a mental disorder; and a one-legged man was assigned to teach physical education. Some teachers said that the newcomers' teaching performance was so bad that they lost the students' respect.[83]

Complaints against transferred cadres reflected the SEB's own criticisms of governments and enterprises ridding themselves of unwanted staff, as well as the agency's observation that some cadres wanted to leave the schools badly. Some senior teachers called the cadres "an old, weak, and wounded troops" unsuitable for staffing classrooms. Others complained that former bank employees "knew nothing about teaching." They observed that some cadres applied for sick leave as soon as they arrived at the schools or claimed to be sick all the time. They told the authorities that both teachers and students in the schools were unhappy with the cadres.[84]

Because of their gender role, former housewives endured gender-specific disrespect from faculty members. Many of these women had not had any previous professional role that could be used to impress their colleagues. Still bound by family responsibilities, they normally did not immerse themselves in their newfound careers. Their lack of professional experience and ambition invited prejudice from a male-dominated and increasingly politicized society.[85] Lumping former housewives together with transferred cadres (specifically those from the People's Bank of China), Zhu Gongzheng, a teacher from the prerevolutionary faculty who joined the Communist Party in the mid-1950s, recalls that "these people did not resemble other teachers [at that time]. They looked like petty urbanites [rather than educators]. The housewives always made a hue and cry [when work was a little demanding]."[86] Another teacher of a similar background, a woman herself, echoes the complaint. "Housewives were relatively naive, not knowing much about politics and society, for they were not in full contact with society. They came to work on time and always tried to leave on time. Most of them did not really care about [political] activities. They liked to dress nicely and fashionably."[87]

Least educated among the newcomers, former workers became easy targets of disdain because they personified what senior teachers regarded as the invasion of the faculty by outsiders. In fact, senior teachers were not alone in looking down upon these people; the sentiment pervaded the entire faculty. None of the retired teachers I met who was not a former worker says anything positive about the workers. One man recalls that these workers "could not keep their heads up. Even if they wanted to teach well, they could not do it. . . . They themselves felt that they were unfit teachers."[88] Another remembers that former workers "were loyal to the party and diligent, doing whatever they were told by the party secretary. But they had no brains. . . . They did not teach well, and they felt inferior themselves. They wanted to return to the factory."[89] It is not clear that former workers were any more likely to fail as teachers than other new instructors, but these opinions do suggest that their presence in the faculty precipitated greater dissension.

Like other newcomers, former workers found it hard to get assistance from their senior colleagues, although they needed professional advice as badly as anyone else. They were quite aware of the tension surrounding their appointments. Yan Lanfen, the woman worker quoted above, says this about her colleagues: "I received no help from other teachers, and I did not ask for help either. On the surface, other teachers were polite to me. But what was in their hearts was not easy to tell."[90] Even those workers who had gone to college before becoming teachers felt rejected by other faculty members. As Tian Yipeng, another worker introduced above, explained: "If you were a worker or a peasant and you became a teacher, your position in the school was shaky if you lacked a bit of knowledge. Other teachers came from generations of scholar families, but our ancestors were laborers. On the surface, they looked up to you. But, in reality, they did not."[91]

It would be a mistake to think that the unemployed intellectuals, transferred cadres, and former workers were simply victims of senior teachers' disdain, or that they were always necessarily nothing but second-class citizens within the faculty. Because the CCP considered political qualifications more important than technical qualifications in the distribution of official authority, the senior teachers, however knowledgeable and experienced in classroom instruction, found themselves losing control of the schools shortly after the revolution. They were forced to work with the new teachers, just as the latter had little choice of occupation due to the disappearance of the labor market. The attack by these middle-class professional educators on their less-qualified colleagues was noteworthy precisely because they had no power to remove this group from the faculty. By contrast, despite lacking academic credentials or teaching experience, some unemployed intellectuals, transferred cadres and, especially, former workers were able to capitalize on their class background, work history, or political performance to promote their own careers. The schism between the senior faculty and the newcomers was therefore not based only on the cultural prejudice of the learned. It also reflected political tensions in the faculty. Such tensions, a key feature of counter-bureaucratic administration, are discussed in the next chapter.

SHORTAGES OF EXPERTISE IN SHANGHAI SECONDARY SCHOOLS

For Weber, recruitment by technical qualification is a central feature of modern bureaucratic administration. It enhances the level of knowledge and skills available to the organization and therefore its efficiency and reliability. Because staff members are selected on technical merit, they tend to share similar work styles, habits, and expectations. This helps strengthen their relations with one another as well as motivation to improve their individual performance and collective performance.

After the 1949 revolution, the CCP adopted the Leninist tactic of exploiting the former elite to help build a modernized socialist society. In Shanghai, however, large numbers of people who were unwilling or unable to teach entered the secondary school faculty. On the frontline of a historic political and cultural mission, the campuses were ironically marred by a serious lack of well-trained instructors. There were three basic reasons for this development: the school system expanded with unprecedented speed; the institutionalization of official job assignment terminated the campuses' right to select teachers; and the state combined teacher recruitment with efforts to reduce unemployment as well as reorganize government and the economy. With increasing numbers of college and teachers college graduates joining the faculty in the early

1960s, the Shanghai authorities envisioned that a breakthrough in the quality of instruction would happen within a short time. The Cultural Revolution, however, dashed any hope of that happening.

The lack of qualified personnel in the teaching ranks affected not only teaching performance, but also faculty solidarity. It pitted well-educated senior teachers against poorly trained newcomers. To senior teachers, the hiring of their new colleagues by the government destroyed the exclusivity or high status of their profession. The new teachers, for their part, resented their senior colleagues for being unhelpful and condescending and casting them as intruders unworthy of respect. The tensions between the two groups resulted in a lack of association and cooperation within the faculty—cooperation that might have helped to raise the quality of instruction or strengthen the schools' contribution to the developing socialist political economy.

The lack of qualified teachers indirectly led to a political problem for the CCP regime. This is because the official decision to permit former KMT agents, business managers, inferior employees, and others who were regarded as politically questionable to be schoolteachers naturally raised an important question: would these people use their capacity as state-appointed educators to sabotage the building of socialism or Communist Party rule? Of course, the regime faced a similar problem when it kept the prerevolutionary faculty in the schools. After all, during the 1930s and 1940s, the CCP had considered these teachers too unreliable to be a force in the revolutionary movement. However, postrevolutionary teacher recruitment intensified the risk of sabotage. In sum, although the CCP greatly expanded secondary education in Shanghai, the price was a decline in teaching performance, faculty solidarity, and official trust in schoolteachers. The risk of political sabotage by the faculty, in particular, was one that the authorities had no choice but to address. The next chapter, therefore, examines how the CCP reformed school management to control the faculty.

3

Political Domination and Its Discontents

> Party branches stink like toilets (*matong*). When you lift
> their lids up, they stink up the entire place. But there are
> people, that is, activists, who hold the toilets to the face and
> then say they don't smell at all!
>
> —a teacher's complaint during the Hundred Flowers

A fundamental objective of the socialist revolutions worldwide was the expropriation of the landlords and bourgeoisie to the extent that they could no longer reproduce themselves as social classes, let alone dominate other classes. From a Leninist perspective, however, the building of socialism also requires "a 'suspension' of the offensive against capital."[1] A brutal suppression of the former elite may well obviate counter-revolution, but it would hinder socialist development, too. In particular, the successful communist regime must utilize the knowledge and skills of the bourgeoisie to keep factories, universities, and other modern enterprises in operation. As long as the Russian working class was not trained sufficiently to manage production and reproduction, Lenin noted, the workers' state should "maneuver, retreat, wait, build slowly, ruthlessly tighten up, rigorously discipline, [and] smash laxity" to keep the bourgeoisie productive.[2] To achieve the latter objective, it must control with "workers' representatives" who would ensure compliance or, better yet, cooperation from the bourgeoisie.

In this chapter I describe the impact of this Leninist conception of politics and production on the development of counter-bureaucracy in Shanghai secondary schools. The Chinese Communist Party (CCP) deployed a heterogeneous group of Communist Party members to control the campuses. Conventionally underqualified to run the schools, these "workers' representatives" recruited a variety of activists from the faculty and staff for political and administrative support. The party further arranged for seasoned instructors, who were mainly from formerly privileged families and considered politically unreliable, to teach senior classes, mentor new teachers, or furnish necessary pedagogical skills. The new authority structure thus reflected the official desire to modernize as well as to tightly control the political economy. It placed political loyalty above technical competence, while legitimizing the importance of both.

The installation of this Leninist counter-bureaucratic structure of authority in the schools, however, caused great damage to faculty work and faculty life. Being representatives of a revolutionary regime, the party members treated their colleagues with suspicion and even contempt. The senior faculty, in turn, despised the party members and activists for lacking the professional qualifications to direct the campuses. They refused to cooperate fully. Unfamiliar with pedagogy and school administration, the party members failed to provide leadership in academic instruction and other matters. Even worse, because of their different backgrounds or training, some of them were unable to work together. Their internecine conflicts further fragmented an already divided faculty.

Put in a different way, for Weber, the technically based hierarchy in modern bureaucratic administrations is a superior feature of organization because it enhances the professional quality of the staff as well as their cooperation. In Leninist thinking, such a feature is but a product and tool of capitalist domination that must be abolished after the socialist revolution. Instead, communist regimes should simultaneously appoint "bourgeois experts" and "workers' representatives" to the workplace. The former would provide the technical leadership needed in production and reproduction; the latter, the political supervision necessary for the evolution toward socialism. Lenin believed that their efforts, when combined in such a manner, would compensate for the shortages of professional expertise and political loyalty in the workplace during the transition to socialism. What happened in Shanghai secondary schools shows that the two hierarchies—political and technical—were incompatible in practice, because genuine cooperation rarely existed between the politically and the technically qualified. Instead, faculty tensions intensified and persisted. In the end, the Leninist order of authority engendered three interrelated and harmful consequences in the schools: faculty conflict and political disaffection, faculty alienation from work, and ineffective campus management.

POLITICAL APPOINTMENT OF PARTY MEMBERS

As soon as the CCP seized Shanghai, it began to take over the public sector and extend political control over private enterprises, including secondary schools. During the 1956 "high tide of socialist transformation," it converted all remaining private campuses, which had for all intents and purposes been under state management, into public schools. The CCP takeover of the workplace involved the appointment of party members to management and the building of party cells for more comprehensive control. In Shanghai secondary schools, a relatively undereducated and mixed group of people came to occupy management positions and staff the party cells. Their ascent severed the positive relation between professional achievement and professional authority that had developed in the schools before the revolution.

Because of their relatively weak bargaining position within the CCP structure of institutions, Shanghai secondary schools had been equipped with fewer party members in the early 1950s than had industry and government in the city. Three years after the revolution, only 55 of the 232 regular or technical schools had the official minimum of three or more party members needed to form a party branch.[3] The rest were mostly what the government called "blank spots" without any party member in the faculty or staff.[4] As a whole, the schools had no more than 300 party members out of a total of 6,500 faculty and staff. By 1956, the number of party members in the schools had roughly tripled; more than 70 percent of the campuses had a party-member principal, and 5 percent of the faculty and staff had joined the party.[5] In the following six years, hundreds of party members were added to the schools annually from the outside and by recruitment of existing faculty members into the party. By the end of 1960, almost 70 percent of the regular schools had a party cell, and 13 percent of the faculty and staff were party members.[6]

The institutionalization of Communist Party control led to dramatic changes in school management composition. Since the party had not courted Shanghai secondary school teachers before the revolution, there were fewer than one hundred party members in the entire faculty on the eve of the takeover.[7] After the revolution, these former underground political agents became the first party members to direct the schools. Too few in number to staff 250 campuses, they were sent to the public schools, top private schools, and a few other campuses the party had chosen to initiate its domination of Shanghai secondary education. Depending on the schools and individual qualification, these party members assumed the posts of school principal, deputy school principal, head of instruction, or deputy head of instruction.[8]

Regardless of their level of appointment, these former underground agents became the most powerful people on campus. Backed by the party, they oversaw curriculum revision, teacher recruitment, student enrollment, and other reforms dictated from above. Having been teachers themselves, they were the most professionally qualified people to head the schools during the entire Mao era. Nonetheless, compared with the management personnel they replaced, they still lacked professional or even academic training. Whatever school management experience they had, if any, was in small or middle-rank campuses rather than the kind of prestigious or large schools most of them took over.

One of the appointees was Duan Lipei, who was originally trained as a primary school teacher. In the early 1940s he became a secondary school instructor as well as a Communist Party member. He later managed a small secondary school in Shanghai, turning it into what the party called a "red fortress." Shortly after the revolution, the party appointed him to take over the renowned Yucai Secondary School, whose former principals, as Duan himself recalls, were "distinguished personages," and whose teachers prior to the revolution were "very notable people."[9] Another appointee was ex-underground operative and college graduate Yao Jing. He received months of political training after the revolution before being assigned to be the deputy school principal and party secretary of a large public school where he had taught.[10] If not for the revolution, people like Duan or Yao, despite being veteran educators, would not have taken control of any of the top or large campuses on the strength of their professional qualifications.

In the early 1950s, the party also appointed some senior high school graduates and college students who were party members to the schools as politics instructors. On paper, these young teachers were there to help students learn about the party, the revolution, and socialism. In reality, they performed critical political functions for the regime. They studied campus physical structures and financial conditions, documented faculty backgrounds and behavior, investigated the student body, and helped organize campaigns and arrest "counterrevolutionaries" in the schools. Where there was no other party member, these young instructors became de facto campus leaders. By the mid-1950s, they began to assume formal positions of authority, becoming party secretaries, heads of instruction, and later school principals.

To tighten control of the campuses, the party inserted more of its own members into the faculty. Between 1952 and 1954 roughly two hundred officials who had joined the party at different times and worked in various agencies were reassigned to be school principals, party secretaries, heads of instruction, or politics teachers.[11] In principle, the school party secretaries supervised political matters and the party-member principals managed academic affairs. In the 1950s, however, this division of labor was rarely enforced. Because of concurrent reforms in various institutions, the party had trouble filling one, let alone both, of these positions with party members. In some schools, therefore, one person occupied the two posts; in others, two people shared the responsibilities. Not until after the Hundred Flowers debacle did the CCP elevate school party secretaries above party-member principals in a wider effort to tighten party control of the workplace.

Data collected by the Shanghai Education Bureau (SEB) on thirty-three party-member officials who became school principals in 1953 indicate that only five had experience or interests connected to education. The rest "lacked readiness" to be educators or would have preferred to join the privileged economic sector.[12] Another set of data on thirty-five party-member principals suggests that the reassigned officials were extraordinarily undereducated by prerevolutionary standards. Within this group, twelve had finished college; eight had some college education; five had some senior high education; eight had been to junior high school; and two had primary education only. Not all of these party members were reassigned officials—only those who did not finish senior high school—because the rest were former underground agents who had acted as teachers or young party members who had recently completed senior high education or attended college. In comparison, within the same survey, nine out of nine principals who were not party members had a bachelor's degree.[13]

Like the transferred cadres mentioned in Chapter 2, the reassigned party members included individuals who had been pushed out by their original workplaces. Some of these people had previously been punished by the party for corruption, insubordination, lack of discipline, or so-called pleasure-seeking lifestyle; others reportedly had had ties to Nationalist Party (KMT) personnel or had family members who had been disciplined by the government. With flawed political records or what the party deemed to be questionable social ties, these party members were no longer seen as adequately reliable by the party superiors in their original workplaces. But thanks to their senior party membership, they obtained top posts in the schools before the mid-1950s.

Wei Xingzhi was one of these party members. A veteran revolutionary with a junior high school education, he had worked in county-level departments of education, culture, and propaganda. The SEB noted that he had many good qualities but was not serious in his work. He had a lifestyle that was far from commendable and had recently been found guilty of corruption.[14] Chao Guoguang was another such party member. His father and grandfather were both labeled by the government as "landlord hegemons," and his mother was under criminal surveillance. He himself had reportedly helped his uncle, a top official in the exiled KMT regime, by delivering letters and money to relatives on the mainland.[15] Both Wei and Chao were reappointed as deputy school principals.

During a large-scale reorganization of the military in the 1950s, some military officers, normally company or battalion commanders, who were Communist Party members were also reappointed as school principals or party secretaries. These officers rarely had school management experience, but their military achievements entitled them, upon demobilization, to comparably ranked positions in the civilian sector. It is unclear how many such officers entered the schools directly; the number is probably not greater than fifty.[16] But as Hong Yung Lee noted, the military preferred to discharge those it found less useful or politically reliable, including ex-KMT officers, older or weaker soldiers, and those who "were low in cultural level."[17] This implies that some of the officers who entered school management also had unflattering political and academic records from the official perspective.

Because the Hundred Flowers debacle precipitated the so-called replacement of white flags with red flags in the late 1950s, large numbers of party members arrived at the schools during this period. Between 1957 and 1960, almost 250 officials became school principals or party secretaries.[18] They were sent to campuses where those posts had not been filled, where the incumbents had been removed, or where reinforcement was considered necessary. As before, these party members were not selected because they had experience running schools, but because they were regarded as politically reliable compared to the majority of the existing faculty members. In fact, for those who were politically eligible to be principals or party secretaries, the SEB only required them to have "a cultural level comparable to that of a junior high graduate" or "the cultural level of a junior high education." By contrast, others who were reassigned to be teachers during this period were required to have "the cultural level of a senior high education" or "a cultural level comparable to that of a senior high graduate."[19]

By the early 1960s, the schools also had a group of young party members who were recent college or teachers college graduates (see Table 2.2). Some of them had already been promoted to assistant heads of teaching-research groups. A Soviet invention adopted by the CCP, these groups brought together several instructors teaching the same subject and served as "the basic units for collective course preparation, teacher training, and mutual supervision."[20] In Chapter 2, I noted that by this time Beijing wanted to invest in the best young teachers to improve the quality of academic instruction in the long run. Young party members had thus been handed the above posts for their professional growth, at the expense of senior teachers whom the authorities considered less politically reliable or professionally promising. But despite the quick promotions, these young instructors did not have the same level of opportunity as young party members had had a decade before. By the time they entered the profession, the top faculty posts had already been filled through persistent state intervention. Although they were given significant responsibilities, their careers could not but unfold under the direction of others whose social backgrounds were quite different from theirs.

On the eve of the Cultural Revolution, Shanghai secondary schools as a whole contained almost four thousand party members in the faculty and staff.[21] Three types of party members dominated management: veteran revolutionaries, ex-underground agents, and reassigned officials or military officers. Other kinds of party members such as recent college graduates and former workers also partook in campus administration. The appointment of all these party members had stemmed from the official desire to tighten control on secondary education. The actual selections, however, had been outcomes of numerous ad hoc decisions made by the authorities in response to changes within and beyond the schools. Although what Susan Shirk has called "virtuocracy" clearly developed on campus—as those who held positions of authority were all party members who had supposedly proved their commitment to socialist development—these people had, in fact, social, educational, and professional backgrounds very different from one another.[22]

Equally important, the appointment of party members to school management turned this elite tier of the faculty into the least educated segment of the profession. Ten years after the revolution, more than two-fifths of all school principals had no college education (see Table 2.3). If principals without party membership, who were usually college-educated, were counted separately from party-member principals, the latter would show even poorer academic achievements. Because party secretaries were all party members, this powerful group of faculty, ironically, contained the least-educated people in the profession. Less than 10 percent of them were college graduates; two-thirds did not have any college education. Within management, only the heads of instruction, a group that included both party members and nonmembers, were more educated than the rank-and-file instructors.

TECHNICAL EXPLOITATION OF THE SENIOR FACULTY

Compared to the school party members and new teachers, the faculty who had started their careers before the revolution were quite educated. But their formal authority was quickly expropriated by the government, which considered them politically unreliable. At the same time, the government tried to utilize these people to strengthen classroom instruction as student enrollments soared, because neither the party members nor new instructors could teach sufficiently well on their own. In effect, the party's usage of the prerevolutionary faculty produced a secondary hierarchy based on professional and academic experience.

Table 3.1 summarizes the academic qualifications of four cohorts of secondary school teachers. The oldest cohort contained the prerevolutionary generation of instructors and the earliest postrevolutionary recruits; half of this group had a bachelor's degree. No more than one-third of the teachers in the other cohorts had finished four-year college. The late-1950s cohort contained many transferred officials and workers due to the replacement of white flags with red flags; this was the least-educated cohort. The figures indicate that when colleges and universities began to mass-produce schoolteachers after the mid-1950s, the majority of new instructors the secondary schools received were from two-year programs rather than four-year programs, which had been the norm before 1949.[23]

From the beginning, the Shanghai CCP authorities intensely distrusted the prerevolutionary faculty because of the latter's middle-class

TABLE 3.1

Educational Attainments of Four Cohorts of
Shanghai Secondary School Teachers

	Time of entry to the profession									
	Before 1952		1952–56		1957–60		After 1960		Total	
	n	%	*n*	%	*n*	%	*n*	%	*n*	%
Four-year college graduates	1,102	48.1	1,600	30.6	1,687	21.2	831	31.5	5,220	28.8
Two-year college graduates or two years of higher education	664	29.0	1,618	31.0	3,045	38.2	1,096	41.6	6,423	35.5
Less than two years of higher education	193	8.4	884	16.9	935	11.7	273	10.4	2,285	12.6
Senior high school graduates	266	11.6	895	17.1	1,726	21.7	286	10.9	3,173	17.5
Less than a senior high education	65	2.8	228	4.4	568	7.1	149	5.7	1,010	5.6
TOTAL	2,290	100	5,225	100	7,961	100	2,635	100	18,111	100

SOURCE: SMA B105-2-425 (1961, 8)

NOTE: School principals or administrators and the part-time faculty were not included.

experience as students, teachers, and residents in the city or nearby areas. They believed that these people's thinking and worldviews were impediments to the development of socialism. A 1951 SEB report on primary and secondary school teachers captures this dissatisfaction:

Schoolteachers are generally complacent and arrogant. They pay no attention to politics. They work for money and hold other kinds of obsolete thinking, and they are incapable of improving the quality of teaching. They measure problems according to their own petty-bourgeois interests. . . . Most of them do not understand what socialism is. But they look down on workers and stress the usefulness of intellectuals. . . . They do not know much about Soviet society and the government there but were displeased that the Soviet Union is our big brother. . . . They share the obsolete mentality of "Love America, fear America, and team up with America (*chongmei, kongmei, qinmei*)." These kinds of sentiment are especially popular in the schools that have been subsidized by foreign money. . . . A minority of teachers in missionary schools are backward Christians. They do not understand the peasantry or peasant rebellions, and they always take the landlords' side. . . . In general, schoolteachers are not eager to learn politics [from a socialist standpoint]. . . . They are afraid of hardships and sacrifice. They wish that China would prosper and socialism succeed so that they can sit idly and enjoy the fruits of others' labor. The average teachers still possess feudal, comprador, and fascist beliefs. Such beliefs are very strong in some teachers. As for petty-bourgeois and bourgeois beliefs, they are even more common.[24]

Because the KMT had penetrated the schools for two decades, concerns arose within the government that some faculty members might sabotage campus reforms or even CCP rule. Results from the 1952 Thought Reform Campaign reinforced this official belief. Implemented nationwide, the campaign targeted what Beijing referred to as intellectuals, that is, people who had controlled the means of reproduction before the revolution. Professors, writers, journalists, teachers, and others were forced to confess and criticize their own backgrounds, beliefs, lifestyles, and political involvements as well as to study Marxist and Mao's writings and to declare support for the CCP regime and socialism.[25] The campaign enabled the Shanghai authorities to collect detailed information on the secondary school faculty.

Nearly the entire secondary school faculty and staff in Shanghai went through thought reform in 1952 and 1953. The SEB reported that at least 20 percent of these people had been active in the KMT Party, state, or military before the revolution (see Table 3.2).[26] A small number had had high-ranking posts under the KMT such as central party committee member or head of a provincial department. There was an ex-minister of police and security of Wang Jingwei's wartime regime—the regime that had collaborated with the Japanese military during its occupation of China. The SEB noted that this man was "a big national traitor, a big

TABLE 3.2

Kuomintang Experience of Shanghai's Secondary School Faculty and Staff
(out of 7,069 people in regular and technical schools), 1952–53

KMT Party or Youth Corps administrators or administrators in KMT-sponsored political organizations (from district to provincial level)	331
High- and mid-level government officials, military officers, or police officers[a]	376
Other officials, military officers, or police officers	316
Group leaders of special agents and group leaders in KMT-sponsored political organizations (proven or suspected)	53
Special agents (proven or suspected)	367
Regular members in the KMT Party, Youth Corps, or other KMT-sponsored political organizations[b]	1,515
Low-level state employees (section chief and below)	600
TOTAL	3,558

SOURCE: SMA B105-1-664 (1952–53)

[a]High- and mid-level officials, military officers, and police officers include heads of province and county; heads of central ministry and county and municipal bureau; section chiefs in district governments; and divisional and regimental military commanders as well as lieutenant colonels.

[b]KMT-sponsored political organizations include the Chinese Youth Party (*Zhongguo qingnian dang*) and Chinese Social Democratic Party (*Zhongguo minzhu shehuidang*).

special-service agent . . . and a big CCP renegade." It also discovered that the ex-secretary of top KMT official Chen Guofu, the former head of civilian officials in the "office of the President [Chiang Kai-shek]," and a former intelligence office chief in the Military Bureau of Statistics and Investigation were among the faculty and staff.[27]

Other people were found to have sat on KMT Party committees of various levels; worked as party organizers, recruiters, or trainers; headed a county, district, or village government; run a government office or police force; or acted as special-service agents or intelligence officers. A minority had worked undercover in the schools to attack campus resistance against the policies or actions of the Nationalist government. The campaign also revealed that there were "local hegemons, landlords, chief members of reactionary religious cults (*daohuimen*) . . . bandits, etc." working in the schools.[28] Not every one of these ex-KMT agents or people whom the CCP found objectionable had entered the campuses before the revolution. In the early 1950s, most private secondary schools in Shanghai did not have CCP members to regulate teacher recruitment. Some of the above people, displaced from their jobs or local communities, had used their personal ties or academic credentials to obtain school positions. Others, as we saw in Chapter 2, were placed in the schools by the SEB through teacher-training programs.

To be sure, the information collected on the backgrounds of the faculty and staff during Thought Reform contained both overstatements and understatements. The process of investigation was marked by powerful pressure exerted on these people to confess their personal information, but also a limited capacity of the government to corroborate the data through thorough investigation. It thus engendered exaggerations of political ties and wrongdoing by individuals under duress, but also concealment of such connections and activities by others who feared that disclosure would do them greater harm. The government was aware that the information was incomplete and would continue to investigate the faculty and staff. Still, the data collected during the campaign formed an important basis for the authorities' treatment of these people.

Even before the campaign, the government had begun to expropriate the formal authority of the prerevolutionary faculty. When CCP members entered the schools, the principals would be pushed out of management practically, although allowed to retain their titles. Adding insult to injury, some party members, out of spite or distrust, reassigned the principals, many of whom were veteran educators, to manage "rear services"—that is, sanitation, building upkeep, and other work not directly related to academic instruction. Seeing their authority usurped by the party members, no fewer than twenty principals resigned in the early 1950s, claiming poor health, senility, or, among other reasons, incompetence to fulfill their new professional assignments.[29] Fearing that they would be unable to find a comparable livelihood, the rest stayed behind, but received what the SEB would call a few years later "nominal appointments" that ill fitted their professional experience or standing.

In the same vein, the government restricted what the heads of instruction could do, although they, too, nominally remained in management. They could no longer oversee faculty work or appraise faculty performance independently. Neither they nor any senior teachers could design study plans, approve textbooks, or organize faculty or student activities without supervision. The government gradually took over such responsibilities and assigned party members or activists to be heads of instruction. In fact, with the rapid expansion of secondary education after the revolution, it appointed many school principals and heads of instruction in the 1950s. Because senior teachers and those who had entered the profession before the revolution were considered untrustworthy, they seldom moved into such posts of authority despite having superior education and professional experience.

Marginalized from management, the senior teachers, nonetheless, acquired a newfound significance on campus. The government tried to exploit their superior academic experience to safeguard academic standards because the party members and new teachers had inferior education. As the new instructors arrived at the schools en masse, many junior high school teachers were reassigned to take over graduating junior high classes or even senior high classes. Likewise, senior high school teachers were reappointed to teach graduating senior high classes or sometimes even transferred into higher education.[30] The rearrangement permitted the new teachers to concentrate on lower-level and easier courses. Ironically, it boosted the academic status of the senior faculty against their declining political status.

In the mid-1950s, as the decline in teaching performance became obvious, the SEB started a faculty program called "learning from senior teachers" (*laodaixin*). The fact that junior and senior teachers had not been cooperating was an additional reason for introducing the program. Veteran teachers were asked to mentor one or more new instructors by helping them prepare lectures, conduct instruction, use teaching tools, and interact with students. By introducing this program, the government, in effect, further acknowledged that veteran instructors, though not to be recruited into management, were essential for the schools and, by implication, socialist development.

Based on the same utilitarian logic, when teaching-research groups were instituted in the faculty shortly after, veteran instructors were tapped by the SEB to be group leaders to help others become better teachers in their own subjects. Because of their middle-class backgrounds, senior teachers seldom became leaders in political studies, as such positions were reserved for party members, activists, or former workers. But they became leaders in history, mathematics, and the rest of the subjects. In some schools, management even knowingly assigned senior instructors who had been guilty of wrongdoing to be group leaders because no one else was sufficiently knowledgeable. For example, in the late 1950s, five of twelve subject group leaders at Yenan Secondary School were what the government called "historical counterrevolutionaries" who had worked for the KMT or Wang Jingwei's collaborationist regime or had been punished by CCP authorities for wrongdoing committed before the revolution.[31]

After Chairman Mao reiterated the need for class struggle in the early 1960s, the role of veteran teachers as educators came under increasing attack. What they had accomplished professionally quickly became less important than their "dubious" class backgrounds or what they had done or failed to do politically before 1949. Two years before the Cultural Revolution, the SEB plainly stated that within the schools "too many teaching-research groups are still in the hands of old intellectuals." The fact that it had not long ago handed these people such responsibilities did not matter anymore. Reacting to political pressure and policy change, it now complained that "too few young teachers" were subject group leaders. Precisely because many young graduates had recently been added to the faculty, it suggested that management should "boldly promote" these junior instructors. Having received secondary or college education entirely under Communist rule, the latter were officially regarded as politically more reliable.[32] The SEB's recommendation fitted the official vision that young teachers should, in the near future, become the cornerstone of the school system. What the agency did not clarify explicitly was nonetheless transparent to the teaching ranks—that senior teachers should expect to finish their careers as rank-and-file instructors.

A DIVERSITY OF TEACHER ACTIVISTS

It is a well-known fact that to facilitate its political domination, the CCP universalized the deployment of party activists (*jiji fenzi*) in the workplace after the revolution. Though they were not party members, these people worked closely with the party and shouldered a wide range of responsibilities. Andrew Walder's study of Chinese industry still provides the most detailed account of the everyday role of activists. They led political study, explained policies to co-workers, and helped organize so-called employee unions that were in fact controlled by management and therefore by the state. They labored hard to set performance standards, worked unpaid overtime, and accepted pressing jobs; and they counseled new workers, reported on co-workers, and ran errands for superiors. Their cooperation with state and management was motivated by opportunities for rewards and advancement as well as by individual political and moral beliefs, exactly what Weber would refer to as material and ideal interests.[33] In Shanghai secondary schools, the teacher activists were a mixed group of people. Their careers oscillated with political change and their own social backgrounds.

When the CCP took over Shanghai in May 1949, it lacked party members to penetrate the schools and hence relied heavily on teacher and student activists to institute campus reforms. Four months after the takeover, it had trained more than 450 people "elected among teacher activists or recommended by progressive individuals" to be politics teachers.[34] Besides teaching mandated classes on socialist philosophy and the Communist movement, these instructors provided critical administrative support to school party members, especially in organizing the faculty and student body according to the new regime's requirements. Their presence on campus helped the authorities bypass the senior faculty in carrying out reforms. In schools where there was no party member, teacher activists became the essential conduit through which new policies were introduced to the faculty.

Like activists in other places, teacher activists were generally young adults. Some had been involved in protest or political study organized by underground Communists before the revolution; others were simply considered not as contaminated ideologically as their colleagues by the prerevolutionary society. It was clear that from the outset the Shanghai authorities wanted to cultivate the support of young teachers but rejected senior instructors. Five months after the takeover, the SEB had established a special "political education and research office" aimed at changing teachers' thinking. After training a group of "middle-aged" teachers, the office issued this scathing criticism of the group:

Politically, most of them are neither very progressive nor very reactionary. But their thinking is rigid and spiritless and their lives undisciplined and leisurely. They are not interested in politics or the mass activities [organized by the government]. They are middle-aged people who think of themselves as sufficiently accomplished or understanding precisely what is right or wrong. They are intellectuals from the past and are unlikely to change the way they think.[35]

Although the SEB also criticized young teachers' reactions to such training, it demonstrated patience and interest in these people to the extent that even those whose fathers were landlords or who had personal ties to KMT personnel were not considered incorrigible to be activists. Teacher Lu Huowen was an exemplar of a young man with "dubious" background who became an activist in the early 1950s. He grew up in a landlord family, and his brother had been in the KMT air force. He graduated from college during the civil war and became a teacher. After the revolution, he dutifully followed the orders of the CCP members who took over his campus. By the time of Thought Reform, the party members were sufficiently impressed by his cooperation to let him assist his colleagues in making confessions and in political study. After the campaign, Lu continued to work with the party members and was promoted to deputy head of instruction during the mid-decade political thaw that led to the Hundred Flowers Campaign.[36]

Since the prerevolutionary faculty had mainly contained middle-class individuals, few teacher activists in the early 1950s were from a worker or peasant family or had a good class background by CCP definition. The Thought Reform Campaign mentioned above greatly helped the government to cultivate activists from this middle-class and otherwise suspect profession. With plenty of records from confessions and political study, the SEB was able to compare individual performances, qualifications, and backgrounds. When the campaign ended, the government recruited almost 1,800 activists among a total of 7,000 faculty and staff. These people were asked by the SEB to take an active role in teaching and political study as well as to assist the work of management when they returned to their campuses.[37]

By the mid-1950s, the CCP began to recruit the best-performing teacher activists into the party and promote them professionally. Compared to the party members who had joined or would join the faculty

from elsewhere, these individuals did not have comparably successful careers in the following decade due to official biases against their
middle-class backgrounds and pre-1949 employment in the teaching
profession. Despite having better teaching experience or education,
they rarely became school principals or party secretaries. Zhu Gongzheng, an activist since the revolution, was one of the first teachers to
join the party. Within his school party branch, he was the most experienced educator but the member with the lowest political standing. He
recalls that having been a secondary school teacher before 1949, for less
than two years, he was nonetheless regarded by the party authorities as
"a petty-bourgeois intellectual" even after joining the party. As a result,
he was not involved in the major decisions of the party cell.[38]

On the whole, the effort to recruit teacher activists into the party
occurred in fits and starts. Recruitment plummeted during the mid-
decade Campaign to Wipe Out Counterrevolutionaries, but surged
afterward due to the onset of the Hundred Flowers Campaign, and
then dipped again when the Anti-Rightist Campaign began. By the late
1950s, still only a small number of activists had joined the party, even
though they had been indispensable to the functioning of the schools.
But this all changed at the turn of the decade because of the ambitious
development goals set by Beijing during the Great Leap Forward,
which included an expansion of the party membership. In 1959, over
five hundred faculty and staff members joined the party; the following
year, another three hundred became party members.[39] Besides young
teachers from the early 1950s, these new party members included some
of the unemployed intellectuals, transferred cadres, and demobilized
soldiers who had been working in the faculty.

Xu Ruhua, a former housewife mentioned in Chapter 2, joined the
party during this period. Because of her working-class background and
support for the party members in her school, she had already been a
leader of a teaching-research group despite being less educated and experienced than other members in the group.[40] With party membership
added to her credentials, she was now an influential instructor. Her
colleagues probably still looked down on her for her lack of education
and cooperation with the party. But they would have been foolhardy
to antagonize this party member whose career was on the rise if they
wanted to preserve their own livelihoods. She was no longer an easy
target on campus as she had been when she first joined the teaching
profession in the mid-1950s.

Likewise, Lu Huowen, despite being the son of a landlord, entered the party during the Great Leap Forward. But, unlike Xu, he found his hopes for a better career shattered shortly after. By 1961, that is, even before Mao proclaimed anew the need for class struggle within state and society, the Shanghai authorities had already criticized themselves for having been too "adventurous," "overhasty," and "sloppy" in recruiting party members during the Great Leap Forward or letting unqualified people, including those of "poor" class backgrounds, join the party.[41] Although Lu's party membership was not revoked, both he and his superiors understood that there would be no promotion for him, politically or professionally, in the near future.

As a new generation of college and teachers college graduates joined the faculty from the late 1950s onward, some of them became activists, too. Thanks to reforms in higher education, quite a few of these activists were from worker or peasant families, unlike most of the teacher activists recruited in the past.[42] College-educated and supportive of party policies and personnel, these young men and women were precisely the people the CCP sought to groom into superior teachers and school administrators for the future. After teaching for two or three years, some of them were picked by management to be deputy heads of teaching-research groups. The official rationale was to help them acquire pedagogical expertise from the veteran teachers who headed such groups and gain administrative experience. As Mao's pronouncements for class struggle intensified in the early 1960s, the future of these activists, indeed, looked very bright.

WORKPLACE ABUSE AND CLEAVAGES
WITHIN MANAGEMENT

From early on, the counter-bureaucratic reorganization of the school authority structure—the installation of a political and a technical hierarchy—strained faculty relations. A schism emerged between party members and activists on the one side and nonmembers on the other. But those who exercised power did not form a coherent force. Like the ordinary instructors we saw in Chapter 2, some of them disliked or distanced themselves from one another. Such faculty strife and tensions continued up to the eve of the Cultural Revolution.

Among the faculty cleavages that developed after the 1949 revolution, the one between party members and nonmembers was most

damaging to faculty solidarity due to the disparity of power and qualifications between the two groups. With the first party members who
took over the schools, the veteran revolutionaries and ex-underground
agents personified the sacrifice, risk, and discipline the CCP had endured to accomplish the revolution. The young party members, too,
demonstrated political courage before and after 1949. Though some of
these people had flawed records, they represented the new regime and
its intent to remake China. By contrast, the ordinary faculty contained
not only members of the upper classes but also quite a few former
KMT agents, business managers, dismissed employees, and lawbreakers. This group of people symbolized the danger of counterrevolution,
criminality, and other problems that would confront the transition to
socialism. In other words, school party members and the ordinary faculty occupied divergent places on the official political spectrum. One
group belonged to a rising elite aspiring to eradicate class exploitation,
bourgeois culture, and moral depravity; the other contained beneficiaries of class privileges, supporters of fallen political regimes, consum-
ers of bourgeois culture, and social deviants.

Official reports during the Shanghai takeover indicate that underground Communist agents and teacher activists wasted no time in demanding "the immediate dismissal of large numbers of public school
principals, the seizure of private schools controlled by reactionary elements, and the audit of profit-oriented diploma mills." These party
members and activists "normally shared such inordinately leftist sentiments of settling accounts" with their colleagues who were KMT appointees, members, and supporters.[43] When Communist Party members entered the schools, a struggle for authority followed. Rather than
"uniting" with the faculty to reform curricula, student enrollment, and
campus management as instructed by higher authorities, the party
members "overemphasized the backwardness" of the faculty and depended on a few activists for assistance. When other teachers expressed
support for social or campus reforms, they were disdained as "oppor-
tunist" and untrustworthy. The young activists wanted the dismissal
of large numbers of their colleagues. Had the regime gone along with
their demands, these inexperienced teachers would have benefited
from a surge in faculty vacancies.[44]

On the other side, ordinary faculty members immediately cast the
party members and activists as usurpers. In the main, they did not
publicly oppose the assigning of the party members, but attempted to

isolate them after their arrival by withholding support. Appealing to the ideal of professionalism, an argument quickly becoming an anachronism, they complained that the activists neglected their teaching responsibilities while working for the party members. When the SEB began to appoint individuals to the schools to teach politics classes, some campuses lobbied for their own choices, who turned out to be people of "inferior qualities" by CCP standards but supported by the original school principals.[45]

A retired teacher explains the hostility directed at the party members, specifically those who acted as politics teachers, and the outcome of the faculty struggle.

The school principals and teachers knew very well that those teachers stood for the party and brought politics into the schools. Some people hence tried to undercut them. Between 1949 and 1951, the school principals did not listen to what these politics teachers said. However, after *zhenfan* (the 1951 Campaign Against Counterrevolutionaries) things started to change. Some principals quit because they did not like [the kind of] politics [the CCP inserted] in the education system. But not too many principals did that. The rest began to discuss matters with or consult the opinions of politics teachers.[46]

As school party members consolidated their power with official backing and activists' support, they displayed little desire to work with the ordinary faculty. They treated these people, who had rejected them, with a suspicion and contempt that caused serious concern for the authorities. In a 1955 report, the SEB stated that school party members had been acting against official united-front policy of seeking cooperation from the former elite.

1. School party cadres and party branches primarily employ the concepts of closing the door [to the ordinary faculty] and stressing homogeneity [within management]. There is a lack of respect, trust, and delegation toward ordinary faculty members. School party members feel that the school principals who are not party members are there for "keeping up appearances," and that schools "will do fine with or without them." . . .

2. Because school party cadres tend to close the door and stress homogeneity, they exhibit impatience and subjectivity. They run things all by themselves, thinking that they can represent everyone else in the schools. Some party members even resort to coercion, commands, and rude and brutal behavior [when dealing with teachers] . . .

3. A major cause of the above problems is that school party cadres are arrogant and complacent. They cannot see the strength or function of the masses or their improvements. They fail to patiently assist others to rectify the weaknesses in their political thinking. Some party-member principals take their work and the faculty seriously, but they do not know how to get the right results.[47]

In numerous campuses, the better-educated and experienced principals who were still in office were forced into insignificant roles by the
party members. At Shanghai Girls' Secondary School Number Eight,
the principal had a master's degree but was now seen as "incapable of
accomplishing anything, but very good at spoiling things." At Girls'
School Number Three or the formerly exclusive McTyeire School, the
principal had been a Ph.D. student at Columbia University and was
now considered "too bourgeois in thinking and too Americanized" to
be given any serious work.[48] The principal of Wu'ai Secondary School
reportedly had "a sluggish style of work and was shallow in his performance." None of these educators received any work befitting their
professional standing.

For ordinary teachers, who had lower social status, public reprimands
and disrespect by party members were commonplace. At Pudong Secondary School, the SEB reported, a party member complained that his
colleagues were all "arrogant on the outside and empty inside." He
therefore lashed out at them publicly and privately to "expose their
emptiness and attack their arrogance."[49] At Xuhui Secondary School,
the party-member principal openly and rudely reprimanded a "backward and incompetent" teacher after he failed to prepare for political
study: "People like you who did not read the books assigned and yet
lie about it . . . do not look forward and upward but are willing to fall
behind."[50] At Qixiu Secondary School, management spurned teachers'
need by putting their lounge "behind a women's restroom and inside a
coal storage room" while converting "a well-ventilated room with large
desks" into an office for students' use.[51]

Pierre Bourdieu suggested that until relations of domination are accomplished by "objective mechanisms" that free the dominant group
from "endless work of creating or restoring [such] social relations," they
would "have to work directly, daily, personally" to reproduce the "conditions of domination."[52] The above behavior of school party members,
which the authorities called "leftist" mistakes, revealed the abusive tactics these people used to maintain their everyday domination on campus *in the absence of* institutionalized practice capable of legitimizing
their authority in the eyes of the ordinary faculty. It is no wonder that
the SEB was especially worried about the situation in private schools,
as the abuse there was "relatively common and extremely severe."[53]
When the campus takeover began, party members with better professional qualifications—and therefore conventional prestige—were inserted into public and top private schools. Because those who were as-

signed to other schools lacked comparable achievement or status, they probably encountered more faculty hostility and thus found coercion a better means to assert their authority. Furthermore, public schools generally had better teachers than private schools despite the decline in teachers' qualifications after the revolution. This suggests that the abuse of the private school faculty was also related to their poorer job performance.

Besides leftist mistakes, the SEB reported that some party members committed "rightist" errors. They were too close to ordinary faculty members, tolerating their attack on the Communist regime and feeling unqualified to command these people. In other words, their mistake was submission rather than coercion. But rightist errors were, too, inevitable with the party members' sudden elevation to management. With their authority sustained by the state but not tradition, some party members tried to cater to and win the approval of their colleagues at the expense of official policies. Both leftist and rightist mistakes were what Bourdieu called *elementary forms of domination* when a system of rule "has not yet developed the power of self-perpetuation."[54] Under this circumstance, the party cadres were forced to re-create conditions for their domination inside the schools continuously. From archival documents, rightist errors appeared to be rather common in the early 1950s. But the charge gradually disappeared as the CCP expanded its controls in the schools and as the political climate tightened. By the late 1950s, the SEB reported that school management personnel "would lean to the left rather than to the right" (*ningzuo wuyou*) in their work with the faculty.[55]

Unsurprisingly, there was strong resentment against party members and activists within the ordinary faculty. Two kinds of people were particularly despised: campus managers who before 1949 would have been considered underqualified to act even as secondary school instructors, and young teachers who were promoted at senior colleagues' expense. These people were not regarded as educators but as political functionaries or, with derision, people who "ate the party's rice" (*chi dangfan*). After brief resistance against use of Communist management, the ordinary faculty were intimidated by the official punishment of "counterrevolutionaries" and obstinate colleagues. They recognized that further sabotage would only jeopardize their own livelihoods. The original school principals and administrators reacted to their marginalization by dissociating themselves from everyday management. The teaching staff expected little advancement unless they became activists. Compliant on the outside, these people were, however, seething inside. They blamed the party and its members as well as the activists for ruining their careers and the profession they had formerly controlled.

No event captured the resentment of the faculty as starkly as the Hundred Flowers Campaign. Encouraged by the state to speak out, some teachers attacked the promotion of party members and activists with little reservation. In essence, they waged a Weberian assault that revealed their desire for technical-based appointment. The following are examples of the many complaints documented by the government.

Party-member principals have titles but not brains. Their knowledge is thin and shallow; their leadership, impotent.

Party members are only useful for weeding out counterrevolutionaries, leading street demonstrations, and reporting on others. Other than that, they are useless.

The party branch is a faculty of toddlers, youth society, youth party, and children's home.

Speaking of the activists, everyone hates them deeply. They are servile and sycophantic, and they do not care about social justice. They use the masses as stepping stones, climbing desperately up the social ladder. Even their facial expressions and demeanor remind you absolutely of lackeys.

Seeing themselves as casualties of institutionalized injustice, some faculty members attacked the ruling regime directly.

What the Communist Party means is one party commandeers all the land under heaven; the Communist Party is a new nobility; the Communist Party manufactures a new class.

With the appointment of school principals and heads of instruction, the leadership only cares about one thing: whether the person is a party member. . . . Political eligibility should not displace other requirements. We cannot idolize party members.

The Communist Party is not working for socialism, but toward a slave society. Under Communist Party rule, people work like oxen, follow orders like sheep, and are slaughtered like pigs.

The Communist Party is cruel and brutal. Indeed, it depends on factional rule [by party members, but says that it is against such rule].[56]

No significant or lasting improvement in faculty relations occurred after the Hundred Flowers Campaign. To the contrary, the purge of intellectuals in the Anti-Rightist Campaign, their assignment to labor education during the Great Leap Forward, and Mao's later reiteration of the need for class struggle harmed schoolteachers' social status and reinforced the belief among party members that teachers should be dealt with harshly. In 1961, the SEB surveyed eight campuses but virtually repeated its criticisms of party members from six years before. The party-member principals and secretaries were overbearing, shortsighted, and inflexible in their work. They ignored the CCP guideline of "uniting, criticizing, and remolding intellectuals" and exhibited "antipathy" toward ordinary teachers, especially former KMT officials or members.

Within one urban district, the SEB discovered that only two out of eighteen original school principals had "important" work related to academic instruction; the rest looked after campus maintenance, meal provision, and other "insignificant" tasks.[57] In two of the schools, some party members remarked that "teachers are the dregs of society" and "criticized, censured, and labeled" these colleagues whenever they were upset with them. On one campus, management had used students to direct the faculty to labor during the Great Leap Forward, which caused the students to yell at and abuse their teachers.[58] By the end of 1962, the SEB issued another report on the work of the school party branches. Although the language in this report was less strident, there was no cause for celebration. Among the two hundred campuses in urban Shanghai, only 20 percent of the party branches were found to have good working relations with the ordinary faculty. Within a small number of schools, the party members were "brutal, tyrannical, and extremely conceited."[59]

We should not assume that because school party members entirely dominated management, they therefore shared close working relations among themselves. In fact, the reverse was often true: they were no more cooperative as a group than the ordinary teachers we saw in Chapter 2. Being in a profession in which conventional qualifications for authority had been invalidated and new norms for office changed with the political climate, school party members tended to emphasize selectively one or more of their various qualifications—college education, teaching experience, revolutionary credentials, class background, or political activism—to legitimize or advance their positions. In other words, they, too, reacted to the institutionalization of the political and technical hierarchies by stressing the personal qualifications that would benefit them personally. What occurred at Guoguang Secondary School, where I interviewed multiple teachers, is instructive. At first, the story seems to be one of simple gender discrimination, but, in fact, it shows the extent to which party members could attack one another despite their collective domination on campus.[60]

Established in 1954, the party cell at Guoguang contained three young party members: a former underground agent, a recent senior high school graduate, and Zhu Gongzheng, the "petty-bourgeois intellectual" mentioned earlier. Two years later, the authorities assigned the ex-underground agent, who had been the party secretary, to further training and appointed the high school graduate as acting secretary. To strengthen the party branch, they transferred the female principal of a nearby school to the campus. A high school dropout, she had joined the party in 1937 and then specialized in organizing rural women. Upon arrival, she acted as if she was the party secretary, despite the fact that she had not been appointed to that post, and the two men resisted. One of them scornfully recalls that "she got here because her husband was a party secretary in a nearby district."[61] The other remembers that she "lacked knowledge and skills" but had "tricks and stratagems."[62] They not only scorned her personally; they criticized her behind her back and yelled at her in faculty meetings. Not backing down, she responded by attacking them in front of the faculty.[63]

Raised in urban Shanghai, both of these young party members came from highly educated families. The family of one owned a top commercial press, and the other's father had taught English in the best schools. The woman did not have the education, refinement, or cosmopolitanism these two men shared. If they displayed an urban, male, and elitist snobbery against her rural, female, and "crass" intrusion, she had political credentials beyond either of them, which turned out to be a more powerful asset than they had expected. During the Anti-Rightist Campaign, she succeeded in organizing the campus to attack the men, focusing on things they had said or done. Both of them lost their party membership and faculty positions and were branded as rightists.

To be sure, what happened at Guoguang, especially the severe penalties meted out, was exceptional. SEB records contain little evidence of open strife between party members. Muted distrust and lack of cooperation, however, were rather common. As early as 1954, the SEB began the complaints and cited Shanghai Girls' Secondary School Number Three as an example. The school principal and the head of instruction there, both party members, "had a considerable gap in their ways of thinking." They had many complaints against each other and even refused to converse. Their mutual dislike, the SEB noted, had not only stalled the formation of "a nucleus of leadership" on campus; it had impaired the work of the faculty.[64] Almost a decade later, the SEB stated that the top party members in twenty-five of two hundred urban campuses "were not united." In some schools, these people "looked down on each other" or even "could not coexist with each other."[65]

Besides engendering faculty conflict, the postrevolutionary change in the school authority structure fostered a faculty retreat from providing leadership in academic instruction. First, the lack of teaching experience among the party members limited their capacity and willingness to provide such leadership. Second, shunned by management, veteran educators were unable to intervene in academic matters. Third, senior teachers, whose cooperation the government badly wanted, acted perfunctorily due to their resentment of the party members and activists. Neither management nor veteran educators were therefore sufficiently motivated to protect the quality of classroom instruction as large numbers of new teachers entered the schools.

In 1953, as the Shanghai government completed the Thought Reform Campaign for the secondary school faculty and staff, the SEB noted that party-member principals "generally did not look after teaching-related matters." They had spent much of their time organizing political campaigns and activities, which had produced "an excess of assignments, organizations, meetings, part-time obligations, as well as documents and forms" for the principals.[66] Even politics teachers, who were mainly party members or activists, had been "overburdened by extra responsibilities."[67] They had difficulty teaching all their classes, let alone in the manner expected by the authorities. The political campaigns and activities, however, were a pretext as much as a cause for the party members' withdrawal from academic leadership and pedagogical duties. Since the party members generally lacked teaching experience, they focused on the work they were familiar with: organizing political campaigns and activities, investigating the faculty, and other tasks related to politics or organization. Providing academic leadership or superior lectures in the classroom was not their priority.

In a 1955 survey of nine schools, the SEB reported that some party-member principals "had not directed teaching at all," while the rest lacked "the level and experience" to fulfill their academic responsibilities.[68] None of these nine principals provided sufficient academic leadership. At Yenan Secondary School, there were already two party-member principals, but they displayed "a lack of concern" for classroom instruction and failed to supervise it "concretely and carefully." One of the principals had a primary education and the other "a cultural level that was not high either."[69] They did not implement pedagogical changes required by the state or had only done so superficially. Rank-and-file teachers complained that even though teaching-research groups had been set up, there was no guidance from management on how they should be run.[70] At Weiyu Secondary School, which the SEB also cited, the new teaching staff received little academic help from management or, for that matter, senior teachers. A young college graduate "ran into obstacles everywhere" with her classes, but had gotten absolutely no useful advice. Consequently, she had to go back to her college mentor for help.[71]

A major development in the workplace after 1949 was the institutionalization of political study that the CCP used to promote its ideas, policies, and political conformity and cooperation. Here the labor force was divided into small groups led by party members or activists to regularly read and discuss selected official documents and political writings.[72] At the faculty level, management was expected to use such activities to strengthen support for the regime. But SEB reports indicated that the party members often failed to organize political study properly. On the one hand, this reflected the fact that the party members distrusted their colleagues and had too many other responsibilities. On the other hand, their lack of academic training and experience limited their ability to turn political study into an asset for the regime.

At Yenan Secondary School, the SEB complained, management merely used such study to convey official plans and instructions and did not even clarify their significance. More important, it did not offer advice to teachers to help them understand or accept official views. At Weiyu Secondary School, the situation was almost identical. The teachers complained that they did not understand the aims, plans, or lessons of political study. They were regularly given materials to read but not told how to handle them. Sometimes, they received the materials right before scheduled discussion and were expected to respond appropriately. When they failed to do so, they were chastised as "shallow and speculative."[73]

Like the teaching staff, school party members gained on-the-job experience that improved their knowledge and skills. From time to time, the SEB sought to remove those who had performed badly. In 1957, it planned to reassign forty-two party-member principals with "poor abilities or cultural level or too many responsibilities."[74] These changes, though helpful, had limited impact on academic leadership. Throughout the 1950s, the repeated insertion of professionally ill-qualified party cadres into management reproduced its withdrawal from such leadership. Furthermore, the successive mobilization campaigns that involved the schools after mid-decade—the Hundred Flowers Campaign, the Anti-Rightist Campaign, and the Great Leap Forward—offered further justification for party members to focus on political rather than academic work.

In a 1961 survey of one school district, the SEB noted that "a considerable number" of party secretaries did not "firmly enforce" education policies. Some spent much effort on political work but did little in other areas; others kept their distance from the teaching ranks and did not help teachers "reform" their thinking.[75] Two years later, the SEB surveyed twenty-three schools in another district and found that nineteen out of twenty-nine party secretaries and seventeen out of twenty-seven principals did not teach. The main reason was not that these people did not have time, but that they lacked teaching experience, which allegedly made them "worry that if their classes did not go well, they would harm their positions on campus." In one school, the principal had held the post for three years, but was "still unfamiliar with professional work" and had yet to observe how the teachers performed in the classroom.[76]

In practice, classroom instruction issues were generally handled by heads of instruction with little help from their superiors. By the early 1960s, these teachers were mainly well-educated party members, many of whom had been activists since the early or mid-1950s, but lacked the political background to be promoted to school principal or party secretary.[77] The rest were current activists or veteran teachers. As Mao's skepticism toward expertise gained strength, young party cadres and former workers who had finished college with state sponsorship assumed stronger roles in academic work, too.

While party-member principals and secretaries failed to provide academic leadership, the veteran educators who had been school principals before the revolution were unable to help even if they wanted to. As we have seen, they were shunned by management and given work that ill fitted their professional experience. In the early 1960s, the government, eager to improve declining faculty performance, occasionally invited the principals who had had especially high status before 1949 to discuss their work in so-called meetings of immortals (*shenxianhui*).[78] Because such meetings occurred after the punishment of dissenters in the Anti-Rightist Campaign, the invitees would have been injudicious to attack the party or school party members. Still, from their testimonials, it is obvious that these educators had been languishing away on campus and were quite angry.

A college-educated man who had thirty years of teaching experience and had managed one of the best schools said this to the authorities:

I am scared of making mistakes. I don't know whether some of my [professional] opinions actually reflect my bourgeois thinking on education. For example, are my opinions on students and student discipline or the work we need at various class levels and areas of the curriculum, in fact, bourgeois thinking? I don't know. That's why I don't dare to offer my opinions. I have many, many opinions. But I feel it's better not to express them. I try to keep them to myself.
—Zhao Xianchu, Nanyang Model Secondary School[79]

Another school principal described her withdrawal from management and her ritualistic compliance. For her, the situation was personally traumatic.

I felt like I was a toddler who wanted to skip school. I was frightened to go through the front entrance of the school every morning when I arrived at work. I did not know what to do during the day. When I was home in the evening, I felt suffocated. I did not accomplish anything and the day had passed me by. But I also felt that I should go to the school early in the morning and leave late in the evening. That was at least my responsibility. . . . In the past I shoved each and every matter to the party-member principal. I did not dare to make any decision at all.
—Wang Peijing, Shanghai Girls' Secondary School Number Nine[80]

In theory, because of their superior education and teaching experience, many of the teachers who had begun their careers before 1949 were excellent candidates for providing pedagogical leadership. By appointing such teachers as leaders of teaching-research groups and promoting "learning from senior teachers" in the 1950s, the SEB demonstrated its willingness to use such teachers to raise instruction quality. But what actually occurred between these teachers and their colleagues suggests that they, too, failed to offer academic leadership. As we saw in Chapter 2, senior teachers clung to their ideals of professionalism and did little to help the undereducated newcomers. With their subjugation to party members and activists as well as scant chance of promotion, they had even less incentive to cooperate with the government.

When young college graduates entered the faculty in large numbers in the late 1950s and early 1960s, they, in turn, had little motivation to work with senior teachers due to the obvious political distrust with which management and the state treated the latter. To protect their own careers from guilt by association, a main strategy of theirs was, in fact, to stay away from such teachers. As early as the mid-1950s, the SEB had remarked that young and old teachers commonly looked down on one another. On one side, the veterans accused young teachers of lacking academic knowledge and skills, thus implying that they should not be promoted. On the other side, young teachers argued that senior instructors were "old and useless," which supposedly justified the opportunities rendered to themselves by the state and management.[81]

From then on, the SEB repeatedly reported similar faculty tensions as the proportion of young teachers rose in the faculty. At Xinchang Secondary School, where the SEB conducted an in-depth study in the early 1960s, the relation between junior and senior teachers was, indeed, very tense. The senior faculty felt that young teachers were openly disrespectful, having "their eyes on the top of their heads, high-sounding expressions, and considered everybody beneath their notice." On the other side, young teachers complained that senior teachers gave them "the cold shoulder and deliberately set obstacles" to hinder their work.[82] During this period, Wang Peijing, the veteran school principal quoted above, explained to the authorities what she could do to improve the cooperation between junior and senior teachers. Her statement not only confirms that she had been languishing in her school; it illustrates the gaping distance between the junior and senior faculty.

People like us should help tackle the tensions between junior and senior teachers. We need to talk to the senior teachers, and we need to communicate with the Communist Youth League committee [on campus that had signed up many junior teachers] as well as to the junior teachers themselves. By doing so, we'll get results. If we can't solve the problem between the junior and the senior faculty, we won't benefit from having teaching-research groups. When I return to the school, I'll take up this job. . . . In the past, I did not do this. I've politely refused to do it and said that the party branch should do it.[83]

The tensions between young and old teachers undermined "learning from senior teachers," the program the SEB promoted to improve teaching performance. Only one out of fifteen teachers I interviewed who began their careers when the program was available recalls being mentored by a senior colleague. Others remember such a program within the school system or even their own campuses, but indicate that they were not participants. With the senior faculty, the only mentors were a small number of teachers not threatened or despised by their younger colleagues and sufficiently confident in their own knowledge and skills. These were normally well-educated party members or teacher activists who had excellent professional experience. Contrary to what the government wished, then, there was limited transfer of pedagogical expertise from the senior to the junior faculty even with the program in place.

COUNTER-BUREAUCRACY
AND "BUREAUCRATISM" ON CAMPUS

Shortly after the 1949 revolution, Chairman Mao began to complain about the spread of "bureaucratism" (*guanliao zhuyi*) within the party officialdom. As he stated, often colorfully, party members were conceited, complacent, subjective, careless, truculent, arbitrary, stupid, confused, and ignorant. Among other deficiencies, they did not understand their work, listen to people, care about reality, or work diligently. They used force to carry out orders, maintained blind control over their subordinates, aimlessly talked about politics, and formed factions and cliques to benefit themselves. Other party leaders, such as Zhou Enlai and Deng Xiaopeng, expressed similar concerns on bureaucratism and, like Mao, believed that such behavior had harmed socialist development by hurting workplace productivity, public support, and the rewards deliverable to workers and peasants.[84]

For Mao and other party leaders who later promoted attacks on the party and state and supported radical political reforms during the Cultural Revolution, the reason why such "evils of bureaucracy" persisted was ultimately because the CCP had failed to eradicate the bureaucratic arrangements carried over from the KMT era and the imperial past. As Mao put it in the early 1960s, "the old society (*jiushehui*) has left us this bad style of work that is bureaucratism. If we do not use our broom to sweep it away once a year, it will sprout when the spring breeze returns."[85] Distinct offices, long-term careers, graded remuneration, and hierarchical authority had been key features in the workplace that were also normalized under Communist Party rule. Mao came to believe that these organizational arrangements not only profit management personnel in capitalist states and enterprises, but also party cadres in the workplace after the socialist revolution. Since the CCP takeover, such cadres had been as strongly attached to the power and privileges proffered by their offices, careers, and compensation as their KMT predecessors had been. They "behaved like overlords."[86] The Cultural Revolution was his grandiose attempt to remove this bureaucratic structure and eliminate bureaucratism from Chinese society, after more than a decade of unsuccessful official effort to check cadre abuse and misbehavior.

From the evidence in this chapter, Mao and others made a major theoretical mistake by seeking the cause of party cadres' arrogance, incompetence, ineffectiveness, and indifference in the prerevolutionary legacy of bureaucratic development, especially under KMT rule. No doubt the irregular rationalization of the political economy amid war and social instability in the 1930s and 1940s had produced large numbers of self-aggrandizing and unfit officials. Like any modern state, the KMT government had its share of red tape and ritualism that impaired the provision of public goods and services. After the Communist takeover, however, the alienation of party officials from their work, their staff, and the people they served was not caused by any further rationalization of the workplace or even continuation of modern bureaucratic structures with state and society, as Mao's argument implied, whether he recognized it or not. To the contrary, such "bureaucratism" must be explained within the postrevolutionary pattern of organizational development, that is, *the growth of counter-bureaucracy,* or politically based appointment, arbitrary discipline, and other nonrational features in the workplace.

Within Shanghai secondary schools, the institutionalization of a political and a technical hierarchy was a main reason for which party superiors exhibited the behavior that Mao called bureaucratism. Having few seasoned educators in its ranks, the CCP selected various party members on the basis of a range of political qualifications to manage the campuses. Although these people represented the revolutionary state, their authority as educators was not widely accepted by the faculty. They thus trusted only a small number of activists within the faculty and treated others rudely as objects of political control. The majority of the faculty, in turn, despised the party members and activists for running the schools without proper professional qualifications. When asked by the state to help raise teaching quality, veteran teachers refused to cooperate. Because of their heavy political responsibilities and lack of teacher training, the party members concentrated on political work. Their lack of concern for academic matters further compromised faculty teaching performance. Because of the differences in their own backgrounds, the party members themselves tended to look down on one another and even struggled against one another.

In other words, the appointment of party members to the schools not only undermined the level of expertise on campus; it fostered conflict within management as well as between management and the rest of the faculty. The outcome was a politically divided faculty led by people with little school management experience. It engendered inefficiencies, indifference, friction, and abuse in the schools, or what Mao and other party leaders suggested, wrongly, were consequences of the workplace having too much bureaucracy. The next chapter will place faculty income within this counter-bureaucratic context of school authority relations and show that the distribution of salaries further deepened faculty tensions and dissatisfaction with the state.

4

Income Inequities

Some senior high school teachers earn less than junior
high teachers, who in turn earn less than primary school
teachers. Those who have more responsibilities are not paid
properly, and the diligent are paid less than the slothful. . . .
These matters are immensely unfair! How can they benefit
faculty performance?

—a teacher's complaint documented
by the Shanghai government[1]

Central to Lenin's critique of capitalism is the understanding that professionals, such as factory managers, newspaper editors, and school principals, are normally well compensated because their work in organizing production and reproduction helps perpetuate bourgeois domination. Remuneration by job responsibility as well as professional qualification, seniority, and performance—a main feature of modern bureaucratic administrations—is a tool that enables the ruling class to reward the "lackeys of the moneybags," "lickspittles of the exploiters," and "bourgeois intellectuals" materially for their cooperation in capitalist rule. The transition to socialism must therefore incorporate a change in professional compensation in addition to the political subjugation of professionals. When Lenin penned *The State and Revolution,* he suggested that the working class would hire its professional workers, including state officials, and pay them "ordinary workmen's wages."

Lenin later indicated that all sorts of professionals or "bourgeois experts" were essential for building a modern socialist society in industrially backward Russia. These people understood modern technology, administration, and management better than anyone else. Their participation in the workplace was the only way to guarantee productivity as well as higher training for workers in organizing production and reproduction. To seek uninterrupted cooperation from "bourgeois experts," the Bolshevik regime must "retain the present higher remuneration" of these people, if necessary.[2] Lenin thus proposed a two-pronged approach to professional compensation during the transition to socialism:

privileged salaries for "bourgeois experts" but "workmen's wages" for the rest of the professional workforce. As we will see in Chapter 7, the Bolsheviks followed this approach only briefly after the 1917 Russian revolution. By contrast, this chapter shows that the Chinese Communists turned out to be better Leninists in this respect.

In this chapter I describe how the Chinese Communist Party's Leninist thinking on professional compensation and economic development in China shaped the development of counter-bureaucracy in Shanghai secondary schools up to the eve of the Cultural Revolution. Shortly after the 1949 takeover, the Shanghai government started to pay middle-class salaries to the prerevolutionary faculty but workmen's wages to most faculty newcomers. It subsequently adjusted faculty salaries according to central policies and local-level decisions. But pay raises were generally small and disproportionately benefited party members and activists. Given the already divisive hierarchical structure on campus, this pattern of remuneration only deepened faculty tensions and political disaffection. School party members and activists were unhappy that the state rewarded the prerevolutionary faculty with better compensation even though they were considered questionable politically and barred from management. Other teachers were angry that their income barely improved with teaching experience, while management personnel rewarded themselves and those who supported them with pay raises. In other words, the system of faculty compensation intensified the perceptions of unfairness and inequity within the faulty that accompanied the enforcement of a political and a technical hierarchy.

A FACULTY INCOME DIVIDE, 1949–1955

During the first years after the 1949 revolution, the logic of faculty salaries reflected three distinct political objectives of the Chinese Communist Party (CCP)—maintaining social stability, co-opting professionals, and pursuing class struggle. The Communist state did not pay the increasingly diverse faculty by seniority, authority, responsibility, or academic or political qualification. The result was a conspicuous schism in faculty income, with the prerevolutionary faculty being the major beneficiaries.

Seizing power after decades of warfare and mass dislocation, the CCP elite were aware that their rule would not be safe unless economic security and stable livelihood were the norm within state and society.

In the wake of the revolution, the regime promoted social stability by expanding employment, job training, educational opportunities, and welfare assistance.[3] The takeover of government and public establishments such as factories, universities, and hospitals was facilitated by an official policy of "no change to appointment and salary" (*yuanxin yuanzhi*) aimed at protecting production and employment.[4] Even the management personnel who were compelled to surrender authority would keep their titles as well as their salaries. Only a minority of people, mainly those who had had close ties to the KMT regime or resisted the takeovers, were laid off by the CCP authorities.[5]

To Beijing, the "no change" policy was only a stopgap measure of pacification. Although it promoted much-needed stability and productivity in government and the public sector, it could not but perpetuate the class inequalities developed before the revolution. Those who received high salaries from the state, such as professors, engineers, and officials, were mainly from upper-class families. By contrast, manual laborers, office assistants, and other low-income employees in government or public schools or hospitals were mostly from the working class. By protecting existing appointments and patterns of income, the policy was therefore politically indefensible from the CCP's own ideological standpoint.

To redress class inequalities, Beijing unveiled a set of salary plans in 1952. It required the local authorities to assign a skill grade to each staff member in the expanding government and public sector and to pay salaries according to standardized scales based on skill grade. In general, the salaries for professional workers were set considerably lower than their previous rates.[6] In particular, high school and college graduates who joined a profession in the public or private sector would start at the bottom of the scales. The plans had profound implications for class reproduction, because professional workers, who were still mainly from middle-class families, would not be able to reproduce their privileged lifestyles when they received smaller salaries or "workman's wages." The plans would also enable the state to save on salaries as it annexed the private sector and pursued industrial growth.

However, the regime feared that the new salary practices would incite workplace sabotage and popular revolts. It therefore decided that existing jobholders' salaries should not be cut when these practices were put into effect. In other words, these people would continue to benefit from the "no change" policy, while their new colleagues would bear the austerity of the new practices. This compromise engendered what Beijing called "salary retention supplements" (*baoliu gongzi*) in the labor force. The beneficiaries received a monthly amount from the state on top of their new skill-based standard salaries to match their previous incomes. The possession of a salary retention supplement indicated that one was paid according to prerevolutionary standards. Since professional workers had commanded high salaries before the revolution, most were entitled to a supplement afterward. By contrast, the new crops of professional workers (surgeons, engineers, editors, and so on) were given much lower salaries. The CCP thus instituted a Leninist system of professional compensation: the "bourgeois experts" and "bourgeois intellectuals" from the prerevolutionary era kept their high salaries, and the rest of the professional workforce received "workmen's wages."

Within the Shanghai secondary school faculty, the use of the "no change" policy and standardized salaries instantly created an income divide that had little to do with professional qualification, authority, performance, and responsibility. The faculty members who benefited were those who had entered the profession before the revolution, regardless of the year, and those who started teaching shortly before the salary reform. Since most schools had calculated faculty salaries according to middle-class income standards, these people continued to receive such levels of compensation from the state afterward. Before the reform, the government surveyed two public schools and found that the average monthly faculty salary was 110 yuan.[7] Shortly thereafter, the SEB reported that 82 percent, 93 percent, and 75 percent of the school principals, heads of instruction, and rank-and-file teachers in all public schools had salary retention supplements averaging almost 20 percent of their standard salaries.[8]

In the early 1950s, the still-private schools usually paid teachers by hourly rates rather than monthly salaries as in public schools. All in all, the incomes of the private school faculty were no less middle class. As these campuses were gradually brought under public ownership, the teachers and administrators hired before the salary reform saw their remuneration protected by the "no change" policy. Because former missionary schools at both the primary and secondary levels had been offered especially generous compensation, over 80 percent of the faculty enjoyed a salary retention supplement after these campuses were seized by the state.[9] In 1955, the SEB reported, 40 percent of the public secondary schools paid their management personnel an average salary of 130 yuan per month.[10] Of the 117 remaining private secondary schools, over 80 percent of the school principals and heads of instruction earned more than 100 yuan and almost 30 percent earned 130 yuan or more.[11] The best-paid secondary school principals earned 150 to 200 yuan per month. As for regular instructors, they normally earned 100 yuan—in the best schools, 140 yuan.[12] In comparison to these middle-class salary figures, the average wage of workers in state-owned factories was 63 yuan per month during the same period.[13]

I have shown in Chapter 3 that the CCP considered the prerevolutionary faculty politically unreliable and kept them out of management after the revolution. It was mostly these people who benefited from the "no change" policy. In the early 1950s, the SEB reported that many of them maintained a comfortable lifestyle. They allegedly lived in "opulently and splendidly" furnished modern apartments resembling "homes of the bourgeoisie."[14] They "frequently" went to the cinema and traveled outside of Shanghai. They dressed well, dined in nice restaurants, and invited families and friends to sumptuous meals at home. Those who had a working spouse often hired servants and had savings for helping friends and relatives who were in need. Even if they had four or five dependents, the rest did better than making ends meet. Most lived "comfortably" and "satisfyingly" in an "upper-middle level" lifestyle.[15] They had no problem paying rent, utility, medical costs, and children's educational fees. If they planned well, they were able to save. If they had financial problems, it was usually only because of personal mismanagement, lavishness, or a hefty medical bill.

Even more ironic, included among the high-income faculty were people who had worked for the KMT regime or acted against the Communist political takeover. Unless disclosure of their past political behavior had led to severe punishment—which in many cases it had not—they were able to keep their original salaries. For example, the government had described teacher Wu Shouzhong, a former member of the KMT Youth Corps, as "an old hand in trickery and deception" who had had "complicated" ties to the KMT establishment, especially the Central Ministry of Education. After the revolution, he had acted cooperatively but was later found to have used "backward" students surreptitiously to attack "progressive" ones. When his campus was taken over by the government, he kept his original salary, a very high 150 yuan per month.[16] Similarly, head of instruction Jiang Shichang was "politically backward" from the CCP's perspective. He grew up in a landlord family and had been a scientist with Wang Jingwei's puppet regime during the Japanese occupation. Some of his colleagues regarded him as a traitor (*hanjian*). As a teacher, he was competent, articulate, and energetic, but "very stubborn, selfish, and individualistic." He was indifferent to "progressive" students and claimed that CCP educational reforms would not succeed. After his school was taken over by the government, Jiang was demoted to a regular teacher but kept his enviable salary of 140 yuan per month.[17]

Among the beneficiaries of the salary reform were the Communist veterans and ex-underground agents who had joined the faculty as overseers shortly after the revolution. Under official auspices, these people, seasoned educators or not, had been receiving salaries comparable to those of the other school administrators. When the salary reform took place, the authorities pressured these party members to give up their salary retention supplements in order to minimize public criticism that the CCP rewarded its own members with high salaries. Few party members, however, were willing to accept pay cuts that would greatly reduce their income.[18] One interviewee, a veteran revolutionary, had earned 200 yuan per month as a school principal since the revolution. When asked to give up his monthly supplement of 70 yuan, he politely declined but agreed that his wife, who had been receiving a salary supplement herself, would forgo hers.[19] Unlike this man, who was a career educator, other veteran revolutionaries who had been in charge of schools were not college-educated. Many were not even academically qualified to be secondary school instructors according to conventional standards. Yet thanks to the salary reform, they were among the best-paid faculty. Timing and state policy rather than academic or professional qualifications determined their salaries.

Compared to these faculty members, other teachers earned significantly less once standardized salaries were instituted. Depending on educational achievement, the unemployed intellectuals who made up the bulk of the new teachers in the 1950s started at 43 to 51 yuan per month in both the public and the private schools. Although they generally received a raise after three months of probation, their postprobation monthly salaries, 46 to 64 yuan, were closer to those of factory workers than to those of the rank-and-file instructors carried over from before the revolution.[20] It is true that the government was not satisfied with the political or academic qualifications of many of these new teachers.

But their low salaries were less a reflection of an unfavorable assess-
ment of their education, teaching experience, or class backgrounds than
of the ideological desire to suppress professional workers' income. The
new teachers were frequently better educated than the veteran revolutionaries who controlled the schools and, in the case of those who had
not worked for the KMT regime, were politically more reliable than the
senior teachers who once had. It was only their untimely entry into the
profession that cost them a better income.

Unless they had secured a teaching position before the salary reform,
the high school or college graduates who joined the faculty after the
revolution also suffered financially. In 1955 the government paid 43,
51, and 59 yuan per month to high school graduates, two-year college
graduates, and four-year college graduates respectively after they had
completed six months of teaching.[21] Many of these young instructors
became party activists, taking on additional responsibilities inside and
outside the classroom. Although relatively well-educated and hard-
working, they were the worst-paid faculty members. Had they entered
the faculty earlier, they would have earned 30 to 60 yuan more per
month.

In its 1955 survey of schools, the SEB reported that 23 percent of the
faculty had "average" or "severe" financial difficulties. Although some
high-income individuals had such trouble because they had too many
dependents or unusual circumstances, the poor ones were mostly former unemployed intellectuals or young graduates with a large family
to support. Those who had "average" troubles, the SEB noted, could
barely balance their income and expenditure. Their family's diet mainly consisted of vegetables "occasionally" embellished by "inexpensive
fish and a little bit of meat." They bought winter clothing only once
every few years and depended on "sewing and mending" for clothing
upkeep. They could not afford reference books or classroom materials
for their children. The situation of the "severely" poor faculty members
was even worse. These faculty members cut expenditure on all fronts
to buy food for the family. They sold belongings or borrowed money
to pay for rent, medicine, and other necessities. Their families, the SEB
concluded, were basically unable to survive on their incomes.[22]

Between the high- and the low-income faculty, there was a medium
group consisting of transferred cadres and demobilized soldiers who
had entered the schools after the salary reform. To alleviate dissatisfaction due to job change, the state generally let these people keep their

original salaries. Sometimes, it even offered them a small raise. Their salaries reflected salary scales in government, industry, and the military rather than their faculty responsibilities, teaching experience, or academic qualifications. As a rule of thumb, transferees from state-owned enterprises (such as the People's Bank of China) earned more than those from government (such as the Shanghai Tax Bureau), who, in turn, earned more than those from the military. This is because the CCP abolished salary retention supplements in government in the mid-1950s, but permitted their continuation in other sectors.[23] By contrast, the military did not offer any such supplements to begin with and paid lower wages. As a result, the transferees from state-owned enterprises kept their salary retention supplements; those from government received standardized earnings based on the government scale; and those from the military earned even lower salaries based on the military scale. In monetary terms, demobilized soldiers normally earned 51 to 74 yuan per month, respectively the salaries of platoon leaders and company commanders; government transferees earned between 70 to 80 yuan; and transferees from state-own enterprises could earn as much as 120 yuan. Overall, the salaries of these transferees were smaller than those of senior teachers.

FACULTY INCOME INEQUALITIES, 1956–1965

The CCP leadership was not unaware that the faculty compensation system described above was counterproductive in terms of faculty cooperation and support for the ruling regime. In the following decade, it carried out additional salary reforms to improve faculty income as well as the distribution thereof. Constrained by poor economic growth, however, its efforts were not sufficiently effective. As a result, the types of income inequality that had appeared in Shanghai secondary schools after the 1949 revolution persisted.

Two major events occurred in the school system in 1956, in the middle of what the state called the "high tide of socialist transformation": the remaining private schools were transferred to public ownership and another salary reform took place. The reform was part of an official initiative to link monetary compensation in nonagricultural work to jobholders' skill levels, a Weberian tactic of organizational rationalization par excellence. By early 1957, all faculty members had an officially designated skill grade indicating their professional standing and stan-

TABLE 4.1

Standard Salaries for Shanghai Secondary School Faculty, 1956

	Skill grade/salary (yuan)				
	1	2	3	4	5
Administrators	163.5	145.0	130.5	116.0	104.0
Teachers	157.5	130.5	106.5	94.5	83.5
	Skill grade/salary (yuan)				
	6	7	8	9	10
Administrators	92.0	82.5	74.0	—	—
Teachers	74.0	65.5	57.0	49.5	45.0

SOURCE: SMA B105-5-1808 (1956, 125–26)

NOTE: Administrators include school principals, heads of instruction, and heads of general affairs.

dardized salary entitlements. This reform helped raise faculty salaries as well as reducing the income inequities stemming from the use of the Leninist salary schemes.

Table 4.1 shows the new salary scale for the secondary school faculty in Shanghai. Faculty members were paid according to their positions in the professional, not the political, hierarchy. Appointments to political offices such as party branch secretary or party branch executive did not in itself bring extra income, although it was an important asset for promotion and pay increase, as we shall see. Theoretically, then, all faculty members were paid according to their levels of professional knowledge, skills, or experience. During the assignment of skill grades, almost two-thirds of the rank-and-file teachers and half of the school principals and heads of instruction saw an adjustment upward—a total of 6,500 people.[24] Not all of them, however, saw their income increase in absolute terms. The state stipulated that any pay raise for people with a salary retention supplement should be used to offset the supplement first, thus making their real earnings closer, if not equal, to the standardized salaries for their respective skill grades. From the official perspective, this regulation served two functions. First, it helped reduce faculty income inequities. Second, by raising the skill grades of some of the senior faculty but not their actual income, the state was in effect approving their work and promoting their cooperation with the local authorities.

After the reform, however, 46 percent of all faculty members still enjoyed a salary retention supplement. With the private schools that had been newly transferred to public ownership, this percentage was often higher. A survey of five such schools revealed a range of 53 to 85 percent. The largest monthly supplement was 63 yuan.[25] Overall, the size of salary supplements had shrunk due to the reform, but still averaged 18 yuan for regular teachers and 22 yuan for school administrators.[26] Most of the people who received real income increases were high school graduates, college graduates, and unemployed intellectuals who had entered the profession after standardized salaries were implemented. Some transferred cadres and demobilized soldiers were also among the beneficiaries. The average rate of increase was substantial: averaging 11 yuan per month for rank-and-file teachers and 9 yuan for school administrators, or roughly what one would obtain with a promotion to the next skill grade.[27] Two groups of teachers, however, did not benefit from the reform at all. They were the unemployed intellectuals and young graduates who had begun teaching shortly before the reform. New to the profession, these people had yet to qualify for salary increases. They therefore stayed at the bottom of the scales (level 8 to 10).

The 1956 reform led to what the SEB described as "a more reasonable and uniform" system of faculty compensation.[28] However, further hope for rationalization, or overcoming the Leninist-style compensation system in the faculty, was dashed by both the onset and the economic consequences of the Great Leap Forward. Originally, the government had planned a further pay raise for 25 percent of the faculty in another nationwide salary reform in 1960. In particular, it wanted to help the teachers who had not benefited from the previous reform or whose salaries had stagnated for half a decade or more. The pay raises would have served to alleviate faculty dissatisfaction toward the regime. Because of the stress on nonmaterial incentives during the Great Leap Forward and the disaster caused by this mass campaign, Beijing was forced to abandon its attempt to increase salaries in the workforce broadly.[29] In the end, less than 4 percent of all jobholders in the educational sector in Shanghai obtained a pay raise in 1960, which averaged a meager 5.1 yuan per month, or about half of the 1956 average increase.[30]

As we have seen, many party officials, or "red flags," were inserted into the faculty in the late 1950s to strengthen political control. These newcomers assumed administrative and management responsibilities. Most of them, however, were not eligible for pay increases in 1960 due to short tenure in the teaching profession. As with previous transferees, their salaries were based on what they had earned in their original workplaces rather than their faculty positions or duties. The salary reform also did little financially for the young college and teachers college graduates who had recently entered the teaching profession. As new teachers, they were not eligible for salary increases, although some would shortly assume administrative responsibilities, if not they had already done so.

The 1960 salary reform, then, not only failed to rationalize faculty income further; it reinforced the two-pronged system of faculty remuneration. Despite adding several years to their teaching experience, the low-income teachers from the mid-1950s saw little or no improvement in their income. By contrast, many senior teachers still enjoyed salary retention supplements in addition to their standardized earnings. The lack of pay raises thus perpetuated income inequalities that had nothing to do with individual qualifications, responsibilities, or performance. The reform also reinforced the dissociation between faculty income and faculty authority that the state had tried to address with standardized salaries. The "red flags" who assumed top faculty posts were not paid according to their new positions; the young activists who gained responsibilities in organizing teaching-research groups or student activities still clustered at the lowest end of the income distribution. By contrast, the prerevolutionary faculty, who had been banished from management for a decade, still received the best salaries in the profession.

As China's economy gradually recovered from the damage of the Great Leap Forward, the CCP conducted another much-needed salary reform in 1963. In Shanghai, the government acknowledged that it was high time to raise faculty and other incomes, especially for the large number of high school and college graduates who had been trained after the revolution and were gaining influence in the workplace. A 1963 report by the SEB noted the following.

In general, the college and technical school graduates who completed probation during or after 1955 have not received any promotion in skill grade or pay raise. Their current salaries are at the bottom of the standardized scale [about 65 yuan per month for college graduates]. The government has further lowered the skill grades of such graduates by one step after 1957 [about 60 yuan for college graduates]. In the last few years, these people have made relatively quick progress. They started to work at different times [between 1955 and 1962]; some are better than others; some have been promoted; but all of their salaries are at the very bottom of the scale.[31]

Thanks to the 1963 salary reform, almost half of the secondary school faculty and staff in Shanghai saw real income growth, while the raise received by another 12 percent of the faculty went to offset their salary retention supplements. But this reform, too, had limited impact on those income gaps that had nothing to do with individual qualifications, responsibilities, or authority. Due to the economic devastation caused by the Great Leap Forward, the government budgeted for even smaller raises than in 1960. The average raise in the secondary school system was a meager 3.5 yuan per month. Some teachers who received a raise were promoted by one skill grade.[32] For low-income faculty, this meant anywhere between 4.5 to a rather substantial 9.5 yuan more per month. Others had 1 or 2 yuan added to their salaries.

Because neither the 1960 nor the 1963 salary reform was particularly generous to low-income teachers, there was a "bunching" of the faculty at the lower reaches of the salary scale after the mid-1950s.[33] By 1964 the average salaries of the rank-and-file teachers and school administrators were 70 and 76 yuan respectively. Both figures had fallen considerably from their mid-1950s averages, which were roughly 100 and 120 yuan respectively. But out of 15,000 teachers in the urban area with a designated skill grade, almost half were at or below the seventh grade with monthly standardized salaries of 65.5 yuan or less.[34] By contrast, shortly before the 1963 reform, almost 4,000 faculty and staff members in the urban schools still enjoyed a salary retention supplement. The average of such supplements was 16 yuan per month; in some cases, they were over 100 yuan.[35] In other words, a faculty income divide still existed.

For many among the less privileged faculty, their perception of the income inequalities was worsened by their own progression in the life cycle. In his study of Chinese industrial workers, Andrew Walder has pointed out that wage austerity under CCP rule was experienced differently in the labor force. Income stagnation did not burden the middle-aged as much as it did young adults. The former had usually gone through some or all of those stages of life in which growing children and aging parents bring about great increases in household costs; young adults, however, had expected a salary increase to offset the cost of marriage and raising a young family. As the expected raises fail to materialize at those critical stages, the young teachers were forced to cut expenses, seek support elsewhere, or adjust their family plans. It was these young victims of extended periods of income stagnation who had the most difficult lives among the faculty.

It is well known that as the CCP consolidated its power, it gradually came to control and distribute other benefits besides salaries through the workplace. Some of these benefits, such as labor insurance and medical care, were provided to all long-term employees equally. The distribution of others, such as financial loans and subsidies, was subject to management discretion. In the schools, this meant that management could reward low-income teachers, especially activists, with the benefits that it controlled, and thus compensate for its inability to raise these people's salaries.[36] As we shall see, management did just that, which added another dimension to faculty complaints about the remuneration system.

Notwithstanding such action by management, only a small number of low-income teachers were able to raise their living standards substantially. The most desirable benefit that they could use to improve their lives—state-allocated housing—was scarcely available. Housing development in postrevolutionary Shanghai was extremely slow vis-à-vis population growth and other capital construction. In fact, per capita living areas declined significantly between 1949 and 1965. Moreover, the state privileged industrial workers and government officials in housing development.[37] As a result, even those teachers who were in dire need of housing, including party members and activists, normally had to endure a long wait for such service from the state. The case of teacher Fang Zuwen illuminates the difficulty. A teachers college graduate and a party activist who began his teaching career in 1956, he shared a room on campus with another teacher for four years and continued to live there after getting married, while his wife lived with her parents. Not until 1963, after teaching for seven years, was he allocated, in his word, "a small flat of six to seven square meters" as a faculty group leader and father of two children.[38]

A CASE STUDY OF SALARY: GUOGUANG SECONDARY SCHOOL

Guoguang Secondary School was one of the oldest private schools in Shanghai before the 1949 revolution. Its graduates had done very well, getting coveted appointments in the public and private sectors and places at overseas and domestic universities. Although its achievements were eclipsed by those of other campuses after the mid-1940s, it remained respectable within the school system. What happened here to faculty salaries after the revolution is useful for further teasing out the

TABLE 4.2

Income Distribution at Guoguang Secondary School and Salaries of
Industrial Workers Before the 1956 Salary Reform, 1953–56

Teacher type[a]	Average monthly wage (yuan)	Number of people
Veteran revolutionaries	140	1
Non-Communist administrators[b]	139	3
Teachers from the Nationalist era	107	12
Teachers hired from 1949 to 1952	109	5
Early unemployed intellectuals (assigned before official use of standardized salary scales)	108	6
Young Communist Party members	66	2
Transferred cadres	59	1
Demobilized soldiers	60	1
College graduates	51	1
Late unemployed intellectuals (appointed after standardized salary scales were introduced)	49	7
Support staff[c]	81	6
School workers[d]	55	11
SHANGHAI INDUSTRIAL WORKERS		
Beijing-controlled heavy industries	70	13,405
Beijing-controlled textile industry	60	92,297
Large, private machine factories	83	11,745
Large, private match factories	51	1,418

SOURCES: SMA B127-1-956 (1955, 1–2) (and another document that cannot be disclosed owing to issues of confidentiality)

[a]Data exclude one teacher-cum-support-staff, two part-time workers, and individuals subjected to disciplinary measures.

[b]Administrators include the school principal, the head of instruction, and the head of general affairs.

[c]Support staff include instruction assistants, librarians, accountants, and clerks.

[d]School workers include cooks, janitors, and carpenters.

political and economic issues associated with faculty remuneration.
Table 4.2 shows the pattern of salaries at Guoguang immediately before the 1956 salary reform. The figures reflect the average earnings of different types of faculty in the previous three to four years. They show a bifurcation of income between those who had entered the school before 1952 and those who arrived afterward or after the state introduced standardized salaries. In the late 1940s, Guoguang's management personnel had had close ties to the KMT regime. Before the Shanghai takeover, the school principal had fled the campus; his replacement and three other faculty members were arrested by the CCP authorities afterward. In the early 1950s, the government appointed a locally respected and "progressive" man to be the school principal to court faculty cooperation. His monthly salary was 141 yuan. The head of general affairs

and the head of instruction, both carryovers from the prerevolutionary faculty, earned 144 and 133 yuan respectively. Although very well paid, none of these people had substantive authority. The teachers regarded the school principal with personal and political skepticism as an "elegant flower vase" (*huaping*) put on campus to make it and the CCP look good. The other faculty member who had a similarly high salary was Chou Liping, the female veteran revolutionary mentioned in Chapter 3 who was embroiled in a power struggle with two younger party-member colleagues. A former deputy school principal elsewhere, she came to Guoguang in 1954. Neither a college graduate nor career educator, she earned 140 yuan per month.[39]

At this stage, the majority of the teaching staff at Guoguang had started their careers before the revolution or the standardization of faculty salaries. They therefore enjoyed a middle-class income. Among these people, a handful were former KMT members. In particular, there was a former district commissioner of the Shanghai KMT. Having lost his job after the revolution, this man registered as an unemployed intellectual and then underwent teacher-training before coming to Guoguang. In 1955, his monthly salary was 110 yuan. Another teacher, a carryover from the prerevolutionary faculty, had held the same kind of political office and earned 117 yuan. These two former KMT members were among the best-paid teachers.

In the early 1950s, the government depended on two young CCP members, Yan Bonan and Chen Yongtong, to control Guoguang. Yan was a former underground agent and a graduate of the local and prestigious Fudan University. Formally a politics teacher in the school, he was practically its head, supervising the organizational changes, political campaigns, and faculty investigation required by the government. When the school established a party branch in 1954, Yan was appointed as party secretary. A year later, he was promoted in the professional hierarchy, becoming an assistant head of instruction. The other assistant head of instruction was Lu Huowen, whom we have also met. He was an activist from the prerevolutionary faculty who had grown up in a landlord family. When Yan arrived at Guoguang, he earned nearly 90 yuan per month based on his teaching hours and administrative duties. When standardized salaries were put into effect, his salary was slashed to 60 yuan. Prior to the 1956 salary reform, he earned 66 yuan per month. By contrast, Lu earned 133 yuan, or twice as much as this party-secretary-cum-assistant-head-of-instruction.

On the surface, Chen Yongtong, the other young party member, taught politics and acted as a political counselor for students. A large part of his work, however, involved what was officially and euphemistically referred to as "personnel matters." He kept in regular contact with the Public Security Bureau, assisted in its investigation of the backgrounds of the faculty, and studied his colleagues' confessions and performance during political campaigns. Sometimes, he traveled to places outside of Shanghai to verify the backgrounds of his colleagues. A security liaison for the state, Chen was a powerful man on campus. When Yan Bonan took leaves of absence, he acted as the party secretary. Chen, too, had earned nearly 90 yuan per month initially but saw his income reduced afterward. Before the 1956 reform, his salary was 66 yuan.

The last and least influential party member at Guoguang was another person mentioned in Chapter 3, Zhu Gongzheng, the young teacher regarded by the authorities as a "petty-bourgeois intellectual" even after he had joined the party. Solely for the reason that he had started teaching at Guoguang before the revolution, his salary was based on prerevolutionary standards. He therefore earned considerably more than Yan or Chen, although neither his educational qualifications nor his party ranking were better than theirs. His salary of 109 yuan per month was the average for those teaching staff whose salaries were protected by the "no change" policy.

Before the 1956 reform, the faculty members who had the lowest salaries were almost exclusively former unemployed intellectuals, including former housewives, who entered the school after standardized salaries were introduced. Most of these people were in their thirties and, except for one person, had attended or finished college before or after the revolution. They started their teaching careers at the junior-high level. Some promptly became homeroom teachers, and others assumed that responsibility shortly afterward. Their initial salaries had been 43 yuan per month. Even with pay raises after probation, their salaries were close to, and in some cases lower than, the pay of school carpenters and janitors. As we can see from the table, despite their college experience and white-collar, public sector employment, former unemployed intellectuals had an average income lower than that of representative groups of low-skilled factory workers.

Though poorly paid, these unemployed intellectuals were not necessarily less educated or less politically desirable than their senior col-

TABLE 4.3

Faculty Income at Guoguang Secondary School before the 1963 Salary Reform, 1957–63

Teacher type	Average monthly wage (yuan)	Number of people
Non-Communist administrators	134	4
Veteran revolutionaries	128	1
Teachers from the Nationalist era, including CCP members	107	10
Teachers from 1949 to 1953, including CCP members	97	22
Transferred cadres	77	8
Demobilized soldiers	77	7
Unemployed intellectuals	65	12
Graduates of the mid-1950s or subsequent years	60	19
Other teachers	72	13

SOURCE: Archived document, Guoguang Secondary School (1963)

NOTES: One case of missing data for graduates during or after mid-1950s. Other teachers include transferees from primary schools and other secondary schools in or after the mid-1950s and one case of missing data

leagues. One of them, for example, had impressive academic and indeed political credentials. He began his college education at the famous St. Johns University in Shanghai before the revolution and finished it at the Shanghai College of Economics and Finance in 1952. After an unsatisfying appointment in Beijing, he returned to Shanghai and enrolled in teacher training for unemployed intellectuals. His class coincided with the 1955 Campaign to Wipe Out Hidden Counterrevolutionaries, and he performed sufficiently well to be appointed as a small-group leader to assist his classmates to go through the campaign. When he arrived at Guoguang, his salary was set at 43 yuan per month. Not until 1963 did he receive a substantial pay raise.[40]

Table 4.3 summarizes faculty income at Guoguang by the time of the 1963 salary reform. The campus had grown dramatically in the intervening years. The faculty now consisted of ninety-six people. Most of the newcomers were college or teachers college graduates, transferred cadres, or instructors acquired from campus mergers. Although the split in faculty income was not as sharp as before, it was still visible between those who had begun their teaching careers before or during the early 1950s and those who started afterward. Due to the salary freeze after 1956, the figures reflect faculty earnings in the late 1950s and early 1960s.

On the eve of the 1963 reform, Guoguang had thirty-seven faculty members who had started their careers before standardized salaries were introduced in the early 1950s. Twenty-eight still enjoyed a salary retention supplement ranging from 1 to 40 yuan per month. Only two of the people who had begun their teaching careers afterward had such a supplement. Both were transferred cadres who had kept their original and higher salaries since joining the faculty. The majority of the beneficiaries of salary supplements had received some college education, but a fifth had never been to college. The average of all supplements was 15 yuan per month. Half of the beneficiaries had a supplement larger than 16 percent of their standardized salaries. The man who benefited the most was the head of general affairs. His standardized salary was 104 yuan; his real salary, 144 yuan. In other words, he was employed only as a grade-5 school administrator, but his salary was equal to that of a grade-2 administrator. There were sixteen faculty members whose supplements boosted their earnings to one or more steps above the standardized salaries for their designated skill grades.

Guoguang's party branch had previously had only a handful of members, but it now included fourteen of the faculty members. But the income gap separating the party members from one another had persisted. Four had begun their teaching careers before or during the early 1950s, and their salaries averaged 107 yuan per month. Among them, one was party secretary Yan Bonan. Even though he had received pay raises in the intervening years, his salary was the lowest of these four party members, at 84 yuan per month. Each of the other three enjoyed a salary supplement, earning 100 to 130 yuan. The rest of the party members had started their teaching careers after the early 1950s. There were five college or teachers college graduates, three transferred officials or workers, one demobilized soldier, and one former unemployed intellectual. Except for one former official, who received a salary supplement, the others saw their income hurt by the standardization of faculty salaries. Their monthly salaries averaged only 62 yuan.

On the whole, the college and teachers college graduates trained after the revolution stayed at the bottom of the salary scale. Ten of the nineteen graduates earned 58 yuan per month, or the standard salary for a four-year graduate after six months of teaching. Five earned a little more by benefiting from the previous salary reforms. The rest earned less than 58 yuan because they were from two-year colleges or had recently joined the faculty. Though poorly paid, these graduates formed an influential group within the faculty. Two were Communist Party members, and twelve were Communist Youth League members. Some had been organizing the campus branches of the league for the faculty and for students; others had been teaching at the senior-high level or heading faculty groups. They were part of the young faculty from which the SEB intended to select the best performers to be groomed as future campus leaders. Fang Zuwen, a teacher activist mentioned above, was the deputy head of the math faculty group. He was a small-group leader in faculty political study, too. A 1956 college graduate with a "good" class background, he was married with two children but earning 65 yuan per month. His poor salary was in contradiction to his desirable political, academic, and professional qualifications.

The former unemployed intellectuals at Guoguang were also poorly paid. There were twelve such people in the faculty, all arriving in the mid-1950s. After gaining seven or eight years of teaching experience, only one of them had moved up the professional ladder considerably, becoming a grade-5 instructor with a salary of 84 yuan per month. Four others earned 58 yuan, the same rate as they had received upon completion of their initial probation as schoolteachers. The rest received 65 yuan per month because they had had a one-step promotion in the 1956 or 1960 salary reform. Mostly in their thirties or forties, this group of teachers had been financially disenfranchised by the CCP policy on faculty compensation.

STRUGGLE AND RESENTMENT OVER INCOME

In general, pay differentials that do not arise from differences in work authority, professional qualifications, seniority, or job performance can easily generate controversy in a modern political economy. Within Shanghai secondary schools, the problem was not only that such differentials appeared shortly after the transition to socialism had begun, but also that they existed within a Leninist division of labor, or the reproduction of a political and a technical hierarchy. The faculty with political or academic qualifications or responsibilities could reasonably argue that they deserved better compensation from the state. After all, the latter stressed the need for political control in the schools as well as students' academic performance. Likewise, the faculty could rely on Leninist or pre-1949 thinking to contend that some of their colleagues were not worthy of their high pay rates. The outcome was a faculty struggle over income, which was exacerbated by China's economic downturn after the mid-1950s, and which intensified faculty disaffection toward colleagues, management, and the state.

Before the 1956 salary reform, the Shanghai government observed that the relations between "old and new teachers" were already quite tense. After standardized salary scales were introduced in 1952, most new teachers had been paid poorly compared with senior teachers, and even those who had gained valuable teaching experience or administrative responsibilities had not gotten any pay raise. At the same time, transferred cadres were paid on the basis of their original salaries, without reference to the standardized scale for secondary school teachers in Shanghai. Faculty compensation, as the SEB conceded, was not only "chaotic and complicated"; it had "severely affected the teachers' unity and the government's ability to motivate the faculty positively."[41]

It should not be surprising that young teachers were particularly dissatisfied with their salaries. As a group, they had been gaining responsibility and stature within the profession because the government kept the older faculty out of management. However, these young men and women received the worst salaries in the profession. There was a great disparity between their influence and their compensation. The SEB noted that some young teachers had "excessively leftist sentiments" toward the prerevolutionary faculty. They complained that they themselves worked long hours enthusiastically only to watch the "unreasonably large" salaries going to the "old wily chaps." They protested that the government "took care of the old but not the new teachers." In defense of their inferior professional qualifications, which might have been alleged to justify their low pay, they contended that the state should not privilege teaching experience or educational qualification in calculating salaries. Rather, it should look at what individual teachers did on campus and their political activism. Besides seeking a pay raise, young teachers strongly wanted the abolition of salary retention supplements from the schools. As one of them put it, such supplements "were unfair [to other faculty members] and should be completely eliminated."[42]

The teachers who were demobilized soldiers and transferred cadres complained about such salary supplements, too, but for slightly different reasons. The SEB noted that the demobilized soldiers were "very proud of their credentials as revolutionaries," as they had served in the

military. They were unhappy that other teachers with much less political accomplishment received salaries two or even three times larger
than theirs.[43] As for the former government officials, they saw no reason for keeping salary retention supplements on campus, because such
benefits had already been abolished in government. If they had enjoyed
a salary supplement while in government, this had been taken away
prior to their transfers into education. Other transferred cadres shared
the sentiment that they were politically superior to the older faculty
and thus deserved better compensation. As for the former unemployed
intellectuals, the SEB observed that they, too, had "a definite degree of
resentment" due to the poor salaries they received.[44]

Although the 1956 salary reform meant generous raises for many
faculty members, it did not improve faculty relations to the extent that
the government had expected. On the contrary, it generated additional
controversies that angered and divided the faculty. Influenced by the
political thaw that subsequently led to the Hundred Flowers Campaign,
the government indicated that school management should meet with
each faculty member and use three criteria—virtue, talent, and experience (*de cai zi*)—to determine his or her skill grade and standardized
salary. Translated into political activism, professional achievement, and
work history respectively, the criteria, as the SEB later acknowledged,
still encompassed "many possible things" that had not been carefully
enumerated, weighed, and explained to the schools. As a result, management by and large conducted the reform as it wanted, while different groups of teachers had different understandings and expectations
about pay raises.[45]

Since many young teachers recognized that the state considered
them politically reliable and indispensable to further campus reform,
they stressed to school management the need to reward political activism and cooperation with the authorities. The transferred cadres from
government argued that their participation in officialdom since the revolution was evidence of their "virtue." By contrast, senior teachers emphasized the books and essays they had published and the classes they
had taught during their meeting with management. In the end, young
teachers and former officials, especially Communist Party members
and activists, or precisely those who had been working closely with
management, benefited most from the salary reform. Many saw a raise
of 10 or even 20 yuan per month, and some were promoted to management. Because of their dubious political or professional backgrounds,

or their perceived lack of *de, cai,* and *zi,* former unemployed intellectuals, including former housewives, generally received little or no pay
raise at all.[46]

To the relief of the prerevolutionary faculty, the state decided to keep
their salary retention supplements intact. But school management personnel often used the salary reform as another opportunity to attack
these teachers' position on campus. The SEB noted that management
"nitpicked" at the lifestyles of the older faculty and was reluctant to
assign them higher skill grades or to consider them for promotion.[47] As
a result, "even though many older teachers had performed well politically and professionally, they still did not get a [skill-grade] promotion"
that might have raised their level of cooperation with the government.[48]
Equally disturbing for these teachers, some of their colleagues continued to lobby management and the state for the abolition of salary retention supplements. On this matter, young teachers were particularly
vocal, challenging what they called the "theory of seniority" (*zige lun*)
used by the government to justify such benefits.[49]

Since the reform did not alter the entry salaries of high school and
college graduates, they continued to be paid poorly compared to other
faculty members. Indeed, the SEB itself voiced grave concerns about
the impact of such "workmen's wages" on young teachers after the salary reform had ended. At the primary level of teaching, such graduates'
salaries were especially poor. But those who became secondary school
instructors did not fare significantly better, for they merely earned 4
yuan more per month. The SEB noted that this problem of faculty compensation was demoralizing potential and existing teachers.

If junior high and teachers' school graduates go to work in a primary school,
they earn 39 and 47 yuan respectively (and they start at 30.5 and 38 yuan). If
they work in a factory or as a bus conductor, they earn more than 60 yuan. A
19-year-old new worker with three years of primary education earns 60.4 yuan
after three months of probation. The minimum salary for a nurse is 51.5 yuan,
but the majority of nurses from nursing school earn 61 yuan right away. The
students in teachers' schools are disturbed after knowing these differences. . . .
Some even try to quit school to become workers.[50]

At the height of the Hundred Flowers Campaign, some teachers,
still very upset by how little they had benefited from the salary reform,
lashed out at their colleagues, management, and the state. The following are examples of their attacks, which indicate both their anger and
their belief that teachers should be paid according to their responsibilities, education, job performance, or other rational criteria.

Salary reform was the most unjust thing on earth. It has violated the laws of
heaven as well as human reason.

There wasn't any standard when teachers were evaluated for pay raises. The
salary reform was a farce, a show. . . . The party used its own incredibly elas-
tic tape to judge teachers' sacred work. Sometimes the measure comes up
long, sometimes mysteriously short. You never knew how it's obtained.

In last year's salary reform, management produced a name list that fully revealed that those who had high salaries would get raises, but those who
had low salaries would get little or nothing. In a word, it was the party and
youth league members splitting the spoils. Those close to management were
promoted by three grades. Old teachers were not promoted, but they kept
their salary supplements.

Teacher salaries are too low, not even comparable to those of cooks or barbers.
. . . A college graduate only earns 42.5 yuan. Nowhere else in the world can
one find such salary standards.[51]

In theory, management could use a welfare fund available to the
schools to help low-income teachers or alleviate faculty dissatisfaction
at income inequality. It did, in fact, do that to some extent. In a survey of
nine schools and four hundred employees between 1953 and 1955, the
SEB found that management doled out financial subsidies almost 150
times to help teachers who were sick, unable to support their families,
or burdened by sudden and costly events.[52] In a 1961 study of one campus, 4 percent of the employees regularly received financial assistance
and another 11 percent obtained it when the need arose.[53] However,
the disbursement of such subsidies, like the determination of salaries,
was marred by political prejudice that engendered faculty resentment
against management and the state.

According to the SEB, the central government noted during the mid-
1950s that "a large proportion" of school welfare funds was "unused,
embezzled, or misappropriated" at the local level. In some areas, the
authorities deliberately hoarded the funds rather than using them to
help the school workforce. It was reported that school management
and local governments imposed "harsh and unreasonable" requirements on faculty members who sought official assistance, and that the
process of "application was complicated and appraisals were untimely
and improper." As a result, the teachers who needed assistance did not
dare to apply for it.[54] Frequently, the authorities allegedly based their
decisions on the "political consciousness and performance" of the ap-
plicants rather than how urgently they needed help. The teachers with
"bad" class backgrounds therefore faced additional obstacles in gain-

ing access to the welfare funds. Sometimes, not only were their requests denied, but they also received reprimands from the authorities during the application process.[55] In Shanghai, the SEB surveyed twenty-eight secondary schools and found that 20 percent of the teachers who needed help did not get what they deserved. One teacher stated that getting welfare subsidies from the government was similar to being tried in court.[56]

After the Anti-Rightist Campaign, the central government no longer stressed individual virtue, talent, and experience in the 1960 salary reform. Instead, school management was asked to decide pay raises *"mainly* on political consciousness and professional ability, while taking into account educational qualification and years of teaching."[57] Official reports indicating the reform's beneficiaries are not available. Given the elevation of political consciousness as a main criterion and the tightened political climate, and the fact that less than 4 percent of the school workforce in Shanghai received a raise, we can assume that school management felt even stronger to reward those who had been supporting its work and restrict pay raises for others, including those with stronger teaching experience. In fact, this was exactly what happened in the following and broader salary reform in 1963.

In the 1963 reform, the last before the Cultural Revolution, the pattern of management discrimination was well documented. Although the official intent of the reform was to alleviate long-standing income inequities in the teaching profession, school management targeted specific groups for pay raises at the expense of state policies. The SEB reported that over 50 percent and 40 percent of the people who joined the faculty in 1959 and 1960 respectively got a raise. But these percentages "greatly exceeded" those that the official budget had allowed for these recent additions to the faculty.[58] As we saw in Chapter 3, this cohort mainly consisted of current college and teachers college graduates, transferred cadres from government, and former workers. Compared to their earlier cohorts of teachers, they had the best political backgrounds. This suggests that school management, once again, rewarded teachers close to it because their cooperation was critical for the political functionaries who made up management to exercise everyday domination on campus despite their unconvincing professional credentials.

By contrast, the SEB reported that school management imposed "higher, stricter, and more" demands on older teachers. It had the idea that it should "equalize" (*laping*) faculty salaries, especially by with-holding raises from those who already had a relatively high salary. Overall, the government had planned pay raises for half of the faculty and staff in the entire school workforce. In the end, however, school management offered raises to only 30 percent with disproportionate concentration among recent entrants noted above.[59] Ironically, the longer one had taught, the less likely one was to receive a raise. Compared to their colleagues, the teachers who had begun their careers before 1954, the SEB noted, were not even half as likely to receive a raise.[60] In the schools, the faculty ignored by management were mainly the prerevolutionary faculty and former unemployed intellectuals, that is, those at the bottom of the political hierarchy.

Because party cadres controlled management, they wielded great influence on the distribution of pay raises and other rewards. Along with activists, they were the major beneficiaries of the salary reforms. However, not all party members benefited equally from their collective domination of the campuses. Just as occurred with faculty promotion, the earlier they entered the faculty, the more likely they were able to take advantage of official reforms to improve their own livelihoods. However, few of the party members who had joined the faculty after the 1956 salary reform were able to gain handsomely from the 1960 or 1963 reforms due to the comparatively meager raises they offered. This development had a particularly poignant impact on younger party members. In his study of Chinese Communist rule, Lynn White has observed that before the Cultural Revolution, party members in industry were overworked and underpaid; "their days were full of pressure and self-sacrifice, not just new power." Grassroots party members, he wrote, "were often no happier than the rivals they had partially displaced."[61] This was an apt description of the lives of the young party members who arrived at the schools after 1956. Despite their important contribution in helping the CCP tighten its control of the schools, most of them stayed at the lower end of the faculty income distribution as they gained teaching experience and administrative responsibilities. Some faculty members of the same rank or even under their supervision earned twice as much as they did. To paraphrase White, these younger party members, despite gaining power or, more precisely, because of it, could not but harbor resentment against their older colleagues as well as the state. They shared "a sense that the CCP owed them more than it was giving."[62]

A COUNTER-BUREAUCRATIC SYSTEM
OF COMPENSATION

In Leninist political thinking, the salary retention supplements the CCP doled out to professional workers were part of the expenditure the regime had earmarked for co-opting "bourgeois experts" and "petty-bourgeois intellectuals" during the transition to socialism. As Beijing realized, their disbursement was also in contradiction to their own socialist philosophy, as they perpetuated class inequalities, this time through the action of the socialist state. Within Shanghai secondary schools, the salary retention supplements turned the faculty whom the regime considered least politically desirable into the most economically secure and privileged employees. Although the CCP leadership had plans for progressively improving its system of compensation for professional workers, the poor performance of the economy in the late 1950s dashed any hope that a more rational schedule of faculty income would be established. The state was unable to raise faculty salaries broadly, and it never reduced the supplementary benefits proffered to the high-income faculty. As a result, a bifurcation of income persisted in the schools amid a fermentation of income inequalities that bore little or no relation to differences in qualification, authority, seniority, and responsibility.

A divisive issue by itself, the problem of faculty income was further compounded by changes in faculty relations and composition. First, the CCP revamped the school authority structure, privileging political biography and class background as criteria for management posts. However, the majority of the Communist Party members who assumed such posts earned less than the faculty members they had displaced. Second, a generation of young teachers whom the state blessed with increasing authority was being paid poorly by the standards of the teaching profession as well as compared to other occupational groups such as factory workers. Third, management used its power to reward people close to it with pay raises but slighted others who had accumulated teaching experience. In terms of human reaction, the outcome of faculty compensation was that low-income teachers resented the state, management, and the activists for having undue influence over faculty income; those who possessed power on campus resented the older and "suspect" faculty for receiving higher salaries; and almost everyone felt that they did not receive what they deserved.

In Weberian theory, rational remuneration is a key component of modern bureaucracy. A well-defined scale of compensation based on technical qualification, responsibility, and performance (or a combination of these factors) helps alleviate staff anxiety over income and livelihood. It can improve staff cooperation and organizational performance. From this perspective and the evidence above, the CCP system of faculty compensation did not provide any well-argued or convincing measure for recognizing technical qualification, responsibility, experience, or performance. Faculty salaries represented a break from the conventional logic of professional remuneration, but they did not reflect the changing authority relations on campus or satisfy the needs of many for pay raises. A counter-bureaucratic feature of faculty organization, faculty compensation was counterproductive to faculty solidarity and work motivations and therefore to the development of education and, more broadly, to Chinese socialism.

5

The House of Deviants

In spring 1953 the Shanghai Education Bureau received a letter from one Wen Haihuan. In his fifties and unemployed, Wen had recently been an instruction assistant at Sanlian Secondary School. In this four-page well-penned letter, he described his misfortunes and implored the authorities to give him work. He stated that he suffered from stomach bleeding, back pains, throat problems, and skin diseases; he had little appetite for food or drink and did not sleep well at night; and the left side of his face was badly swollen. He mentioned that he had been moving in and out of run-down hostels and that he got out of bed every day in pain to clean himself and cook. He indicated that the Shanghai Education Bureau (SEB) was his last resort for improving his life for his few remaining years. Within days, the reply arrived. The SEB rejected his request for a job.[1]

What is remarkable here is not the official denial of assistance to a destitute, forlorn, and sick man, which was apparently at odds with the well-documented expansion of social welfare under the rule of the Chinese Communist Party (CCP) in the 1950s. Wen was a serial child molester whom the authorities had described as "depraved, rotten, and incorrigible." A former teacher, he had been demoted to library clerk and then instruction assistant before being forced out of the campus. The fact that he could still approach and even bargain with the authorities for a job challenges the dominant scholarly image of criminal justice under Mao. For decades, research has stressed the abusive nature of the Chinese Communist state or how it bludgeoned society into submission with labor reform, incarceration, and capital punishment.[2] The kind of leniency Wen the recidivist had received for assaulting school-girls until his expulsion, and the fact that a criminal like him was not imprisoned, is rarely mentioned, still less explained.

Within Shanghai secondary schools, the leniency enjoyed by Wen was far from exceptional. The government never leveled an all-out assault on the faculty found guilty of wrongdoing. To the contrary, convicted counterrevolutionaries, rightists, and criminals often served out their sentences on campus. A major reason for this was that the state needed teachers to cope with increases in student enrollment. That is to say, the same Leninist utilitarianism informing the use of former KMT agents in the teaching ranks also led to the keeping of deviants. But this pattern of official discipline—conviction followed by retention—had a major impact on faculty composition. It created campus pariahs who were stigmatized both because of their offenses and on account of the state's restrictions on their freedom and entitlements. This produced yet another faculty cleavage on top of standing political, social, and economic divisions.

To put this differently, it is well known that the CCP regime not only punished individuals for unsatisfactory job performance, but also targeted political expressions and private behavior that were unacceptable by official standards. As the state probed into and denounced personal thinking and lifestyles, it created what Sidney Greenblatt called an "epidemic of deviance" within state and society.[3] Previously normal people became suspects of wrongdoing and even crime; some were then punished officially. Within the schools, however, a kind of leniency persisted behind this intrusive, anti-Weberian discipline. The state let faculty members convicted of offenses such as counterrevolutionary acts, theft, and child molestation remain on campus, often to the dismay of management and other faculty members. The wrongdoer, in turn, endured strict supervision, reduced income and privileges, mandated labor, and low social esteem as punishment. In effect, the schools were integrated into the penal system, which could not but have serious implications for both faculty solidarity and faculty reactions toward the state. Before examining how faculty punishment reinforced the schools as counter-bureaucratic administrations, a discussion of the CCP system of penalties is in order.

THE STRUCTURE OF FACULTY DISCIPLINE

After the 1949 revolution, the CCP quickly abolished the judicial system and legal instruments established by the KMT. In the early 1950s, military control commissions, ad hoc people's tribunals, government departments, and the police shared the judicial function, meting out sentences to convicted wrongdoers.[4] The lines of authority or spheres of responsibility among these organizations were not always clear. In Shanghai, the SEB was primarily responsible for discipline in primary and secondary schools. In theory, it only administered sentences for what the state regarded as unlawful but not criminal conduct; the latter, a more serious category of wrongdoing, was under police or court jurisdiction.[5] But a formal code distinguishing the two types of illegal conduct was not strictly enforced. As a result, the SEB disciplined professional impropriety such as slothfulness and insubordination as well as graver offenses such as embezzlement, sexual assault, and even "counterrevolutionary" acts.

As Jerome Cohen observed, the sentences delivered by extrajuridical organizations (such as the SEB) were based on "the miscellany of isolated published proscriptions" and unpublished official policies, instructions, reports, and regulations. Because such material changed and accumulated over time, local officials did not distinguish unlawful conduct from criminal wrongdoing with consistency. The distinction between the two kinds of offenses was further complicated by the principle that factors related to the perpetrators (such as class background, job performance, prior offense, and extent of remorse) could be used to determine whether they were guilty of a crime or a lesser unlawful act. The judicial process thus "neatly meshed" the punishment of unlawful conduct with that of criminal conduct. Extrajuridical organizations often punished acts considered criminal and punishable by the court in other countries.[6]

In the mid-1950s, the CCP tried to establish "an orderly system" of criminal justice by copying legal procedures and instruments from the Soviet system. The reforms reduced the judicial role of extrajuridical organizations but did not eliminate them completely, as "certain relatively severe sanctions . . . continued to be meted out by agencies other than courts."[7] By the late 1950s, China's political break with the Soviet Union and added reemphasis on the "mass line" ended the legal reforms. As local control of the judicial process increased, the SEB regained its judicial authority and, once again, became the primary disciplining agency in the school system.

Officially, the SEB meted out administrative sanctions (*xingzheng chufen*) but not criminal sanctions (*xingshi chufen*), which were the prerogatives of the court and the police. There were eight types of administrative sanctions available to the SEB: (1) criticism-education, (2) warning, (3) record of error, (4) demotion, (5) dismissal from office, (6) expulsion from education, (7) supervised labor, and (8) reeducation through labor. The first five were enacted in the schools. Criticism-education (*pipan jiaoyu*) meant that management, usually the party secretary, would verbally admonish the wrongdoer. If the SEB preferred, it could issue a formal warning (*jinggao*) to the wrongdoer verbally or in writing. These were the lightest penalties; nothing about the misdeed would be recorded in the wrongdoer's dossier.

The SEB could choose to mark an error (*jiguo*) or a severe error (*jidaguo*) in wrongdoers' dossiers while reducing their salaries and state subsidies. From here onward, the process of punishment was quite conspicuous. The wrongdoers had to produce written confessions and self-denunciation, which could be posted on campus with announcements of the imposed sanctions.[8] Sometimes, management would hold employee meetings or even invite students to denounce the wrongdoers in person. With demotion (*jiangzhi*), the SEB would reduce the wrongdoer's professional rank by one or more grades and cut his or her salary accordingly. Alternatively, the SEB could hand down a dismissal from office (*chezhi*). For school administrators, this meant that they would be demoted to teaching or lower positions. Dismissed regular teachers would become clerical assistants, library workers, or menial laborers.

The rest of the administrative sanctions took effect outside the schools. With expulsion from education (*kaichu*), wrongdoers would be put in a lowly position in a factory or other enterprise. In the first years after the revolution, they were let go without any reappointment, which was what happened to Wen Haihuan. Supervised labor (*jiandu laodong*) was similar to expulsion from education, as the wrongdoer would perform manual labor in a factory or farm under its management's supervision. The harshest administrative sanction meted out by the SEB was reeducation through labor (*laodong jiaoyang*). Here the wrongdoer was sent to a labor camp for people whose offenses were "between crime and error." These people would live and work under conditions often as onerous as those in labor camps designated for criminals.[9]

For wrongdoers, none of the above sanctions was irreversible. Their behavior during the sentences and the state's adoption of new disciplinary rules often helped these people to terminate or reduce their penalties. In the mid-1950s, Beijing promulgated *Provisional Rules for Annulment of Administrative Sanctions for Primary and Secondary School Teachers and Staff Members*. These rules permitted those who had received a warning or record of error to apply for its annulment six months after the sanction. Those who had been demoted or dismissed from office could apply for annulment, too.[10] An annulment did not erase the offense from the wrongdoer's dossier but restored some or all professional privileges, including eligibility for teaching posts, pay raises, and promotion. Although the provisional rules did not apply to those who were removed from the schools, expulsion from education, supervised labor, or reeducation through labor did not necessarily end teaching careers. The SEB still maintained the authority to decide the convicts' future with these sanctions. Good behavior during a labor sentence would aid the wrongdoer's cause when seeking to return to the school system. Alternatively, the SEB could find positions elsewhere for convicts or let the correctional facility where they had served out their sentence decided their fate.[11]

Like every adult, schoolteachers who were guilty of wrongdoing could be subject to criminal sanctions (*xingshi chufen*) meted out by the court or the police. In these cases, the SEB had already turned these people over to the above authorities for investigation and decision. The lightest criminal sanction was called "control" (*guanzhi*). It was designed to expose the convicts' identities socially while keeping them productive in the workplace. In the early 1950s, the CCP used this sanction widely to rein in former KMT agents who were branded as "counterrevolutionaries." The "controlled elements" would carry on with their work and lives, but under official restrictions and surveillance. Public meetings were held to announce their sentences, and representatives were chosen in their places of work and near where they lived to monitor their behavior. Among the restrictions, the convicts could not travel or move without approval. They had to report to the local police regularly and work for the local neighborhood. Their salaries and benefits were also cut.[12] Those who were schoolteachers were not eligible for management positions and could not be homeroom teachers, politics teachers, or student counselors.[13] A form of criminal punishment, control was, in fact, less taxing physically, financially, and emotionally than the harsher kinds of administrative punishment.

The other noncapital criminal punishments the government could hand down to schoolteachers were labor reform (*laodong gaizao*) and imprisonment. In these cases, the convicts were sent to labor camps or prisons for a fixed term. But their sentences were sometimes suspended so that they could continue to work in the schools under management supervision. In such cases, the schools virtually became the probationary agency of the convicted, who would definitely be demoted and whose salaries and benefits would be cut. As long as the convicts were obedient on and off campus, they would be eligible for permanent or better posts in the schools after completing their sentences.[14] In addition, the SEB could retake released inmates into its fold and appoint them as administrative assistants, library clerks, or even teachers. Although the central government sometimes encouraged labor camps to hire or retain released convicts at or near the camps,[15] the SEB did bring some former inmates back into the schools in the 1950s.

Besides the above sanctions, Communist Party members in the school system were subject to special party disciplinary measures (*dangji chufen*). Due to a lack of data, this chapter does not examine the punishment of school party members. Suffice it to mention that the disciplinary process for party members was "often handled in semi-secrecy" to protect the party's prestige. In practice, however, it engendered popular suspicion that party members were able to get preferential treatment.[16] From what we saw in Chapter 3, with veteran party members guilty of wrongdoing taking up school leadership positions, it would appear that wrongdoers who were party members received lighter sanctions.

It must be noted that some people who were accused of wrongdoing would use their informal ties to those in authority positions to influence the sentencing process. The way the CCP judicial system was set up, with both decentralization and an unclear division of labor, encouraged and facilitated such backdoor maneuvering. The presence of this informal influence in penal procedures, like the opaque process of disciplining party members, only complicated issues of fairness and justice with official punishment, which involved decisions by extrajuridical organizations to begin with. As a result of formal and informal favoritism, more rather than fewer wrongdoers were kept in the schools.

In sum, the structure of faculty discipline, too, reflected the Leninist utilitarianism that informed teacher recruitment and assignment. It revealed the party's desire to exploit "bourgeois" knowledge and skills during the transition to socialism. There were, to be sure, periodic variations in disciplinary practice, but there was no question that the faculty system promoted the retention or reinstatement of wrongdoers. It is time therefore to look at how the SEB actually deployed punishment in the schools for disciplinary *as well as* staffing purposes.

LENIENCY IN THE THOUGHT REFORM CAMPAIGN

In his pathbreaking research on Thought Reform under Communist Party rule, Theodore Chen exposed the various tactics deployed by the state to compel intellectuals to take part in confessions and political study. Even though few intellectuals were actually beaten, the means were "often violent and painful" or "semicoercive or covertly coercive," and physical force was "always around the corner."[17] Chen's study, however, begs the question of punishment: how did the state penalize those found guilty of wrongdoing? In fact, the Thought Reform Campaign of the early 1950s set a trend of lenient punishment of intellectuals that persisted throughout the 1950s, because this social group was deemed to be useful for the development of socialism. In this respect, Thought Reform was quite different from the Campaign to Suppress Counterrevolutionaries that had started a year before and encompassed the entire society, as many so-called counterrevolutionaries had been imprisoned or even executed by the state during this other campaign.[18]

As we saw in Chapter 3, Thought Reform demonstrated to the Shanghai authorities that secondary schools contained an abundance of politically unreliable or even threatening people. At least 20 percent of the faculty and staff had worked for the KMT regime, of whom a minority had been ranking officials and hundreds had been political, intelligence, police, or military officers. Some had worked undercover in the schools; a few had even killed Communist Party members or soldiers. There were former landlords, religious cult leaders, sex offenders, drug traffickers, and thieves among the faculty and staff.

As the first group of almost four thousand faculty and staff completed their Thought Reform in the summer of 1952, the SEB cautioned against harsh punishment. "Be strict on repudiating bourgeois and erroneous thoughts; be lenient on punishment. Be stricter on disciplining individuals with historical and political problems; be lenient on personal depravity, degeneracy, and corruption. Use the method of 'bringing down one man to warn a hundred.' Discipline a few and educate the majority. Do not hurry to punish, but mete out sanctions gradually and group by group."[19]

There were three reasons for this policy. First, teachers were badly needed in the schools. In 1952 alone, there was a 43 percent growth in student enrollment. In comparison, the number of teachers had increased by a mere 5 percent since the revolution (see Table 2.1). Cleansing the teaching ranks was not a real option for the government, because it would have removed teachers from the classroom. Second, because the almost concurrent Five-Anti Campaign had led to massive layoffs in other sectors, the authorities did not want to exacerbate unemployment and increase the chance of social unrest by dismissing teachers. Third, there was concern that the use of harsh sentences would dissuade the faculty and staff who had yet to undergo Thought Reform from disclosing their backgrounds, beliefs, and lifestyles. Without such disclosure, the SEB would have difficulty comparing these people and recruiting among them activists who would support the work of school management and the implementation of campus reforms.

Table 5.1 summarizes the penalties for the 252 people who were convicted as counterrevolutionaries among the 4,000 faculty and staff. As Julia Strauss has noted in her research on the Campaign to Suppress Counterrevolutionaries, Beijing did not have clearly defined rules for designating a person as a counterrevolutionary in the early 1950s.[20] In general, four factors shaped the authorities' decisions vis-à-vis the secondary school faculty and staff in the 1950s: what the wrongful conduct was, who the wrongdoer was, how the wrongdoer responded to the charges, and the prevailing political climate. Whether one was convicted of unlawful, criminal, or counterrevolutionary conduct, however, could have very different implications. Whereas unlawful conduct was punishable by administrative sanction and crime by criminal sanction, a counterrevolutionary was, by definition, a political criminal.

During Thought Reform, four kinds of people were classifiable as counterrevolutionaries: those who had held important positions in

TABLE 5.1

Sentences for Counterrevolutionaries in Shanghai
Secondary Schools, July–September 1952

Deserve capital punishment	2
Deserve arrest	16
Criminal control	20
Collective training	15
Political education	46
SUBTOTAL	99
Special cases for investigation	6
No need for immediate action	147
TOTAL NUMBER OF CASES	252

SOURCE: SMA B105-1-665 (1952–53, 27)

the KMT establishment, especially in planning or executing attacks on Communist Party members; those who were "blood-debt elements" (*xuezhai fenzi*) guilty of violent crimes or murders; those who had recently engaged in political activities against Communist political rule; and those who had adamantly resisted cooperating with the authorities during the campaign or who had urged others not to cooperate.[21] Overall, 60 percent of the above 252 counterrevolutionaries had been ranking officials in the KMT Party or Youth Corps; another 30 percent had been special-service agents. There were thirteen local tyrants (*eba*), one occult leader, and six perpetrators of unspecified crimes.

Remarkably, 60 percent of the counterrevolutionaries escaped punishment. The SEB recommended the execution of two people, incarceration of sixteen, and criminal control of twenty. It wanted to put fifteen people in what it euphemistically called "collective training," which involved further interrogation through threats or coercion. Forty-six would undergo further political study, and six others would be further investigated. Whether those who underwent further interrogation, investigation, or education would return to the schools depended on the outcomes of these processes.

Cooperation with the authorities was the best policy for avoiding harsh punishment. According to SEB instructions, those who had been guilty of political sabotage but who cooperated during Thought Reform, *even though not fully,* should be subject to collective training or investigation rather than incarceration. "Blood-debt elements" would not be arrested so long as they confessed their crime *partly* and there was no "mass outrage" (*minfen*) against them in the local community.

Those who had been guilty of *serious* sex-related, economic, or other offenses would be demoted or transferred to another campus if they cooperated with the authorities during Thought Reform. The people in this last category were usually those who had stolen large sums of money, molested schoolchildren, or used drugs or prostitutes multiple times. The SEB instructed that "only in a few extremely severe cases" should the perpetrator be dismissed from office or expelled from the educational system completely. It indicated that consideration should be given to one's job performance, relations with "the masses," local reputation, and social status.[22]

When another group of faculty and staff, some eight hundred people, participated in Thought Reform in the autumn of 1952, the government, facing high unemployment and severe shortages of teachers, wanted wrongdoers of all kinds to be kept on campus. Only the worst offenders should be removed:

Insist on not arresting those who could either be arrested or let go. Make sure that those who are arrested have committed crimes deserving five years of imprisonment or more. For individuals whose crime warrants less than five years of imprisonment, suspend their sentences, put them under criminal control, or keep and monitor them in the schools. Employ the method of "few arrests and more training; few incarcerations and more criminal control."[23]

Because professional knowledge and skills were badly needed in the expanding school system, special consideration was granted to faculty with professional training or experience. The SEB stated that former "core" KMT officials and "regular" special-service agents who were well educated and had cooperated in the campaign should not be removed from the classroom, so that they could "atone their guilt with contribution to socialist development" (*ligong shuzui*). More remarkably, even those who were guilty of serious crime, who had yet to "confess completely," and who had aroused mass outrage were eligible for leniency—if they were "proficient in a line of work" (*yiji zhichang*). These people would not be put straight into labor camps but into collective training to see whether they were salvageable for the schools.[24] In stark contrast to the Cold War image of a highly repressive CCP regime, the authorities actually went to some lengths to avoid punishing the faculty and staff. "Even objectionable elements (*elie fenzi*), such as those who have raped female students or trafficked in drugs, need not be dealt with at once. Only when it is absolutely necessary should we use the law against them. Whenever we can use some leniency, use it!"[25]

By the time the third and final group of some 1,500 faculty and staff took part in Thought Reform, the policy of leniency had become public knowledge. The SEB reported that many of these people came prepared. Some had their personal biographies written; others readily recited their confessions when asked, detailing "erroneous" beliefs and conduct. These participants merely wanted to finish Thought Reform safely and return to work. For the government, the policy therefore engendered an unexpected development, as some people exploited the leniency by providing perfunctory confessions without laying out all that the authorities wanted to know. Lacking resources, the SEB could not verify the validity of hundreds and hundreds of confessions, at least not immediately.

After the Thought Reform Campaign, the SEB continued to investigate the existing faculty and staff as well as new teachers. By the end of 1954, the government had arrested 891 people from Shanghai's primary schools and 456 people from its secondary schools since the 1949 takeover.[26] However, it had permitted a larger number of people whom it considered politically questionable to stay on campus. According to official but "incomplete statistics," there were 1,774 counterrevolutionaries and "special-service agent suspects" in the schools. In addition, the SEB estimated that 8,200 people, or 20 percent of the primary and secondary school personnel, had "ordinary political and historical problems or were subjects of registration or investigation."[27] Many were former KMT members or officials; others included members of outlawed religious cults, ex-convicts, and former military police.

LENIENCY IN THE CAMPAIGN TO WIPE OUT HIDDEN COUNTERREVOLUTIONARIES

Ferociously launched nationwide in mid-1955, the Campaign to Wipe Out Hidden Counterrevolutionaries, or *Sufan*, briefly mentioned in Chapter 2, penetrated officialdom, industry, and other sectors. The central government saw the campaign as a means of tightening political controls within state and society, as well as furthering the pursuit of agricultural collectivization and the nationalization of industry and education.[28] Within Shanghai secondary schools, the pattern of punishment during *Sufan* did not indicate an all-out state assault on alleged political enemies. Rather, it suggested that the state's continual drive toward industrialization and modernization, which demanded more schooling opportunities for teenagers, helped many faculty and staff to escape jail sentences and stay in the schools.

Within the schools, four kinds of people were targeted for investigation, public criticism, and formal punishment: (1) those who faced new accusations or evidence of "counterrevolutionary crime" committed before the 1949 revolution; (2) those who allegedly had not honestly disclosed their political activities or ties to convicted counterrevolutionaries or former KMT special-service agents; (3) those who had been spreading harmful opinions about the party despite having received leniency for wrongdoing; and (4) those whom the police suspected of being engaged in counterrevolutionary activities.[29] In short, the targets were the dishonest, the unreformed, and saboteurs. Convicted counterrevolutionaries, criminals, and wrongdoers who had been working properly were not formal targets.

The campaign began with the government evaluating the management of each school to see whether it was politically qualified to carry out the campaign. If not, local officials or faculty members from elsewhere would be assigned to the school. In principle, each campus was to have had a "three-person nucleus" to run the campaign, with activists providing support. The faculty and staff were divided into groups to take part in political study, confessions, and reporting on others (*jianju*). On the basis of the information so collected and faculty and staff records, the authorities on campus then decided whom should be investigated further. They would join force with the SEB and the police to conduct the investigations.

The SEB later admitted that in the heat of the campaign there had been excessive attacks on faculty and staff, because its own personnel had not "sufficiently understood the difficulties and complexity of the campaign or completely grasped its policies, objective laws, or special aspects." As a result, some cadres had been "too subjective, rash, and rude" in dealing with some faculty and staff. They had not "calmly or carefully analyzed the material" gathered on these people, but had been "too anxious to get results and therefore intensified the struggle."[30]

When *Sufan* ended in early 1957, the SEB had apparently rectified such excesses by limiting the extent of punishment. It stated that in the nineteen schools it directly operated, a total of 2,377 faculty, staff, and school workers took part in the campaign. Among them, 111 people turned out to be "subjects of investigation," and 35 had been targeted for removal from the schools. In the end, 21 were sentenced as counter-

revolutionaries, including 12 former KMT special-service agents, 6 former KMT officials, and 1 blood-debt element.[31] Based on this conviction
rate, there would be fewer than 150 people (1.2 percent) in the secondary school workforce sentenced as counterrevolutionaries. Another report indicates that 600 counterrevolutionaries and criminals (*huai fenzi*)
were "weeded out" from the primary and secondary schools.[32] If these
people were proportionately distributed in the two types of schools
according to the sizes of their workforces, some 200 faculty, staff, and
workers in the secondary schools were convicted as counterrevolutionaries or criminals.

Because *Sufan* overlapped with the political thaw that would lead to
the Hundred Flowers Campaign, many of the convicted escaped severe
penalties. In late 1956, Beijing issued a decision to limit punishment in
the campaign. It indicated that the struggle against counterrevolutionaries had "already been won" and the leadership wanted to "mobilize
all forces that can be mobilized" to build socialism.[33] Once again, the
building of socialism, which required political compliance *and* technical expertise from a Leninist perspective, was a key consideration in the
determination of sentences. Sanctions up to imprisonment and even
execution were, so to speak, negotiable on the basis of one's job performance and willingness to admit guilt. Reductions of, or even exemp-
tions from, punishment were accorded when individuals decided to
"thoroughly confess" their social backgrounds and political activities or
had established "merit" in their work. Even those "against whom there
was great popular anger" were eligible for leniency when they admitted guilt.[34]

Within the schools, the decision to be lenient provided much relief
to the targets of punishment. In its final reports on *Sufan*, the SEB noted
that among the convicted counterrevolutionaries, "a minority had been
sentenced according to criminal law, and the overwhelming majority received lenient treatment and remained in the schools."[35] Gong Shouzhi
and Xia Lei were both former KMT Party officials who were convicted
and punished as counterrevolutionaries during *Sufan*. The punishment
they received illuminates not only how penalties were meted out, but
also the lengths to which the authorities went to keep wrongdoers on
campus.

According to the SEB, Gong, a teacher at Fuxing Secondary School,
had been concealing his political identity before *Sufan*. He had worked
for the KMT for three decades, holding district- and city-level posi-

tions since the 1920s. During the Japanese occupation, he was a traitor working for an intelligence agency set up by Wang Jingwei's regime. He was an instructor and recruiter in the agency and its liaison officer in the schools. He went on to become the KMT Party secretary of Jiangsu Province and sat on the executive board of the Bureau of Social Welfare under the puppet regime. During *Sufan*, the school party branch indicated that Gong's performance as a teacher had been good and that he had not been linked to any illicit activity since the revolution. The authorities decided not to prosecute him for his dishonesty and lengthy political career under KMT regimes. It demoted him to the post of clerical assistant to the principal and recorded "severe error" in his dossier.[36] Because Beijing announced the rules for the annulment of administrative sanctions shortly after, Gong was therefore eligible to apply for the termination of these minor penalties and regain some of his professional privileges, including teaching responsibilities.

Similarly, Xia Lei, a teacher at Girls' Secondary School Number Four, had been hiding his past. The SEB noted that he was a former special-service agent in the KMT's Central Bureau of Statistics and Investigation. He had also been a district-level KMT Party secretary in Shanghai, Hankou, and Yichang. During his tenure, he recruited two to three hundred party members, quashed a theater company run by the Communist resistance, and attempted to arrest underground Communist Party members. According to SEB records, he had been giving "reactionary" lectures and talks to students since the revolution despite warnings from school management. His uncooperativeness was a major reason that he received much harsher punishment than Gong, even though both teachers had been involved in similar types of political activities before 1949. Xia was arrested by the police, removed from the school, and sentenced to seven years in prison.[37]

Archival records suggest that the government arrested three kinds of people from the schools: formerly convicted counterrevolutionaries who had been insubordinate in the schools; former ranking officials or blood-debt elements who had been hiding their identities since the revolution; and others who were charged with sabotage or a serious crime. Thanks to Leninist utilitarianism, even these people were not all imprisoned or put into labor reform—only the worst and unreformed offenders were. Some arrestees who were experienced teachers were exiled to remote provinces such as Ningxia or Qinghai that needed teachers badly. Compared to those who would be incarcerated, these people had probably shown some degree of remorse or cooperation before or after being convicted as counterrevolutionaries. They would become schoolteachers in those provinces but under harsher physical conditions and would have little chance of returning to Shanghai during the Mao era.

In June 1957, the central government ended the Hundred Flowers Campaign due to what Chairman Mao called "wild attacks against the working class and the Communist Party." It initiated the Anti-Rightist Campaign to reassert political and ideological control within state and society. In Shanghai, the municipal government exhibited resolve to punish those faculty and staff who had taken aim at the party. Paradoxically, however, the campaign added another relatively large group of deviants—rightists—to the campuses.

By April 1958, as the Anti-Rightist Campaign was ending, the SEB reported that 3,086 people in primary and secondary schools, including adult schools, had been convicted as rightists. On top of this figure, 1,175 people had been convicted as counterrevolutionaries and 194 people as criminals in the schools after the *Sufan* campaign.[38] In Wangpu district, for example, there were 58 rightists in 12 secondary schools, and 12 other people were labeled counterrevolutionaries or criminals. As a whole, the SEB stated, more than 10 percent of the teachers were rightists, counterrevolutionaries, or criminals.[39]

Table 5.2 shows the penalties meted out to some of the rightists, counterrevolutionaries, and criminals in the secondary schools during the Anti-Rightist Campaign. The offenders were overwhelmingly teachers and male; 2 percent were Communist Party members.[40] Because the data are from an undated document, it is not clear how representative the penalties were. But the relatively large numbers of punishments suggest that they included the majority of the penalties meted out in the secondary schools during the campaign.

As before, the wrongdoers were either removed, permanently or temporarily, from the schools or punished on campus. The authorities generally removed permanently from the campuses those on whom criminal discipline, reeducation through labor, or agricultural labor had been slapped (1, 2, 4a, and 5a in Table 5.2). Almost half of the offenders were therefore removed permanently. The majority of them were

TABLE 5.2

Sentences for Rightists, Counterrevolutionaries, and Criminals (huai fenzi)
from Shanghai Secondary Schools During the Anti-Rightist Campaign

Sentences	Count	Percentage
1. Criminal discipline[a]	244	19.6
2. Reeducation through labor		
a. Discharge from state employment	31	2.5
b. Suspension of state employment	42	3.4
3. Removal from office and supervised labor	151	12.1
4. Removal from office		
a. Agricultural labor education	182	14.5
b. Labor education in school	63	5.1
5. Suspension of teaching position		
a. Agricultural labor education	120	9.6
b. Labor education in school	158	12.7
6. Demotion and pay cut	193	15.5
7. Exemption from sanctions	62	5.0
TOTAL	1,246	100

SOURCE: SMA A23-2-1398 (n.d.)

exiled from Shanghai; the rest were reassigned to factories or farms in or near Shanghai. Though banished from the schools, some of these people would be able to teach again after serving their sentences. Those whose eligibility for state employment was not formally terminated (2b, 4a, and 5a in Table 5.2) could be appointed to teaching posts at or near their places of exile depending on the demand for teachers there and their behavior.

The other half of the offenders remained in the schools or returned there after a labor sentence. Twelve percent of the wrongdoers were sentenced to farm or factory labor that would last from one to three years (number 3 in Table 5.2). Within this group, those who behaved well would return to teaching; the rest would assume technical or clerical duties in the schools. Another 18 percent of the wrongdoers were given reeducation through labor to be carried out on campus (4b and 5b in Table 5.2). They were usually not allowed to teach and reassigned as administrative, technical, or library assistants. These people would also be able to regain teaching privileges based on their behavior. Another 16 percent of the wrongdoers were demoted but kept their teaching privileges (number 6 in Table 5.2). Finally, 5 percent were simply labeled as rightists and exempted from other sanctions.

In August 1958, the Shanghai government announced that 6.1 percent of the faculty and staff in primary and secondary schools had been convicted as rightists. Over 1,900 people were removed from the campuses permanently or temporarily. The rest, more than 1,100 people, stayed behind. The school faculty also consisted of 361 of the 1,352 counterrevolutionaries convicted during *Sufan* and the Anti-Rightist Campaign. Despite the removals, the report noted that "there is still a large number of former counterrevolutionaries, criminals, and other kinds of reactionaries [in the schools]." In addition to the above people who were still in the schools, there were those convicted before *Sufan* but who had not been affected by *Sufan* or the Anti-Rightist Campaign. They, too, remained on campus. The government estimated that the schools still retained more than 3,600 counterrevolutionaries and other offenders. Altogether, they made up 5.2 percent of the existing school workforce.[41]

At the secondary level, many of these people continued to teach, due to the lack of teachers. In October 1958, the SEB reported that more than 60 percent of the counterrevolutionaries, criminals, and rightists, or almost seven hundred people, were classroom instructors. About three hundred taught literature, history, and geography, courses that the state preferred to be taught by politically reliable instructors. In fact, one hundred people who had been convicted as "serious" (*yanzhong*) counterrevolutionaries were instructors of these or other subjects, and almost one hundred wrongdoers were homeroom teachers, heads of faculty groups, or heads of instruction. A few still had the ceremonial title of school principal.[42]

Case records are useful in illustrating further how the Shanghai authorities dealt with deviant teachers during the Anti-Rightist Campaign. Zhen Zhaoquan was a physics teacher. According to the SEB, he was a secretary of captains in a KMT army division in the early 1940s. He carried a handgun and often followed his superiors when they undertook activities that included extortion and plunder. In 1945 he was a section chief in the areas of organization and training in a division of the KMT Youth Corps. He became the chief editor of a newspaper established by this division, promoting "counterrevolutionary propaganda." Then he became the executive secretary of the Quell Rebellion and Build the Nation Committee in Songjiang County near Shanghai, forcing people to enlist in the military and engaging in blackmail and extortion. After the revolution, Zhen confessed his previous political activities. His work as a teacher was reportedly acceptable. However, he took part in attacking the party and the state during the Hundred Flowers Campaign. The authorities demoted him and sentenced him to three years of criminal control, but did not remove him from the school.[43]

By contrast, Chen Dejiong, a chemistry teacher with a rather poor political record, was not only spared from punishment; he was able to exploit the campaign for his career. The SEB reported that Chen had been a section chief in a provincial education bureau during the Japanese occupation, which made him a national traitor. He came to Shanghai after the war and changed his identity. In the early 1950s, he confessed what he had done to the authorities. Since then, he had been "actively and positively" doing his work and participating in school activities. When the Anti-Rightist Campaign began, Chen adopted a "clear-cut and firm stand," condemning and "struggling against" the rightists. As a result, the school party branch requested permission from higher authority to put Chen in a small group of faculty and staff that had been helping with the campaign on campus.[44]

These and other cases from archival records suggest that the people who were imprisoned, put into labor reform, or removed permanently from the schools during the Anti-Rightist Campaign were only the so-called extreme rightists (*jiyou fenzi*) or "current (*xianxing*) counterrevolutionaries."[45] They had usually held important civilian or military positions in the past or had used their offices or authority to thwart the Communist movement.[46] The harsh sentences these people received, however, were not directed at these past actions. After years of Thought Reform and investigations, the SEB had excellent knowledge of the social and political backgrounds of the faculty and staff, yet had chosen to keep many counterrevolutionaries on campus. The "extreme rightists" and "current counterrevolutionaries" received harsh punishment because they had continued to offend the authorities despite having been treated leniently. Their dissent in the Hundred Flowers Campaign was therefore used as evidence of their unceasing opposition to Communist political rule and socialist development. Had they remained discreet throughout their teaching careers or even during the campaign, they would probably have escaped punishment. Had they received moderate support from management for their political and professional performance, they would have received lighter sentences or even remained in the schools like other rightists. They were removed from the schools because their behavior, cumulatively, breached the limit of Leninist utilitarianism that the Shanghai government deployed to staff the secondary schools.

PUNISHMENT OF LUST AND GREED

With help from school management personnel, the SEB also investigated and punished sex and economic offenses committed by the faculty or staff after the 1949 revolution. Romance with adult students, adulterous affairs, and promiscuity were formally punishable. In general, the guilty did not lose their jobs but received a warning or record of error or were demoted. Sexually harassing a colleague or molesting or raping a student was punishable by demotion, dismissal from office, or expulsion from education. As for rape, the SEB only handled what was referred to as "rape by enticement" (*youjian*), that is, when the perpetrator used extra lessons, money, or other means to lure a minor into sexual intercourse. In the case of "rape by force" (*qiangjian*), the SEB would deliver the rapist to the police for prosecution. Embezzlement, fraud, and theft were not uncommon on campus. The majority of the perpetrators of these offenses were clerical employees responsible for collecting fees, accounting, or purchasing, but some teachers were guilty of such wrongdoing, too.

Table 5.3 summarizes the penalties for seventy-seven sex offenses and sixty economic offenses that occurred in Shanghai secondary schools between 1952 and 1957. Whether this documentation on such offenses and their punishment is exhaustive for this period is not known. Similar documentation for the periods between 1949 and 1952 and after 1957 is not available. From the documented cases, however, we have an unprecedented picture of how the government punished

TABLE 5.3

Punishments of Sex and Economic Offenses in Shanghai Secondary Schools, 1952–57

	Warning or less	Error or demotion	Dismissal from office	Expulsion from education	Total
SEX OFFENSES					
Sex with students	—	1	2	2	5
Harassment	1	3	1	—	5
Adultery	7	17	4	2	30
Molestation	4	7	3	6	20
Rape or attempts	—	1	12	3	16
ECONOMIC OFFENSES					
Theft	—	6	—	1	7
Corruption	—	7	2	4	13
Embezzlement	6	19	3	12	40

sex and economic offenders found in the schools. As with the punish-ment of political deviance, mitigating or aggravating factors affected the sanctions. When the wrongdoer did not cooperate during investi-gation, was guilty of other offenses, or had "poor" class background or poor job performance, the SEB imposed a harsher sentence.

Besides the offense and the offender, timing was a key factor in the determination of the penalty. SEB records show that cases settled in 1952 and 1953 resulted in relatively light sanctions that were consis-tent with the leniency deployed during the Thought Reform Campaign. Harsher penalties were then meted out until the mid-decade political thaw. For example, only one of eight cases of child molestation in 1952 and 1953 led to the offender's expulsion from education. But five of seven cases in 1954 and 1955 saw the offenders expelled. In 1956 and 1957, none of the five cases of molestation led to an expulsion. In fact, none of the nine perpetrators of rape or attempted rape in 1956 and 1957 was expelled from the schools.

The economic offense case settled in 1952 is quite telling about the le-niency allowed during Thought Reform. The school clerk had collected bribes and gifts and stolen money totaling no less than 20,000 yuan. This was a very large amount, as anyone who earned 100 yuan per month was regarded as well paid by Shanghai standards. The perpetra-tor reportedly also had a "bad" class background and had taken drugs and visited prostitutes. In spite of these circumstances, the SEB did not hand him over to the police or expel him from the campus. Rather, it kept him in the school as a manual laborer.

The following case illustrates anew the leniency of punishment in the early 1950s. In May 1953, the police arrested secondary school teacher Wang Lexian for raping a fourteen-year-old boy. A few days later, it passed Wang's case to the court and notified the school to pick him up from the station. The faculty and staff then held a meeting with Wang on campus and pressured him to make a confession. Wang admitted to using the boy as well as other boys to help him masturbate, but denied sodomizing them. His colleagues were not satisfied with his confession and felt that he was not remorseful. Three days later, he was compelled to confess again, but his colleagues were still dissatisfied. They wanted him out of the campus because he had "an indecent, indulgent lifestyle" and had "severely harmed the mental and physical health" of his vic-tims. Meanwhile, neither the police nor the SEB found any evidence that Wang had, in fact, sodomized the boys. The SEB concurred with the faculty and staff that he was guilty of sex offenses. But it maintained that his confessions were sufficiently honest and that some faculty and staff did not have full knowledge of the offenses and had become "confused." It emphasized that he had not assaulted any student on his own campus and therefore rejected the campus's recommendation that he be expelled. In the end, Wang, a serial child molester, was let off with a record of error.[47]

In 1954 and 1955, the SEB was quite harsh with wrongdoers who had multiple offenses, showed little remorse, or had a "poor" class background. The number of dismissals and expulsions shot up as rapists, molesters, embezzlers and, frequently, adulterers were dismissed from office or expelled from education. The SEB turned many over to the police or the court for criminal prosecution. By contrast, the ensuing political thaw produced a dramatic relaxation of punishment. Among the sixteen cases for which information is available, only one economic offender was expelled from education and two were dismissed from their posts. Other perpetrators received punishment that did not revoke their teaching or administrative privileges. This leniency was continued into 1957 until Beijing launched the Anti-Rightist Campaign.

SEB records show that significant discrepancies often existed between the sanctions wanted by the schools and those meted out by the SEB. The latter had the obligation to staff the schools, while school management had an interest in maintaining a politically and morally desirable workforce. As a result, management often wanted tougher sanctions than the SEB was willing to render. Sometimes, the SEB rapped wrongdoers over the knuckles with a record of error despite management's request for expulsion from education; on other occasions, it issued a warning when the faculty wanted the wrongdoer to be dismissed or demoted. Rarely did the SEB mete out sentences harsher than those requested by management.

There was closer agreement on sanctions between the SEB and the faculty and staff in 1954 and 1955, when they all wanted to rid the campuses of the worst offenders. But whatever influence over sanction decisions the schools had gained by 1955, it was wiped out in 1956. In thirty-seven cases in which both the sentences suggested by the schools and those handed down by the SEB are available, the SEB favored lighter sanctions in twenty-two cases. In some cases, there was a huge discrepancy. For instance, one school wanted to revoke the teaching privilege of a teacher who was guilty of molestation, but the SEB decided that he should receive education and criticism—one of the lightest sanctions available. In another case, the school wanted to expel a former labor-reform convict for sexually harassing his colleagues, but the SEB imposed nothing harsher than a record of error.

There is a lack of archival data on faculty punishment from the early 1960s to the eve of the Cultural Revolution. During this period, the SEB's sentencing decisions were probably influenced by contradictory developments. On one hand, the arrival of large numbers of college and teachers college graduates at the schools made the service of wrongdoers less important. This would have freed the SEB to deploy harsher sentences to cleanse the faculty. On the other hand, the political thaw of the early 1960s helped convicted rightists to return to the schools and probably had a moderating effect on punishment. Due to the tightening of political climate, harsh penalties were apparently more common after 1962. In 1964, for example, the SEB launched a campaign targeting rapists and other sex offenders in primary and secondary schools for severe punishment. What these people had perpetrated was no longer a mere sex crime. With Mao's reemphasis on the importance of class struggle within state and society, their offenses were reinterpreted as bourgeois revenge on socialist youth.[48] The chance that the authorities would treat sex offenders leniently had disappeared. But the government certainly did not compensate for its previous omissions in punishment by proceeding to purge the faculty of deviants. As we shall see in the next chapter, evidence from the Cultural Revolution indicates that convicted counterrevolutionaries, rightists, and other offenders continued to work in the schools, and even teach, up to the eve of the social upheaval.

AN EPIDEMIC OF DEVIANCE

For the Chinese Communist state, faculty discipline was aimed at exacting behavioral compliance with official political, professional, and moral standards. Besides punishing criminal and improper workplace conduct, it targeted prior political activities and current dissent, as well as adultery, gambling, and other lifestyle issues. As the government probed deeply into the lives of the faculty, an ever-increasing number of them were found politically or morally wanting. A look at some of the labels the SEB attached to faculty members—historical counterrevolutionary, current counterrevolutionary, key suspect, backward element, Trotskyite, CCP renegade, reactionary Christian, rightist, bad element, and former landlord—confirms that what Sidney Greenblatt might have called an "epidemic of deviance" flourished in the schools.[49]

An equally important aspect of faculty discipline was the retention of wrongdoers. For staffing and other reasons, the state practiced on-campus punishment of many of its former political enemies, as well as wrongdoers. Only those who were regarded as the worst offenders were removed permanently; the punishment of the rest stopped at physical, financial, and professional penalties. Over time, the number of faculty still on campus who had been disciplined by the state increased, because new deviants were continually created by the political campaigns that penetrated the schools. As we saw in Chapters 2 and 3, other establishments also took advantage of the schools' weak bargaining position and sent them politically undesirable cadres during transfers. Furthermore, as official job assignment replaced the labor market, however badly faculty who had been disciplined wanted to leave campus, they could do it only at the risk of unemployment. The outcome was an accumulation of deviants on campus.

The presence of retained wrongdoers on campus had a grave impact on faculty relations. As we have seen, school party members were generally dissatisfied with their nonparty colleagues and kept their distance from these people. The suspicion, contempt, and abuse that they directed against this section of the faculty were partly because there were all kinds of deviants among this group. Some party members understandably felt that convicted counterrevolutionaries, rightists, child molesters, and other wrongdoers were not qualified to be teachers. From their perspective, these people would have been removed from the campuses by management but for the party's leniency. The unwelcome participation of these deviants in the faculty thus exacerbated the tension between party members and nonmembers.

Even the most mundane events illustrate party members' distrust of, or disdain toward, the deviants. In the early 1960s, the SEB reported that management at City West Secondary School had warned a young teacher against "problems in his private life," most likely having to do with drinking, gambling, or sexual behavior of which the authorities disapproved. On the teacher's wedding day, a party member, acting on behalf of the campus branch of the Communist Youth League, sent him a mirror as a gift. This gesture, traditionally deemed to be mean and inappropriate for such an occasion, suggested that the teacher "should take a hard look at himself and reflect on his personal problems." Even the SEB authorities felt that the party member and Youth Leaguers had acted improperly.[50] Insults like this did not imply that school party members led morally irreproachable lives themselves. Some of them were guilty of womanizing and other misbehavior that led to censure by the party. The episode, however, illustrates how little solidarity existed in this faculty, for a universally celebratory occasion had become yet another opportunity to attack a colleague.

As I noted in Chapter 3, by the late 1950s, school management, responding to change in political climate, would rather commit what the state described as "leftist mistakes" than "rightist mistakes." It was in management's interest to avoid being seen by higher authority as weak in front of subordinates. There is evidence to suggest that school management treated convicted wrongdoers worse than before, specifically, denying these people any financial assistance even when official policy allowed it. The SEB noted that during the 1963 salary reform, management was unwilling to recommend pay raises for those who had at some time been disciplined by the government and those who had worked for the KMT regime.[51] For example, a primary school head of instruction had been demoted in 1956 after being caught having illicit sexual relations. According to official records, he had been "performing well politically and professionally" since then. Compared to his thirty-five colleagues with the same official skill grade, he was the best teacher on campus. Yet management, not willing to appear soft on wrongdoers, did not give him a raise because of his mistake seven years before.[52]

The campus retention of wrongdoers divided the teachers, too. The child molesters, embezzlers, and thieves who had victimized the schools or specific faculty or students were understandably shunned by their colleagues. More important, as Ezra Vogel has pointed out, party members and activists or, in general, anyone with a proper work record, tended to avoid people who had "problems in their background," as the government frowned on any "budding friendship" that involved those who had been disciplined or had "bad" class backgrounds.[53] The official rationale was that former KMT agents, landlords, and convicted wrongdoers should not be allowed to influence others' thinking or behavior.

Of course, there were those who believed that some convicted wrong-doers were innocent or had been unfairly punished by the state—for criticizing management or official policies, for example. However, these skeptics would have been foolhardy to show their sympathy by public-ly befriending the convicted. Management could easily single them out for attack in the next political campaign or refuse to recommend them for a pay raise, promotion, or even urgent financial subsidies. Despite their indignation over unjust punishment, therefore, most sympathiz-ers were reluctant to risk their careers or livelihoods. Innocent or not, the wrongdoers were forced to endure social isolation.

The intense isolation of these people was evidenced by the two CCP members at Guoguang Secondary School whom we met in Chapter 3 and who were branded as rightists. One compares his experience as a rightist to that of "the untouchables in India." He recalls that "friend-ship was broken *overnight*": his colleagues would not talk to him, and he would have risked further punishment had he tried to befriend other rightists or convicted wrongdoers on campus. After stints of la-bor reform inside and outside the campus and clerical posts within it, this once young and promising party member had his rightist label removed in the early 1970s, some fifteen years later. Although he re-turned to teaching at Guoguang, the stigma continued to affect his life and even conjugal choice. Considered undesirable in the marriage mar-ket, he eventually tied the knot with someone he called another "un-touchable," a woman whose father was a convicted counterrevolution-ary, whose sister had been a rightist, and who had no legal residence in Shanghai.[54]

The other rightist explains why people like him had trouble getting married.

When I was branded as a rightist, my salary was cut from 107 to 44 yuan and my party membership was stripped. I didn't want to harm my girlfriend. It was very hard for anyone who had a rightist in the family, so I broke up with her. There were rightists who married other rightists, workers, and so on. But their families did not have pleasant experiences, anyway. When my rightist cap was removed, I still had trouble getting married. I was in my late forties but earning 44 yuan per month. It was not good for people that age to be earning that little.[55]

By and large, then, faculty wrongdoers led a marginal and some-times even precarious existence on campus. They could not escape from being shamed or from the lowly status imposed upon them by the state, as public stigmatization was part of their punishment. They had poor career prospects and were vulnerable to renewed attacks in every political campaign initiated by the party. With nowhere to go or hide, they were pariahs in the schools.

COUNTER-BUREAUCRATIC DISCIPLINE ON CAMPUS

For Weber, rational discipline is a critical feature of modern bureaucratic administrations that can enhance staff commitment to work and support of management. In principle, formal punishment is meted out only when one fails to perform one's official duties. Weber did not specify what constitutes inappropriate conduct or reasonable punishment. His discussion of modern bureaucracy, however, suggests that such conduct and punishment should be determinable on the basis of impersonal rules transparent to both management and staff. He emphasized that rational discipline is different from traditional punishment, the exercise of which is based on personal discretion with severity circumscribed only by tradition.

Within Shanghai secondary schools, the 1949 revolution ushered in Leninist-style discipline. Faculty members were punished not only for unacceptable professional conduct such as theft or child molestation, but also for their political biography and opinions, personal association, and lifestyle. The KMT had targeted and fired teachers resisting its political rule before the revolution, but full-fledged Leninist-based discipline penetrated the school system only under Communist Party rule. The penalties for deviance of any kind, be it slothfulness, insubordination, rape, or attack on the party and the state, fluctuated with the political climate and with the offender, as offenders would receive considerations based on background, job performance, and cooperation with the authorities. As a result, the same offenses often led to widely different sentences.

The technical demands associated with China's rapid modernization and the CCP's Leninist-based ideology led the Shanghai authorities to keep as many wrongdoers on campus as the political situation permitted. Over time, the schools thus saw an accumulation of deviants among the faculty and staff because their professional experience was hard to replace in the skill-starved economy. Counterrevolutionaries, child molesters, thieves, and others whom management would have removed from the schools served their sentences on campus while taking part in "building socialism." To put it simply, the Leninist approach to punishment both created and preserved an epidemic of deviance among the faculty and staff. It was counter-bureaucratic in three ways: it invaded the private lives of the workforce, deprived management of the right to reject employees, and denied the disciplined the freedom to seek other positions.

This development further damaged relations in the already divided faculty. Some Communist Party members found wrongdoers objectionable and treated them with strong suspicion and contempt. Even those who might have thought more charitably about these people would ultimately prefer to make a less career-threatening "leftist" error rather than a "rightist" mistake, when dealing with the wrongdoers. To protect their own welfare, other faculty members generally dissociated themselves from the wrongdoers or avoided being seen as too close to them. With their stigmatization and subjugation within the schools, the wrongdoers constituted a highly repressed group. As the Chapter 6 shows, they participated actively in the violence of the Cultural Revolution. They were ready to avenge their subjugation as soon as they were free of it.

Before we go on, it is necessary to mention the CCP discourse of Red and Expert (*hong yu zhuan*), which permeated state and society in the late 1950s, based on what we have learned in this and the previous chapters. Initiated by Mao, this discourse exemplified official desire to enhance workplace relations and productivity after the Hundred Flowers Campaign revealed debilitating tensions within schools, universities, factories, and other establishments. The party insisted on strengthening professional training for those with political qualifications (the Reds) to help them undertake further technical responsibilities. At the same time, it intensified the pressure on those with academic qualifications (the Experts) to reform their political consciousness through political and labor reeducation. The party leadership imagined that this two-pronged approach to reform would raise the workforce's professional skills as well as political commitment to socialism. Lingering into the early 1960s, the reforms engendered many debates under official auspices about the proper relationship between the two groups.[56]

The Red and Expert discourse, however, was grossly insufficient for addressing the multidimensional workplace problems produced by counter-bureaucracy. It epitomized the leadership's failure in understanding the tensions ripping apart the workplace. As we have seen, the problems that plagued Shanghai secondary schools in the 1950s and early 1960s extended far beyond veteran educators lacking political dedication or party members lacking professional skills. Because of official policies, the faculty was divided socially, politically, economically, and morally. The party's reductive dichotomy of Red and Expert and preferences for the relationship between the two groups not only ignored the social heterogeneity of the faculty; the discourse failed to address the underlying Leninist tactics of organization responsible for producing the schisms, tensions, and resentment in the schools in the first place. The Red and Expert discourse was not an antidote for workplace disorganization but another manifestation of the party's Leninism.

6

Campuses in Distress

I now recognize what the Cultural Revolution was truly
about in my school. The student rebellion and teachers'
factional strife were mixed together. We, the students,
became the tools used by others.
—Feng Jicai, famous Chinese writer[1]

In June 1966, students all over China began to attack their teachers. Until then, the Cultural Revolution, an idea of Chairman Mao's, had been
restricted by Premier Zhou Enlai and other members of the central government to the criticism of literary and academic works against Mao's
wishes.[2] The students' rebellions transformed the restrained campaign
into a violent popular movement against intellectuals, traditions, and
the political authorities. Two months later, when student Red Guards
frantically occupied Tiananmen Square to salute Mao for his political
leadership, thousands and thousands of teachers had already been
abused, assaulted, tortured, or even murdered. Within schools and colleges, Leninist-style management and workplace practices were either
overturned or severely challenged by the political uprising. For the rest
of the Mao era, Maoist organizational practices shaped faculty life. Unlike Leninist tactics that stressed domination by party members and the
cooptation of "bourgeois intellectuals," the Maoist practices were based
on principles of popular management, egalitarianism, and asceticism,
as well as a virulent anti-intellectualism. Major organizational changes
thus occurred in education because of the Cultural Revolution.

This chapter extends my analysis of counter-bureaucracy under Chinese Communist rule to the Cultural Revolution (1966–69). I draw on
archival sources and research on the Cultural Revolution in Shanghai
and in Beijing, where the student rebellion started, to contend that because of accumulated tensions and resentment, the faculty *at all levels*
coaxed, assisted, and rallied students to attack other faculty members.
There are two reasons for expanding my discussion beyond Shanghai

secondary education. First, my aim is to show that after nearly two decades of Leninist workplace reforms, faculty solidarity in terms of management and the teaching staff supporting one another in time of crisis, or even each group closing ranks to defend against the other, was practically nonexistent. Instead, teachers were as eager to attack management, or help it attack other teachers, as management personnel were willing to sacrifice their colleagues and subordinates to protect themselves. The Cultural Revolution laid bare the tensions and resentment that had been poisoning the entire teaching profession.

Second, it is still relatively difficult to research the Chinese Cultural Revolution. The schoolteachers whom I met discussed their experience prior to the mass movement openly; most, however, were reluctant to talk about themselves in detail during the upheaval. Their reactions probably were results of psychological pains and guilt and perceived risk of punishment by the government for relaying confidential information to an overseas researcher. Furthermore, the Shanghai Municipal Archives, which allowed me to study large amounts of records from the 1950s and early 1960s, still strictly controls access to documents compiled during the Cultural Revolution. I have therefore combined various kinds of data to highlight that some faculty joined the Red Guard movement, sought control of the campuses, or even vied for political power. This picture of faculty activism, although quite incomplete, is critical for correcting what has been an influential but partial view that teachers and, more broadly, intellectuals (*zhishifenzi*) were mainly victims of the student uprising. Faculty activism was, in fact, a catalyst of the student rebellion, particularly of its brutal attacks on the faculty itself.

The other half of this chapter describes the reproduction—or, more precisely, intensification—of counter-bureaucracy in Shanghai's school system under Maoism. We shall see that as management by Communist Party members lay in ruins, primary and secondary schools were controlled by a variety of soldiers, workers, peasants, students, and teachers. This heterogeneous group of people had one thing in common: they had little or no experience in managing educational establishments. Due to another expansion of schooling opportunities, meanwhile, the number of teachers increased dramatically. The newcomers came from many walks of life and lacked teaching credentials. Furthermore, faculty income inequities and arbitrary and repressive discipline persisted, despite the fact that Maoism espoused egalitarianism and popular control of the workplace. That is to say, the rise of Maoism not only reproduced but also intensified political domination, shortages of expertise, income inequities, and arbitrary punishment in the schools.

In his influential work on organizations under the rule of the Chinese Communist Party (CCP), Harry Harding is right that even though the Cultural Revolution engendered significant reforms, strong continuity persisted in the constitution of the workplace—for example, there was still a formal hierarchy of offices, formal rules and regulations, distinct careers, and rank-based salaries and wages after the mass movement waned. However, he is wrong to conclude that the movement ultimately re-created modern bureaucracy in another guise, just as those whom he criticizes are wrong in asserting that the uprising led to the elimination of modern bureaucracy from China.[3] Both interpretations of the Cultural Revolution presume incorrectly that work organizations had shared the rational-legal characteristics of the Weberian bureaucracy before the mass movement. The previous chapters have shown that Shanghai secondary schools had been organized as counter-bureaucracy before 1966. Evidence below suggests that they were still counter-bureaucratic afterward. For the schools, the entire Mao era represented the reproduction of counter-bureaucracy through and through.

VICTIMS AS VICTIMIZERS

The Red Guard movement of the Cultural Revolution has been a major research topic in Chinese studies. Why did apparently ordinary youths brutally assault their teachers, party and state officials, as well as one another? Why did they not stop when enjoined by Mao or other political leaders? Research has rightly focused on political and social life under CCP rule, especially the intense political socialization of the students, their class backgrounds, life chances, and ties to powerful officials, as well as the career and other opportunities created by the movement itself. It has, however, largely left out the role of the faculty or merely depicted their victimization by the students.[4] The fact that next to families and friends, teachers had had the closest relations with the students before the mass movement was apparently immaterial to the development of their uprising. Likewise, the prior complete control of the campuses by the faculty has not been theorized as having any particularly noteworthy impact on the uprising, besides turning the faculty into its first victims. From the early 1980s onward, this image of passive, maltreated faculty in research on the Cultural Revolution has been reinforced by memoirs and stories by Chinese intellectuals recounting their sufferings and by official interpretations of the mass movement written to discredit Maoism.[5]

The fact is, however, that as soon as popular mobilization replaced the repressive state during the Cultural Revolution, the tensions that had been tearing the faculty apart since the 1949 revolution erupted into faculty attacks against colleagues and campus officials alike. Suzanne Pepper is correct when she suggests that most teachers "also rode out the storm as more or less active participants rather than victims."[6] No understanding of the Red Guard movement is complete without addressing the impact of such faculty activism on the youth. In Shanghai, in particular, it was the top school and college officials who dealt the first blows of the mass movement by targeting subordinates. Their actions ignited the student rebellion, which, ironically, would turn them into its main targets.

As a popular movement, the Cultural Revolution began in late May 1966 within the famed Peking University. By then, Chairman Mao firmly believed that a new bourgeoisie whose interests were "in absolute conflict with the working class and poor peasants" had emerged in China. This new class of exploiters consisted of mainly party cadres, including ranking party officials, who had benefited from the redistribution of power, prestige, and wealth since the 1949 takeover. Mao contended that members of this "bureaucratic class" had been taking "a capitalist road" in the workplace rather than building socialism. They had produced and countenanced social inequalities that benefited themselves. They would have to be defeated in order to save the socialist project. To cripple their capacity to do further harm, he wanted these "capitalist roaders" in the party and the "ox ghosts and snake demons" who resisted socialism to be turned into "targets of struggle and revolution."[7]

After failed maneuvers within the party, Mao and his allies in the political leadership turned outward and launched a popular movement to achieve political change. Their initial targets were Peking University and the Beijing party apparatus. On 25 May 1966, with Mao's clandestine blessing, Nie Yuanzi, a party secretary in the university's philosophy department, and six instructors displayed a "big-character" poster on campus. This *dazibao* accused Lu Ping, the university party secretary and president, of suppressing the Cultural Revolution. Startled and angered, Lu contacted officials in the Beijing Party Committee and quickly mobilized the Communist Youth Leaguers on campus to denounce Nie and her group as "party renegades" and "antiparty elements."[8] The attack and counterattack between Nie and Lu foreboded a wider struggle among educators.

On 1 June 1966, the national radio broadcasted the entire content of Nie's *dazibao*, which also appeared the following day in the official *People's Daily* and other newspapers.[9] On 3 June, Lu lost his university positions, and other professors and officials in the university were denounced publicly by teachers and students for thwarting socialist development. The upheaval rapidly spread to other schools and colleges in Beijing. The swiftness of the denunciation of campus administrators and teaching staff by their colleagues, practically within hours of the poster's publication, is perhaps the ultimate testimony that little social solidarity existed in the faculty. Faculty tensions descended into vehement political attacks.

In Shanghai, school and college management did not tumble immediately as some of them did in Beijing. Rather, a top-down campaign that resembled the Anti-Rightist Campaign but was broader and more violent and threatened more people took place in the following weeks. Within two days of the publication of Nie's poster, the Shanghai Municipal Committee, seeking to control the Cultural Revolution in Shanghai, named nineteen people in academia and the cultural sector as "key subjects of criticism and struggle." Most of these people were professors; at least three were Communist Party members. They were labeled "bourgeois academic authorities" and "ox ghosts and snake demons."[10] What they had done professionally and politically before and after 1949 was now used against them as "evidence" of their misdeeds or ill intentions against socialist development.

School and college management all over Shanghai then followed suit, selecting older teachers and convicted counterrevolutionaries, criminals, and rightists for attack. The targets of attack quickly spread to the faculty of "bad" class background. Heretofore the most powerless people on campus under the normalization of counter-bureaucracy, they were reclassified into the "five bad categories" (landlords, rich peasants, counterrevolutionaries, criminals, and rightists) of antiparty, antisocialist forces that, once again, deserved public repudiation. In his eyewitness account of the Cultural Revolution in Shanghai, Neale Hunter indicated that college officials used a three-pronged strategy— target prominent academics, attack ordinary teachers, and offer mild self-criticism—to protect themselves from teachers' and students' attacks. Their targets included some CCP members, who were now denounced as "bourgeois representatives who had infiltrated the party." These party members had probably had disagreements or disputes with management in the past and were instantly cut off by the powerful faction of party members. To avoid being criticized by students and teachers for suppressing or controlling the rebellion, some campus officials deliberately refrained from naming targets openly. Rather, they used trusted teachers to put up *dazibao* or hinted who within the faculty should be denounced.[11]

At the Shanghai Institute of Finance and Economics, the SEB reported, sixty-nine people were named as targets on 3 June 1966. At Teachers' College, sixty-one teachers were named on the morning of 4 June 1966, of whom forty-three were older teachers and eight were Communist Party members.[12] At Guoguang Secondary School, nineteen people shared the ill fate.[13] A former college student interviewed by Anne Thurston confirmed that campus management quickly targeted subordinates in these early days of the upheavals:

At the beginning of the Cultural Revolution, they plotted among themselves, deciding which of the intellectuals should be thrown out. They wanted to divert the spearhead of the movement away from themselves, so they threw out some intellectuals as butts of the Cultural Revolution—like meat to hungry dogs, to satisfy their hunger. And then, when they decided who they wanted to throw out, they instigated the Red Guards, with the sons and daughters of high-ranking cadres as the core, and told them to persecute those people, to ransack their houses.[14]

Thanks to its previous investigations, interrogations, and Thought Reform activities, management had plenty of materials on file to use publicly against the rest of the faculty. Under the intensely paranoiac political climate promoted by Mao and his supporters, the students were generally both shocked and enchanted by statements asserting that their esteemed teachers had been former KMT agents, embezzlers, or adulterers, or that they were reproachable in other ways.[15] Two days after Nie's poster was published nationally, the SEB reported that physical abuse of teachers by students had occurred on a few campuses. The victims were beaten or forced to kneel, don dunce caps, or endure other corporal and psychological torments.[16] The behavior of management had unquestionably accelerated the outbreak of student violence against the faculty. A former Red Guard remembers the amazement he felt after the mobilization of students had begun:

It seemed that every day good people were exposed as evil ones lurking behind Revolutionary masks. Friendly people were hidden serpents, Revolutionaries became counterrevolutionaries, and officials who usually rode cars to meetings might actually be murderers. It was confusing because the changes came so fast. . . . [Many students felt that] the Cultural Revolution was a wonderful thing, because when our enemies were uncovered China would be much more secure. So I felt excited and happy, and wished I could do something to help.[17]

It is widely known that in his effort to preserve the political structure the CCP established after 1949, Chief of State Liu Shaoqi, who would perish in the mass movement, dispatched "work teams" to some campuses in Beijing, Shanghai, and elsewhere to direct the student uprising. His action temporarily helped many college presidents, school principals, and campus party secretaries stay in office.[18] Although many of these people were forced to "step aside" as the work teams took over the administration of the campuses, they worked closely with the newly arrived authorities to limit the assault on themselves—by continuing to attack their subordinates. By 30 June 1966, the SEB reported that only nine out of twenty-eight colleges had demonstrated "good progress" in the revolution. The management personnel of the remaining campuses had failed to "set themselves on fire"; that is, they refused to acknowledge their political or ideological mistakes as campus officials and tried to block teachers and students from criticizing them.[19] The report therefore suggests that some SEB officials clearly understood that the targets in education were not the ordinary faculty but party members within campus management.

At the Maritime College, the SEB noted, management insisted that "there were not too many problems" among its personnel and kept attacking the teaching staff.[20] At the College of Chemical Engineering, students complained that only denunciations of "nonparty bourgeois academic authorities" were permitted. They wanted the government to replace the management personnel with a work team, not knowing that it would barely advance their rebellion.[21] On other campuses, management continued to search for targets. At the College of Foreign Languages, campus officials had attacked ten out of two hundred party members. All ten had held ranking posts such as head of a party subcommittee or head or deputy head of an academic department. All were from bourgeois or landlord families, and six had allegedly committed "serious mistakes" in the past.[22] They were for all intents and purposes cut off from the party to be consumed by the roaring fury of the student movement.

Research has shown that students from the so-called five red categories (that is, those who had grown up in the families of workers, poor and middle peasants, party cadres, military personnel, and revolutionary martyrs) were particularly active and violent in attacking the faculty during the early stage of the campus uprising. Whether they were trying to defend the ideals of socialism, protect their own privileges, or settle personal grudges against their teachers, their activism helped management to retain control of the campuses temporarily. Relying on what Maoists later denounced as "hitting at many to protect a few," campus officials found their shock troops among these students when attacking their colleagues. Like party leaders in other sectors, they believed that Beijing would sensibly terminate the struggle against party personnel and the Communist authority structure.[23] They thus continued to attack their subordinates and colleagues in the hope that they themselves would emerge unscathed from the mass movement.

Looking back, these campus officials had acted on a faulty political logic. In early August 1966, the CCP Central Committee, controlled by Mao's allies, effectively legitimized attacks on local party committees in its "Sixteen Articles." The more faculty management had denounced as antiparty or antisocialist, the more its own personnel were now liable to attack. In student rebels' eyes, these school officials had knowingly permitted large numbers of "class enemies" to teach the youth. They were therefore more antiparty and antisocialist than the faculty they had denounced. Furthermore, as the political climate turned against management, some of the people who had been attacked sought to avenge the assaults. In the end, none of the 5,300 top officials in the primary and secondary schools in Shanghai was spared by the uprising. All of them were attacked or persecuted by the rebels. They suffered confinement, humiliation, segregation, physical assault, and other punishments. Seventy of them died, in addition to 550 teachers who committed suicide or were persecuted to death.[24]

Although the victimizers in the faculty were ultimately turned into victims, some of them continued to struggle against their colleagues. The rapid political changes that occurred at the central and local levels during the Cultural Revolution due to power struggle created plenty of opportunities for the victims, if they had survived persecution, to become victimizers again. At Wenzhi Secondary School, the SEB reported, the party-member-principal-cum-secretary was attacked and deposed by rebels in the autumn of 1966. He left the campus but then returned the following spring to organize others to fight against the rebel organization that had been dominating the campus.[25]

Once popular mobilization began in June 1966, teachers at all levels and of different backgrounds rebelled against management. Some of them attacked other teachers or even took their activism beyond the campus. Their actions were connected to prior schisms and resentments in the faculty and profoundly influenced the student rebellion.

As soon as Nie Yuanzi's poster was publicized nationally, some teachers in Shanghai openly or secretly worked against management's attempt to control the uprising on the campuses. They apparently recognized that the target of the political movement was not the ordinary faculty, but management. At this stage, when both the objectives and tactics of the campaign were still ambiguous, these teachers were gambling a great deal with their safety and livelihoods. SEB reports show that at the College of Traditional Medicine, a former KMT Youth Corps member telephoned another college multiple times to gauge developments there and informed his students that classes were suspended on that campus and demonstrations under way. He urged his students to put up *dazibao* and showed them the one that he had already written. At Bi'le Secondary School, a teacher told his students to cover the principal's office with *dazibao* and ask the party secretary why no one had been denounced yet. He had already started rumors among the students that management considered putting up *dazibao* "silly and riotous."[26] Although we only have limited information on these teachers' backgrounds, it is clear that they had little sympathy for the superiors they wanted the students to attack, probably because their careers had suffered under the current administration.

At the College of Foreign Languages, management could barely control the campus because some teachers were leading the opposition. On 7 June 1966, a young teacher attacked the deputy president, a Communist Party member, in a *dazibao*. A group of English teachers then put up their own *dazibao* to denounce the president. Other teachers worked overnight to produce their denunciations. Before sunrise, some of the teachers visited the home of the college party secretary to demand an open meeting. When the secretary arrived on campus later, he was confronted by "upset and emotional" students who pressed for the meeting. They called the president a counterrevolutionary and wanted her stripped of her party membership immediately. In the following days, more than three hundred *dazibao* appeared on campus, the "overwhelming majority written by teachers." The college party committee decided that it wanted nothing to do with the president. It stated that she was "an unreformed bourgeois intellectual" and that she had been brought up by an uncle who had been a ranking KMT official.[27]

It remains unclear whether the event was orchestrated by the campus party secretary for self-protection or whether the teachers genuinely acted against management. Either way, their actions directed the students' attention on a specific faculty member. A retired secondary school teacher remembers that her colleagues, indeed, played the most important role in identifying targets when the uprising reached her school. At first, the students did not know how to act or whom to attack. "They fumbled as if they were blind." But when management and the teaching staff started to attack their colleagues, the situation changed immediately. "The targets suddenly became clear to the students. . . . Some teachers had been close to certain students and told them whom to attack and what they should do. The students were happy to know what they should do."[28] Although political socialization had stirred the students into action, the power struggle among the faculty played an important role in defining whom the students would actually attack.

Throughout the Cultural Revolution, most teacher rebels were young instructors, a group whose social background, professional status, and income differed significantly from those of their senior colleagues, as we saw in previous chapters. As with student Red Guards, what motivated their rebellion was a mixture of political idealism, grievances, and self-interest. Since these teachers still lacked managerial experience and professional achievement, they were seldom attacked by others as "capitalist roaders" or "reactionary academic authorities," the targets that topped the list in the "Sixteen Articles."[29] But their careers could quickly benefit from the demise of their superiors and other teachers. Some of them were genuinely dissatisfied with the management personnel and resented the senior faculty's privileged lifestyles. They thus also identified with the Maoist critique of both groups as obstacles to socialist development. Other young teachers were unhappy that despite having been educated under CCP rule and working hard, they earned the lowest salaries in the profession. Above all, Mao's clarion call for the youth to rebel against "degenerating" school and political authorities powerfully legitimized their attacks on the senior faculty.

At Shanghai Girls' School Number Two, the municipal government noted in the early days of the uprising, twenty of the first one hundred rebels were young teachers.[30] The rest were presumably a mixture of students and other personnel. At Communications University, a young instructor wasted no time in profiting from his attack on a colleague by seeking party membership from the school authorities.[31] The promulgation of the "Sixteen Articles" in early August furthered young teachers' activism. In Shanghai, "secondary and college students and some young faculty established numerous rebel Red Guard organizations" across the city and "took their 'rebellions' to various party and administrative offices of the education bureaus for primary, secondary, and tertiary education." They even "traveled to various places to link up (*chuanlian*) with other Red Guards." By mid-October 1966, Shanghai's primary school teachers had established their own rebel headquarters. Several rebel outfits formed by secondary school teachers then appeared across the city.[32]

Evidence suggests that from early on, some teachers took their activism beyond the campuses, leading or assisting in the Red Guard movement that culminated in the seizure of power from local governments in January 1967. Their actions further fueled the growth and violence of the mass movement. In her well-known autobiography, Nien Cheng describes the ransacking of her luxurious home in Shanghai the autumn before. Besides students, the perpetrators included two older men and one older woman, probably the "teachers who *generally* accompanied the Red Guards when they looted private homes."[33] Official regulations around that time also enabled teachers to venture beyond their campuses. As large numbers of students began to travel to Beijing to salute Mao and to other places to "exchange revolutionary experiences," the SEB initially established a special office to look after such travels. Based on central instructions, it decreed that each hundred students should be accompanied by one teacher, probably for ensuring student safety.[34]

In a rural Shanghai county, when 1,100 students went to Beijing that autumn, 117 teachers, of whom 69 percent had "good" class backgrounds, went with them.[35] In general, traveling teachers assumed various roles. Some retained substantial authority over the students, advising or guiding them throughout their journey. Others had little control over the students or mainly took care of logistics.[36] As the mass movement intensified, especially after Mao condemned local use of class background to block mass participation in early October 1966,[37] schoolteachers were virtually free to move in and out of the campus with or without students, except the most "notorious" faculty, who had been kept on campus by the Red Guards. Young teachers, in particular, continued to travel to "exchange revolutionary experience."[38] Even middle-aged instructors had the choice of staying home or traveling to other places.[39] In any case, the experience traveling teachers acquired seemed critical to their further action in the mass movement. When the above teachers and students from rural Shanghai returned home, the SEB stated, many had been radicalized. They used harsher and more violent means of struggle against "class enemies" or "counterrevolutionaries." At Anting Normal School, the returnees felt that they had been too lenient on the targets of attack. The very night they came back, they forced these people to wear placards on their necks and punished them physically.[40]

The uprising at Peking University suggests that at the college level, midlevel middle-aged party cadres sometimes formed another formidable group of faculty rebels. In particular, Nie Yuanzi's background reflects the frustration these cadres had endured in the faculty organized on the basis of counter-bureaucracy. A longtime CCP member but relatively undereducated, she had been a departmental party secretary at the famous university since the mid-1950s. The campus party secretary, Lu Ping, a highly educated man, had privileged academic achievement in promotion, thus limiting her chances. In this respect of organization, tertiary and secondary schools were apparently different. Due to higher technical requirements in operating colleges, academic credentials were regarded more favorably than in secondary schools. As a result, veteran party cadres like Nie, with impressive political but not academic qualifications, had been feeling that they deserved more from the university.

A year before the Cultural Revolution, a disgruntled Nie had publicly challenged Lu's academic policies for harming the chance of working-class students in attending the university. But she did not obviously hurt his reputation.[41] The onset of the Cultural Revolution, by contrast, provided Nie and people like her with an immediate opportunity for upward mobility or domination over her better-educated colleagues. By mid-July 1966, Nie had practically taken over the university. She became the head of the first Red Guard outfit that was established on campus. As a former teacher of the university recalls, this organization was dominated by "party cadres and students and teachers from peasant or worker backgrounds."[42] Faculty presence was so strong in the rebel outfit led by Nie that some students were angry about its role in the campus uprising.[43]

Convicted counterrevolutionaries, criminals, rightists, and teachers with "poor" class backgrounds became the first targets of attack in schools and colleges, but they did not solely remain victims of abuse. As the campus authority structure collapsed in autumn 1966, some of them exploited the heretofore unimaginable opportunity to vent their resentment against other faculty and even vie for power. Freed from daily subjugation, especially after Beijing's October announcements, these teachers found support in the large number of students of similar situations. Due to their "poor" class backgrounds, the latter had recently been attacked by fellow students or forbidden to join the uprising. They were now encouraged by the state to take its cause. Suddenly empowered, the unfettered teachers, like the "freed" students, provided some of the high drama of the mass movement.[44]

The Red Teachers Union at the prestigious Qinghua University in Beijing was a remarkable example. Led by an engineering professor of landlord background who had been a KMT political officer, it contained faculty members "who had been isolated, oppressed, and attacked" before the mass movement. They now publicly maintained that they had been unjustly persecuted by corrupt authorities and that the "revolutionaries of today must be sought among the dissidents of yesterday." They advocated "a complete overthrow of the old Qinghua." In the winter of 1966, the union, capitalizing on the mass movement's damage to the party and the state, took its struggle outside of the campus. The teachers rampaged through an asylum to free a colleague who had been incarcerated for his dissident views. With the support of hundreds of students, they attacked the police headquarters and stole secret files and even urged prisoners to rise up and break out of the municipal jail.[45]

Had this event taken place before 1966, the teachers would have been arrested quickly, tried for counterrevolution, and imprisoned or executed by the state. In the midst of the Cultural Revolution, however, they reached further political height after their frontal attacks on the authorities. In the spring of 1967, the Red Teachers Union was able to insert itself into the formal political process, after Mao decreed the formation of "three-in-one" committees (see below) to replace party committees in the workplace. Despite opposition, the union's leader acquired a seat on the new committee at Qinghua University. He was supported by the campus's strongest rebel organization, which also put him on its executive committee.[46]

In Shanghai, various retired teachers remember that some of the faculty who had earlier voiced dissatisfaction against management or had political problems in their personal backgrounds turned into rebels as the political tide changed in autumn 1966. At Guoguang Secondary School, the most violent and feared teacher rebel was a former soldier who had been disciplined by the military and had taught physical education in the school before becoming a politics instructor. Once he dragged a Buddhist monk onto the school playground and, together with some students, beat him to death.[47] Another teacher who had been confined and beaten by rebelling students for his "connections to Taiwan" later became a rebel himself. He allegedly used "force and persuasion" on a female party member to extract the "inner secrets" of the party branch, aiming to use the information against its members. Because of his "poor" social background, this teacher rebel had difficulty finding allies among students, who deeply distrusted him.[48] By contrast, the SEB reported later that at Sanlin Secondary School, a former KMT Youth Corps member, with support from some teachers and school workers, gained control of the "rebel brigade" on campus.[49]

Besides top-down and bottom-up, faculty attacks also occurred laterally among rank-and-file teachers, reflecting their disdain of one another. These assaults were generally less open or vocal than the vertical kinds, even though they required no less cooperation from students. A former party-member principal explains why: "Ordinary teachers did not stand out and attack other teachers. They stayed back and provided 'black' [that is, incriminating] material to students. They did so because [it gradually became clear that] the official target was not the masses [to which regular teachers belonged, but rather leaders]. When you wanted to attack other teachers, it was better to encourage students to attack them [rather than doing it yourself.]"[50]

As the Cultural Revolution progressed, Shanghai schoolteachers, like other social groups, splintered into factions and groups that reflected their identities or interests. At Luonan Secondary School, the majority of its twenty-one employees joined a "teacher-worker rebel brigade."

But three teachers who had been assistants to the party-member principal and had been "surrounded and attacked" by the rebels wielded "substantive influence" in an opposing organization.[51] At Nanyang Secondary School, over 70 teachers and workers joined "revolutionary organizations" inside and outside of the campus.[52] In the Xujing Commune in rural Shanghai, 96 of the 121 primary school instructors joined a teacher revolutionary outfit, while 3 teachers decided to work with a rebel organization formed by peasants.[53] In urban Shanghai, according to one observer, primary school teachers were gradually separated into two main factions. One group recruited students to become "little red soldiers"; the other, "red successors."[54]

Compared to decades of research on student behavior during the Cultural Revolution, the evidence on faculty activism is still exploratory. It will take many years before any account on faculty activism achieves the reasonable degree of reliability and understanding now common to research on student activism. Nevertheless, existing evidence indicates that faculty activism was, in fact, a catalyst of student violence. To be sure, some of the assaults were rituals aimed at self-preservation; others stemmed from unavoidable obligations that had developed among faculty. What I have shown, however, is not about halfhearted aggression, which no doubt requires its own sociological analysis, as much as deliberate attacks on colleagues as a result of what Weber would call the material and ideal interests of the faculty. The swiftness with which management targeted subordinates, the rebels' enthusiasm in attacking power holders, and the revenge sought by convicted wrongdoers can be traced to prior tensions and resentment in the schools and colleges. That the faculty splintered as soon as popular mobilization began is perhaps the best evidence that the counter-bureaucratic reforms in education had failed to instill solidarity in the teaching profession. As mass mobilization replaced the repressive state, faculty cleavages descended into life-and-death attacks among faculty.

MAOIST DISORGANIZATION OF CAMPUS MANAGEMENT

The ascent of Maoism during the Cultural Revolution led to a wholesale reorganization of the workplace. With Shanghai's primary and secondary schools, the reconstruction of authority structure only intensified their counter-bureaucratic characteristics. The Maoist emphasis on popular control heightened political domination in practice and further weakened the role of expertise in management. Maoism destroyed any basis of social trust and administrative efficiency in the faculty.

In February 1967, the central government attempted to reassert control over schools and colleges nationwide. The campuses had been in turmoil for more than half a year, as the Red Guard movement mutated into an uncontrollable political force as well as factions with their own agendas and alliances within and outside of officialdom. The government ordered teachers and students, many of whom had been traveling to "exchange revolutionary experiences," to return to the campuses and "make revolution by going back to classes" (*fuke nao geming*).[55] With management by party cadres widely discredited and large numbers of party secretaries and leaders of work organizations deposed in the previous months, Chairman Mao had put forth an idea called the Great Alliance (*da lianhe*) to reform workplace authority structures. The central premise was to enhance popular management of the workplace, not through a Paris Commune style of egalitarian participation, which Mao had rejected, but through the establishment of so-called revolutionary committees. The latter's composition was to be based on a "three-in-one principle" requiring the appointment of "the heads of the revolutionary mass organizations, local military representatives of the People's Liberation Army, and leading revolutionary cadres"—in short, mass leaders, members of the military, and former leaders.[56] The revolutionary committee would replace existing management.

In practice, the makeup of the committees depended on local political situations and power struggles. In Shanghai, where Maoist influence reigned, the first group took the most seats on the school-level committees. It mainly contained students, teachers, staff members, and school workers who had rebelled against management. The second group rarely contained more than a handful of soldiers or citizen militiamen assigned to the campus by the military. The last group generally included one or more party cadres drawn from the deposed management personnel; their appointments had to be approved by members of the other two groups. For example, as of mid-1968, one of the secondary school committees contained nine students, three teachers, three staff members, two school workers, a deputy school principal, and a militiaman. The head of the committee was a twenty-six-year-old man who was a politics teacher and Communist Youth League member, most probably a leader of the most influential rebel organization on campus. Six of the ten nonstudent committee members were under twenty-five.[57]

Within the school system, the Great Alliance was anything but what its name implied, that is, a broad cooperation among students and staff to rebuild the campuses for genuine socialist development. To the contrary, its enforcement engendered further friction in the schools, because opinions differed sharply as to who should join the revolutionary committees and how authority should be divided. To be sure, disagreements on the distribution of authority on campus had been commonplace since the 1949 revolution. But the CCP, through empowering school party cadres, had reproduced a relatively stable authority structure by repressing opposition. With such cadres now deposed, other faculty were much more assertive in pushing their agendas.

A month after Mao's announcement of the Great Alliance, the SEB reported that about 60 percent of the primary schools in urban Shanghai had reopened for classes, with classroom instruction limited to a maximum of two hours per day. In those schools where teachers had established only one revolutionary outfit, the situation seemed manageable, with a semblance of normality restored. However, in the schools where there were two outfits of comparable strength, the teachers continued to fight among themselves. On one campus, the SEB noted, one group of teachers felt that the deposed principal should be brought back and given a seat on the revolutionary committee, but another group of teachers continued to attack this party cadre. In another school, one group of teachers controlled thirteen classes and taught on Monday, Wednesday, and Friday, while another group controlled eight classes and taught on Tuesday, Thursday, and Saturday.[58] At Guoguang Secondary School, there were three factions of teachers at this stage—those of "good" class background, those with party membership, and those who opposed both these groups—and they all wanted seats on the revolutionary committee.[59]

The conditions in rural schools were similarly intractable after the Great Alliance was announced. In Luodian Commune, the SEB discovered intense dissension in the faculty. At Luodian Secondary School, teacher rebels had been split into two factions and refused to work together. They took over different classrooms, with one faction controlling the financial resources and the other claiming administrative authority. At Luodian Central Primary School, the teacher rebels had taken over management and, against some of their own members' advice, refused to follow Mao's three-in-one principle and to share power with others. As a result, the rebels had been fighting among themselves. At Zhengge Primary School, the rebels refused to let the deposed party secretary return to management. They were at loggerheads with other teachers who condemned the practice of "squeezing out and striking down everyone."[60] In Fengxian and Baoshan counties, the SEB stated, some teachers were unable "to come off their high horses" to work with students on an equal basis within the revolutionary committee.[61]

Former school party secretaries and principals were the primary losers in the Great Alliance. Their election to the revolutionary committees as "leading revolutionary cadres" was heavily contested by both teacher and student rebels, some of whom continued to attack these party cadres. By November 1967, after more turmoil, including armed struggles, in schools and colleges,[62] over half of the urban primary schools in Shanghai had successfully established a revolutionary committee. But the cadres displayed little enthusiasm for this new arrangement for several reasons: their return to management was still not welcome by some of their colleagues; they were upset that they had been attacked by students and teachers; and they did not know what they should do in their new roles. As the SEB put it: "They fear that if they make a mistake, others will not let them get off easily. Some merely sit back and watch. They cannot let go of their doubts and devote themselves to work. Some acknowledge that they have made mistakes, but they do not really understand what they have done wrong. Instead, they feel that they themselves have been wronged."[63] The conditions in secondary schools were even worse. The SEB stated that "not too many" school party secretaries or principals had returned to work, let alone participated in the Great Alliance.[64]

In reality, the formation of the revolutionary committees was not based on social cooperation among faculty and students, but forged by the military presence on campus.[65] By late 1967, when the military began to leave, on-campus fighting and disorder intensified once again. In urban Shanghai, secondary schools reportedly "fell into various degrees of anarchist conditions." In Nanshi district, violent clashes between different rebel groups occurred "frequently" on the majority of the fifty-seven campuses and "daily" in seven schools. About twenty other schools were practically deserted by faculty and students. As a means of restoring order in the school system, what the central government advocated, "make revolution by going back to classes," had fallen into "paralysis."[66]

The SEB indicated that by the spring of 1968, teachers, students, and school workers were still divided into two main factions. In many schools, members of both factions had been formally elected to the revolutionary committees but refused to work with one another.[67] The committee at Bi'le Secondary School, for example, had never had a meeting with all of its nineteen members present. The campus was run by merely three or four people.[68] In Hongkou district, twenty-five of the forty-eight secondary schools had set up a revolutionary committee, but seven of the committees exhibited "poor basic understanding" of their functions, while fierce struggle between rebel groups still raged on thirteen campuses.[69]

To quell ongoing violence and exert further control in schools and colleges, the central government, on the basis of Mao's idea, began to dispatch workers and peasants to urban and rural campuses respectively in the summer of 1968. The Maoist political leadership presented the deployment of these official Worker and Peasant Mao Zedong Thought Propaganda Teams as the ultimate control of the educational system by the working class. These teams would remain on campus "for a long time" and "always exercise leadership," on the three-in-one management principle, to prevent the campuses from being captured again by class enemies and bourgeois intellectuals.[70] By the early 1970s, about 80 percent of the heads of schools in urban Shanghai, and one in fifteen faculty and staff members, came from such worker propaganda teams. Overall, the teams were composed of almost nine thousand people. In rural Shanghai, peasants headed all of the campuses, and their propaganda teams boasted more than thirteen thousand people.[71]

With high-level backing, the workers and peasants gradually restored order to the campuses. Because of this, they probably enjoyed some faculty and student support. But the institutionalization of campus management by workers and peasants ultimately engendered further faculty tensions and dissatisfaction—as the school workforce had not engaged in life-and-death struggle to let others take over the schools. Despite the official myth that workers and peasants had superior political and practical knowledge to supervise future developments in education, existing teachers and party cadres deeply distrusted those who took over the campuses. After all, workers and peasants traditionally had had inferior social status, and their occupational backgrounds were well outside the teaching profession. The resentment felt by the faculty was not unlike that experienced by schoolteachers and administrators when party cadres seized control of campuses after the 1949 revolution.

This time, however, both party cadres and the ordinary faculty, including the rebels, were more or less united against the newcomers.

The following are some themes of the complaints from faculty and students nationwide documented by the SEB. They reflect a sharp dislike of management by workers and peasants. The political leadership branded these objections to workers' control of school management as "absurd theories" (*moulun*) opposing genuine socialist development. But these thoughts were so common by late 1968 that Beijing was forced to engage with and debunk them publicly in major newspapers.

Every society requires a division of labor—schools should be managed by intellectuals.
Laymen should not exercise leadership over experts.
Why should workers be sent to the schools when there are already party members there?
This is the very first time that country bumpkins lead a revolution in education.
Schools do not absolutely need the workers; people who can properly grasp Mao Zedong Thought can head the schools, too.
Our understanding of class struggle is not at all inferior to that of workers.[72]

Though armed with official authority, then, the workers and peasants would seem to have enjoyed limited support from their colleagues.

The workers' and peasants' performance as school managers was impeded not only by their lack of academic experience and support from faculty and students, but also by other conditions surrounding their appointments. In Shanghai secondary schools, members of the worker propaganda teams were not selected primarily on the basis that these people had the experience, ability, or even desire to manage schools. Rather, the teams' composition reflected political struggles within those factories that had been designated by the government to take over individual campuses. Sometimes, the winning factions in the factories sent their own members, including party cadres, to the campuses as a way of rewarding themselves; other times, they took the opportunity to get rid of their enemies or people they did not want. Moreover, some schools received personnel from one factory, while others were taken over by people from two or more factories. Sometimes, the entire team on a campus was replaced.[73] The workers and cadres from factories were never the loyal campus unifiers and overseers that the Maoists expected or portrayed. Their assignments to the campuses were shaped by the same divisive politics that characterized other events of the Cultural Revolution.

Because of political struggles within factories and within government, large numbers of workers who had entered the campuses left before acquiring school management skills. Others returned to the factories due to dissatisfaction with campus duties. There were still others who moved back and forth between factories and schools. This high turnover of workers further lowered their ability to cope with the challenge of managing the campuses. Like the party cadres who had taken over school management in the early 1950s, they concentrated on fulfilling Beijing's mandates for political campaigns and suchlike (in other words, the things they could do best) at the expense of developing pedagogy or improving classroom instruction.[74] Their choice of actions confirmed to their better-educated and experienced colleagues that they were not professionally qualified to be school managers.

In rural Shanghai, where peasant propaganda teams had taken over the schools, the development in pedagogy and administration was similarly bleak. Unlike the workers, who were appointed to the campuses on a full-time basis, the peasant team members, whether they were direct producers or accountants, technicians, or physicians from nearby villages, kept their original posts. That is, besides lacking experience or enthusiasm in managing schools, these people lacked time to devote to the complex business of reforming the campuses as well as to the shifting demands from Beijing. The result was devastating. According to one observer, under peasant control, most of the rural schools "existed in name only, as they were in utter disorder." Some teams of peasants not only failed to put "the work of education" onto the daily campus agenda; they used the classrooms or allowed them to be used for unrelated meetings and casually stopped lectures or closed the schools for holidays. Their actions led to a "severe interruption" of academic instruction.[75]

MAOIST REPRODUCTION OF COUNTER-BUREAUCRACY

In Shanghai, the Maoist reorganization of schools not only weakened the capacity and enthusiasm of their management personnel; it reproduced their other counter-bureaucratic characteristics. After the mass upheaval, new instructors from many walks of life joined the faculty and further lowered its professional quality. Despite Mao's emphasis on egalitarianism and asceticism, the level of faculty income inequity had not decreased but, ironically, had increased. Furthermore, intrusive and arbitrary discipline persisted along with the retention of wrongdoers in the faculty. For many, faculty life had only grown harder and more uncertain compared to what they had endured before the mass movement.

Because Maoism stressed the expansion of schooling opportunities more strongly than past CCP Leninist policies had done, student enrollment in Shanghai escalated after the Cultural Revolution. At the secondary level, enrollment increased 70 percent between 1965 and 1975 to almost 1 million students. The number of teachers increased even faster. Within ten years, it had almost doubled, to fifty-two thousand people.[76] Behind this quantitative success, which rivaled the 1950s development of the school system, history repeated itself at the familiar expense of faculty composition and qualifications. We saw in Chapter 3 that after a decade of CCP control of teacher recruitment, which had resulted in a variety of ill-qualified people entering the teaching ranks, college and teachers college graduates returned as the main source of new instructors in the late 1950s. By the mid-1960s, their recruitment had significantly raised the faculty's overall level of education. The SEB had expected that the classrooms would in time be staffed largely by such graduates, some of whom would also head management. The rapid expansion of the school system after the Cultural Revolution, however, erased the improvements in the academic qualifications of the faculty. At both the primary and secondary level, teachers' qualifications, for one observer, "dropped continuously to the extent that they became shocking."[77]

Statistics on teachers' qualifications from the Cultural Revolution to the end of the Mao era are not available. Data on teacher recruitment, however, suggest that it adversely affected such qualifications. It is true that at the secondary level, one group that entered the faculty after the mass movement consisted of cadres and employees from local government offices, enterprises, and other establishments. Compared with others who became teachers during this period, these people were well educated and had worked in professional capacities, including teaching. In the summer of 1969, for example, the government reassigned three thousand cadres from the SEB, People's Radio Station, New China Bookstore, *Liberation Daily,* and other cultural and educational establishments as secondary school instructors. Most of these people had attended senior high school; many had studied in college.[78] As with the members of the worker propaganda teams that had arrived on campus, their reassignments resulted from power struggles within their original workplaces. Some of them were happy with the change; others were bitter at having been forced out of their jobs.

In comparison, the largest group that became secondary school teachers in Shanghai after the Cultural Revolution was selected from the student population that had been ordered by Beijing to labor in the countryside, after the Red Guard movement was terminated. More than ten thousand of these former students entered the profession. On paper, these were "educated youths" (*zhishi qingnian*) who had gone to high school or even college and therefore were marginally or indeed adequately qualified to be secondary school instructors. In reality, however, many of them had had a large part of their senior high or college education disrupted by the mass movement. Their level of academic knowledge was not commensurate with their formal qualifications. In this respect, they were comparable to many unemployed intellectuals who assumed teaching positions in the 1950s, as their professional qualifications were impressive on paper only. Nonetheless, after a brief period of pedagogical training, mostly on political issues rather than professional skills, these young men and women became secondary school instructors.[79] For many of them, this was a welcome change compared to an arduous life in the countryside.

A third group of new teachers consisted of so-called social youths (*shehui qingnian*). These were young jobless adults in urban Shanghai, many of whom had recently returned from the countryside without official permission.[80] To forestall a rise in urban unemployment and thus popular dissatisfaction, the government virtually resuscitated the teacher recruitment policy that had allowed the hiring of unemployed intellectuals two decades before. With assistance from local resident committees, some of the unemployed young adults were absorbed into the faculty to alleviate both joblessness and the teacher shortage due to school expansion. To cope with the inexorable rise in student enrollments, the government also brought back another recruitment tactic from the 1950s: promoting primary school teachers to the secondary level. By 1975, no fewer than seven thousand such teachers had joined the secondary school faculty.[81]

In rural Shanghai, the authorities expanded *chan shazi*, or "the insertion of sand particles," to strengthen its control in the schools as well as to reform the curriculum. In addition to the deployment of peasant propaganda teams at the management level, thousands of peasants and demobilized soldiers were recruited as teachers. Their selection pre-cipitated a further decline in faculty qualifications in the rural campus-es, which had had less educated teachers than urban schools to begin with. Many people who had not graduated from primary school be-came primary or even secondary school instructors.[82] In Jiading County, for instance, 73 percent of the secondary school teachers were college or technical college graduates in 1963, an impressive figure within the entire Shanghai municipality. Due to Maoist educational policy, the ra-tio apparently dropped precipitously after the Cultural Revolution. By 1980, it was on the way to recovery, but still 59 percent of the teachers had not been to college.[83]

It is well known that under the anti-intellectual influence of Mao-ism, school syllabi were dramatically transformed, simplified, and shortened. On the surface, the elimination of more complex materials from the syllabi should have helped inexperienced and undereducated teachers cope with their teaching responsibilities. But the transforma-tion, which varied across localities and persisted due to political chang-es, also created a lack of standard pedagogical tools such as textbooks, teaching guides, and class routines upon which regular instruction could be based. As a result, not only junior but also senior instructors were forced to improvise in the classroom.[84] Teachers often encoun-tered very unruly, if not hostile, students who had been radicalized by the official and popular attacks on schoolteachers during the Cultural Revolution. With rich professional experience, the veterans, if they were not intimidated by the circumstances, could perhaps have turned the shifting requirements of the syllabi into meaningful lessons for the students. But the newcomers still faced great obstacles in their teaching, even if we assume that they did not lack motivation for the task.

I suggested in Chapter 5 that Leninist-style discipline had dominated schools and colleges prior to the Cultural Revolution. The government had had full control of the penal process. It had punished the faculty ac-cording to fluctuating criteria of wrongdoing and local assessments of the wrongdoers, but retained the service of large numbers of convicts. As soon as campus mobilization began in the summer of 1966, state-controlled discipline collapsed. Within days or weeks, intense vigilan-tism by teachers and students permeated the campuses. On the basis of dubious or exaggerated charges, large numbers of people were turned into political criminals who had allegedly opposed and sabotaged socialist development. They endured public humiliation, confinement, searches of their homes, hard labor, and corporal punishment. Some were tortured to death; others committed suicide. For two years, official and systematic investigation, state-sanctioned leniency, and the exploitation of the labor of wrongdoers—hallmarks of Leninist discipline—were unenforceable. The faculty was subject to popular justice characterized by arbitrary and violent punishment.

In urban Shanghai, the arrival of worker propaganda teams at schools and colleges after the summer of 1968 finally curbed student abuse of the faculty and the armed struggles raging on some of the campuses. From then on, punishment was once again the state's prerogative, even though the central government, now firmly dominated by Mao and his supporters, encouraged the masses to participate in the penal process by providing information and attending public meetings. For those teachers and students who had desired to rid the campuses of "class enemies," the Cultural Revolution's outcome was ironic indeed. Still repressive and arbitrary, the official sanctions meted out by the worker teams were light compared with the violence perpetrated by the mass movement. Alleged wrongdoers and political suspects of various kinds were permitted to stay on campus in diminished political or professional capacities. Others were subject to interrogation and investigation on campus until a penal decision could be made, while they were put into manual labor. In other words, Leninism was once again informing faculty discipline, restoring it to counter-bureaucratic form. The Cultural Revolution did not cleanse the faculty politically. Quite the contrary, it increased the number of deviants.

The Clean-the-Class-Rank Campaign that took place in late 1968 was the watershed that restored Leninist discipline in schools and colleges. Beijing asked the worker propaganda teams to separate "true revolutionaries" from "sham revolutionaries," with assistance from "the masses."[85] According to the SEB, the official targets of the campaign were

the small number of traitors who have infiltrated the party, special-service agents [from Taiwan or foreign countries], the small number of stubbornly unremorseful power holders who have taken the capitalist road, ox ghosts and snake demons within society (that is, the landlords, rich peasants, counterrevolutionaries, bad elements, and rightists who have not reformed themselves), and the running dogs of U.S. imperialism, Soviet revisionism, and other forces.[86]

Faculty members were required to hand in their diaries, letters, written works, and photographs for evaluations. Special groups were set up to investigate people who were designated as "key targets." Unlike the charges, countercharges, and physical and other abuse that had been symbols of the mass movement, the campaign delivered official verdicts and penalties.

In Shanghai alone, almost twenty thousand primary and secondary school teachers (22 percent) were "investigated and persecuted" during the campaign.[87] According to the oral evidence I collected, most of those who were found guilty by the worker teams were demoted or reassigned to menial positions in the schools. Others were transferred to factories or farms to complete labor sentences before becoming eligible to return to the campuses. Only a small number of the faculty were expelled from campuses or arrested by the police. There were also "key targets" whose cases remained unsolved for years due to a lack of evidence to support either conviction or exoneration. These people generally spent the interregnum in lowly positions and under surveillance inside the schools.

This pattern of punishment reflected Mao's instruction that "the target of attack [in the campaign] must be narrowed, and more people must be helped through education." Lest popular justice persist, he emphasized that the penalties should be based on "the weight of evidence" and the use of political study.[88] For Mao, popular justice was no longer tolerable. The Clean-the-Class-Rank Campaign signaled that faculty discipline would return to normalcy: in other words, the state would decide whom and what to punish as well as the punishment's intended outcome.

Although there are no official figures on faculty discipline from the early 1970s to the end of the Mao era, it is hard to imagine that large numbers of wrongdoers were expelled from the schools, against a twenty-year-old practice of keeping these people working on campus. In particular, the increase in student enrollments renewed the pressure on the government to staff classrooms and hence to keep the service of the wrongdoers. Even though additional deviants had been created or reindicted in the official political campaigns of the 1970s, the percentage of teachers expelled from the schools is unlikely to have been much greater than that in the 1950s. As Leninist-style discipline reemerged after the Cultural Revolution, the schoolhouse resumed its place in the penal system as a site where formal punishment was administered to the faculty.

During the Cultural Revolution, the issue of fairness with salary retention supplement, the monthly amount the state paid to some employees to match their prerevolutionary salaries, came to a head at last. But the mass movement did not therefore lead to a more rational structure of faculty salaries in the Shanghai secondary school system. Shortly after popular mobilization began in the summer of 1966, the Shanghai government reported that "the working masses" demanded reduction of the earnings of those who had a salary supplement.[89] In fact, as the rhetoric of class struggle intensified in the previous years, some people, especially Communist Party members, had realized that they were taking substantial political risk by accepting such a supplement and had given it up. As rebels gained power, the distribution of such supplements was suspended in many places. But the cuts did not completely satisfy popular desires for more equal compensation. Some rebels forcibly reduced even the standard salaries of better-paid colleagues, most of whom were in professional positions.[90]

The radicalism against the state payment of salary supplements and high salaries, however, was short-lived. As the mass movement proceeded in an uncertain political climate, such supplements were unevenly resuscitated across the city. Government reports mention that those who had had their earnings cut were able to compel management to "sign and agree to reinstate" salary retention supplements and other original salaries. These people were probably acting within rebel organizations against faltering management. By the spring of 1967, all salary supplements were restored within Shanghai's telecommunications sector, including the government offices that controlled the industry. They were also reinstated in the factories overseen by the Electrical Bureau.[91] The reinstatement also occurred at Guoguang Secondary School and other campuses.

At this stage of the Cultural Revolution, the Shanghai municipal authorities, unsure how any of their actions would affect the movement and their own well-being, adopted a wait-and-see attitude. They did not do anything on the issue of salary cut or restoration, leaving the substantive arrangements to individual organizations.[92] As a result, salary practices varied widely in the city, depending on the internal struggles within such organizations. In some places, the original salaries had been restored; in other places, salary supplements had been abolished or a leveling of income had occurred compared with the previous income structure.

By the early 1970s, the incomes of Shanghai's secondary school faculty, including salary retention supplements, were mostly restored to their original levels. It is not clear whether the government had acted on Beijing's initiative or its own accord or had bowed to popular pressure regarding salary arrangements. But within the faculty, salary cuts were primarily used, as before, as a means to punish convicted wrongdoers, criminals, or so-called key suspects.[93] Equally important, the restoration was followed by a freeze in faculty salaries for the rest of the Mao years. This meant that in the mid-1970s many teachers received exactly the same amounts that they had been getting before the Cultural Revolution. In rural areas, some teachers, especially newcomers to the profession, were less fortunate. Instead of being paid the standard salaries based on their skill grades, they were forced to take the lower compensation calculated for peasants.[94]

In practice, then, the system of faculty salaries was as counter-bureaucratic as it had been before the Cultural Revolution. The mass movement did not lead to any fairer distribution of salaries on the basis of authority, responsibility, or qualification. By the early 1970s, large numbers of faculty had not received any pay raise for almost ten years or more. Their expectations of a better livelihood had been seriously violated by the CCP regime. Furthermore, the generational difference in income that had nothing to do with professional authority, experience, or performance, which had first appeared in the 1950s, still existed. In financial terms, Shanghai schoolteachers fared badly under Maoism. As one observer put it, compared to other segments of the Shanghai labor force, primary and secondary school teachers were in "particularly dire" economic situations in the 1970s, so that even "the masses sympathized" with them.[95]

On the whole, the changes in faculty composition, management, discipline, and income, reproduced the schools as counter-bureaucratic administrations. Indeed, the campuses were more counter-bureaucratic than they had ever been because of the institutionalization of Maoism. None of these four aspects underwent any rationalization in the Weberian sense after the mid-1960s. To the contrary, the lack of pedagogical expertise, political domination, income inequities, and arbitrary, repressive discipline intensified in the faculty. It is therefore hard to imagine that faculty relations improved significantly after the Cultural Revolution, even without taking into account the tensions caused by the life-and-death struggles among faculty. But the terms of faculty strife had definitely been transformed by the mass movement. The CCP cadres who had headed the campuses no longer dominated decision making. The teacher rebels who had created havoc could not also impose their will on campus because of the teams of workers and peasants put in charge by the state. But this did not necessarily mean that members of such teams had absolute control of the campuses. The seesawing political struggles within both the central and the lower-level governments continued to provide opportunities for faculty members to advance their interests or pursue a realignment of allies within the faculty. In the 1970s, some teachers cooperated with local leaders who tacitly opposed Maoist rule to strengthen academic learning and the use of exams in the schools; others continued to support the Maoist anti-intellectual agenda in education.[96] In the end, Maoism, even more so than Leninism, normalized a politically and socially divided faculty. Briefly induced into a revolutionary fury during the Cultural Revolution, faculty distrust and indignation were renewed and reencapsulated in the schoolhouse under late Maoist rule.

FACULTY ACTIVISM, CULTURAL REVOLUTION, AND COUNTER-BUREAUCRACY

Compared to the student Red Guard movement, faculty activism in the Chinese Cultural Revolution is a poorly understood topic. What kinds of teachers were involved? How did they cooperate or struggle with one another? What kinds of relations did they forge with students? How did they adjust their alliances or behavior according to the changing political climate? What were the outcomes of faculty activism? Much more research is needed before we can understand faculty activism with the same refinement as has been achieved in studies of the student rebellion. The expression of faculty activism on any campus depended on many factors: faculty and student composition, management style, outcomes of previous political campaigns, reactions of local party leaders, the element of fear and uncertainty and the desire for survival and so on. One thing is clear, however. Faculty members at any level were not merely victims of student violence. To the contrary, they participated and even provided leadership in the making of such violence.

In practice, faculty activism and the student rebellion were inseparable. Students initially followed the lead of campus officials in targeting faculty members. At this stage of mass mobilization, a minority of teachers were already using students to plot against management. Later on, faculty members with "poor" class background and formerly convicted wrongdoers and victims of attack were able to find support from students and engaged in attacking colleagues and even the political authorities. To be sure, faculty members did not control the student rebellion and ultimately suffered as much as other social groups during the upheaval. But it does not follow that they were merely targets of attack. Between Mao's call for a popular rebellion and the students' frenzied responses, teachers served as catalysts of the student rebellion. Their participation was an important reason why some of them were beaten, maimed, or even killed by their own students.

A key precondition of faculty activism had been the post-1949 reproduction of schools and colleges as counter-bureaucratic administrations, which engendered severe schisms in the faculty with the result that little solidarity existed among its members. When the central government and local authorities incited students to attack their teachers, members of the faculty had no qualms in providing public and tacit leadership in the assaults. The charges and countercharges they deployed, and the ties and alliances they forged with students, powerfully induced the latter to resort to violence. As pointed out in previous research, young teachers were particularly active during the Cultural Revolution. But campus officials were the ones who dealt the first blows against their colleagues. The balance of power then shifted in favor of the young faculty as well as enabling previously marginalized or criminalized teachers to ally with students to attack the school and higher authorities. In the end, students and teachers, whether they were attackers or victims of attack or both, joined forces, split up, and reconnected in diverse ways to pursue their personal or collective interests in the course of the mass movement.

The Maoist reconstruction of the schools after the Cultural Revolution did not alleviate the cleavages or resentment in the faculty. The assignment of workers and peasants to school management engendered further dissatisfaction toward the state. Together with further employment of undertrained instructors and wrongdoers, it reproduced a politically and socially divided faculty. The salary freeze perpetuated existing income inequities in the faculty, while the continuation of arbitrary and repressive discipline compelled the faculty to keep their feelings of resentment to themselves. The Maoist reforms of the schools thus intensified their counter-bureaucratic characteristics. In fact, the institutionalization of Maoism on the campuses reflected their reorganization on the basis of Leninist thinking in the 1950s, as experienced school managers were removed from their positions, poorly prepared teachers entered the profession en masse, and income inequities and arbitrary discipline reemerged.

It would be simplistic to characterize Maoism as antibureaucratic. As an ideology, Maoism no doubt deserves this label, because it abhors modern bureaucracy. At the school level, however, the label does not capture the organizational changes following the Cultural Revolution. In the areas of faculty authority, skills, income, and punishment, Maoism virtually returned the schools to the onset of the Leninist reforms two decades earlier and initiated the process of change all over again. In his political thinking, Lenin envisaged that organizational rationalization, that is, an increase in professional and administrative skills and in staff homogeneity, would take place as the transformations that he recommended moved forward. That was precisely what the SEB noted was occurring in Shanghai's school system by the early 1960s. The Cultural Revolution and ascent of Maoism not only prevented such rationalization from proceeding further; they turned the clock back. The schools had not been modern bureaucratic organizations before the Cultural Revolution, but they were even more counter-bureaucratic afterward.

7

Unsustainable Socialist Systems

The previous chapters have focused on the reproduction and consequences of counter-bureaucracy in Shanghai secondary schools in the Mao era. From a Weberian perspective, politically based authority and other nonrational features of the campuses betrayed that they were not modern bureaucratic organizations. Instead, the schools had been constituted on the basis of Leninist and Maoist thinking, which fundamentally rejects modern bureaucracy. In this chapter I draw on existing scholarship to explicate the formation and domination of counter-bureaucracy in two of the most privileged institutions among actually existing socialisms—heavy industry under Lenin's and Stalin's rule and officialdom in Mao's China. It is well known that the Bolsheviks disproportionately invested in heavy industry to expedite the modernization of Russia. After the 1949 revolution, the Chinese Communist Party (CCP) provided better recruitment and administrative support to various levels of government than it ever did to the above schools, because officials were responsible for planning, supervising, and enforcing the transition to socialism. Counter-bureaucracy, however, not only penetrated these two bellwether socialist institutions; its reproduction gravely damaged the official effort to build a sustainable socialist society.

As we shall see, counter-bureaucracy was an extremely powerful political instrument that enabled the Soviet and the Chinese Communist Party to transform even their grandiose or atrocious projects—specifically, the Soviet industrialization drive and Great Purges, and the Chinese Great Leap Forward and Cultural Revolution—into official policies and local practices. Politically, it was thus no less effective than modern bureaucracy, which Weber called "a power instrument of the first order."[1] However, because counter-bureaucracy was founded on a systematic disregard of technical expertise and other rational organizational practices, the outcomes it engendered fell far short of those desired by the political leadership. Neither the Soviet nor the Chinese Communists produced a cooperative and efficient socialist society. Instead, the societies under their rule were afflicted with social friction, political resentment, and economic problems. This places the development trajectories of Mao's China and the Soviet Union in sharp contrast to their postwar neighbors such as Japan, Taiwan, and Germany. The successful development of these other countries, especially in production and education, partly stemmed from their embrace of modern bureaucracy. To borrow a phrase from Pierre Bourdieu, the historical relationship between counter-bureaucracy and socialism was that "the means eat up the end."[2]

In particular, I show that the Soviet industrialization drive of the 1930s prefigured the catastrophe that would happen in China during the Great Leap Forward, which made the latter all the more tragic. Both state projects to raise production at unprecedented speeds resulted in the setting of unrealistic targets, rejection of technical requirements, inflated local reports, and thus an extreme waste of human and material resource, because both governments pursued their goals through counter-bureaucratic administration. Likewise, the horrific Great Purges perpetrated by Stalin's regime and the Chinese Cultural Revolution that happened thirty years later shared important similarities, even though one was tightly controlled by the state and the other engendered innumerable local uprisings—the counter-bureaucratic nature of the workplace fueled the violence of both campaigns. If the Soviet industrialization drive and the Great Leap Forward exposed the wastefulness of counter-bureaucracy as a political instrument, the Great Purges and the Cultural Revolution exemplified this instrument's failure in cultivating social solidarity in socialist Russia and China.

THE HIGH TIDE OF COUNTER-BUREAUCRACY IN SOVIET INDUSTRY

In the Soviet Union, the 1930s presented an apparently spectacular and promising picture of socialist development. This picture impressed the CCP leadership so much that it would draw on this Soviet model of development after 1949. Under Stalin's rule, the Soviet Union recorded a sharp increase in gross industrial production, particularly in heavy metals and capital equipment. Opportunities for the working class were plentiful, as joblessness was practically eliminated. Over 20 million people were added to the wage- and salary-earning workforce. The number of college-educated engineers skyrocketed to a quarter million. Among the ranks, there were large numbers of people born to workers' families, if not former workers themselves.[3] And the payment of pensions became official policy. The main reason for many of the improvements was the state's focus on developing heavy industry to modernize the economy. Extraordinary amounts of resources were injected into construction, manufacturing projects, and technical education. By contrast, the peasantry was squeezed, while the state reduced funding for urban housing, social services, and consumer goods production.

Closer analysis indicates that the rapid industrialization that took place under Stalin's rule was executed through counter-bureaucratic rather than modern-bureaucratic administration. The CCP's failure to see through the Soviet facade of success for its immense costs would lead the party to repeat this organizational mistake at much greater expenses to the Chinese population during the Great Leap Forward. Within the Soviet industrial enterprise, political domination, disrespect of professional skills, and state violence intensified during the industrialization drive, while the workforce was subject to tremendous pressure to accomplish complex and unfamiliar production tasks. Looking back, the outcome was predictable: poor efficiency, excessive waste, workplace conflict, and political disaffection accompanying rapid industrial growth. Stalinist industrialization was at the same time industrial disorganization.

The Emergence of Counter-Bureaucracy in Russia

As a form of factory administration, counter-bureaucracy began to take shape in Russia after the 1917 October Revolution, when the Bolsheviks pursued the nationalization of industry during the civil war period (1917–21). Within the factories controlled by the regime, the most salient development was the formation of workers' committees to oversee production and operation. These committees were normally composed of Communist Party members and sympathizers who were workers or labor union officials. Existing management understandably fought against such populism, to the extent of closing factories. Factory engineers resisted, too, as their national union initially forbade its members to work with the committees. With the new government forcibly taking over factories, the opposition by management and engineers eventually collapsed.[4] Following Lenin's instructions, the Bolsheviks ordered factory directors, engineers, and technicians, or the group they called "bourgeois specialists," to remain on the job as state employees. Some specialists had been arrested or even executed for political opposition. Others who had done the same were treated with leniency because their exploitable skills outweighed their political wrongdoing from the party's perspective.[5] To promote production, the new government granted factory directors and engineers some of the work authority they used to have and paid them handsomely, as they normally earned at least five times as much as skilled workers.[6]

These Leninist tactics of domination and accommodation vis-à-vis the technical and managerial professional in industry engendered the kinds of conflict that we saw in the preceding chapters. Motivated by resentment predating the revolution and their newfound authority, the Communist Party members and activists in the factories assailed management and the technical personnel as "class enemies" who had had complicity in exploiting the working class. They even assaulted these people physically, which in some cases led to murder or suicide.[7] But the Bolshevik regime, especially Lenin, was adamant about harnessing expertise for developing a modern socialist society. It harshly criticized such "specialist-baiting" and its underlying assumption that the working class could take over and operate the system of production and reproduction right away. In fact, less than six months after the revolution, the regime began to curb workers' control of factories, which led to workers' opposition to the party's support of "bourgeois specialists."[8] As the civil war wore on, the working class bore the greatest casualties in battles and suffered greatly from the collapse of the economy. Workers organized strikes and even revolts against Bolshevik rule.[9] In these circumstances, the counter-bureaucratic arrangements that granted workers unprecedented prestige but little work authority or comfort failed to elicit their political support while upsetting managerial and technical personnel. These arrangements were therefore politically unsustainable.

After winning the civil war, the Bolsheviks introduced what came to be known as the New Economic Policy (1921–29) for their own political survival. Besides losing working-class support, the regime had antagonized the peasantry through forced grain requisitions and conscription. Peasants had thus been staging chronic disturbances in the countryside.[10] The adoption of the New Economic Policy signaled that the new government was willing to loosen its control over the economy to stimulate economic growth and raise living standards. The Bolsheviks legalized private manufacturing, trading, and farming and abolished grain requisitions, but continued to direct the so-called commanding heights: large factories, mining, banking, and foreign trade. The private sector rebounded so quickly that by 1924 private enterprises produced more than 50 percent of the national income, and agriculture "was almost entirely in private hands."[11]

Within industry, the regime's desire to raise production strengthened the position of the "bourgeois specialists." These people were incorporated by the government into high-level planning commissions to help rebuild the economy. Even within state-owned factories, which hired the majority of workers, prewar patterns of authority reemerged, as technical directors and engineers were given authority to set piece rates and other work conditions. Physical attacks against such people were now treated officially as "terrorist attacks" rather than mere criminal assaults.[12] To be sure, the regime also initiated legislation, such as limitation on work hours, prohibition of child labor, paid vacations, and health insurance, to protect the working class.[13] However, following the October Revolution, its rationalization of industrial authority based on prerevolutionary trends or precedents was an obvious political contradiction from the working-class perspective. By the mid-1920s, the lots of workers had not improved substantially compared to what workers had endured before the revolution; unemployment was still high due to the overall slow recovery of the economy. By contrast, their "class enemies," the bourgeois specialists, were well protected and supported by the regime. They had "emerged from the revolution and civil war with losses, but largely intact, still struggling for many of the professional interests and allied values that had concerned it during the Tsarist period."[14]

This honeymoon for the "bourgeois specialists," however, was short-lived. As Stalin gained greater control over industrial appointments, Communist Party members and activists who were relatively undereducated and inexperienced in industrial management were transferred from the military, government, and elsewhere into factories to replace the technical directors as factory heads. In 1923 and 1924, almost six hundred such people were appointed to "some of the highest positions in industry." A 1928 survey of some seven hundred factory managers found that over 70 percent had only an elementary school education, and that the percentage of those with higher education dropped from 11 to 9 percent between 1926 and 1928. The large majority of factory directors and important industrial officials were now Communist Party members, while the recruitment of engineers and technical personnel still favored individuals from "nonproletarian backgrounds."[15]

The counter-bureaucratic appointment of "red directors" heightened tensions in the industrial enterprise, just as the use of CCP members to take over Shanghai secondary schools would later induce intense friction in the faculty. But with the Bolsheviks' insistence on accommodating the professional personnel for the sake of production, a "division of labor and an uneasy truce" developed within the industrial enterprise: the red directors would normally not interfere in production decisions but instead concentrate on political and personnel matters.[16] On the shop floor, however, the situation remained tense. Workers continued to complain about the high salaries earned by the engineers and attacked their political and class backgrounds. Some still engaged in specialist-baiting.[17]

Historians will continue to debate whether the New Economic Policy represented a temporary Bolshevik compromise in the socialist project or whether gradualism in developing socialism was preferred all along by the Bolshevik leadership until Stalin pursued a more radical course.[18] One thing is clear, however. The Bolsheviks did not eliminate unemployment or class exploitation during the New Economic Policy years, let alone poverty in the city or countryside. In fact, the working class, the revolution's putative beneficiary, gained little from the industrial reform. The party's use of very well-paid "bourgeois specialists" to manage workers was perceived, both inside and outside the party, as inconsistent with the revolutionary goal of liberating the working class from capitalist domination. In its historical context, the policy was thus untenable.

At heart, the New Economic Policy was about the role of modern bureaucracy in an emerging socialist economy, which Lenin had settled on paper (in *The State and Revolution*) but was forced to reexamine the issue by Russia's economic decline during the civil war. Within the industrial workplace, the policy tried to boost productivity by restoring some of the modern bureaucratic arrangements that Lenin himself had rejected as symptomatic of capitalist domination, such as the distribution of authority on the basis of technical merit and compensation by technical qualification and responsibility. But this return to modern bureaucratic practices in postrevolutionary Russia was precisely the Achilles' heel of the policy. The original rationale for the socialist revolution was based on Leninism, an anti-Weberian ideology that rebukes modern bureaucratic administration as a tool of class domination. By bringing back modern bureaucratic arrangements, the policy represented Leninism against itself. It could not but invite fierce political opposition.

Counter-Bureaucratic Industrialization under Stalin

By the late 1920s, the controversial New Economic Policy had run its course. With Stalin in control, the Bolsheviks launched the First Five-Year Plan. Unlike the New Economic Policy, the latter prescribed central planning of production and rapid growth in heavy industry and marked the beginning of what Robert Tucker and others have called "the revolution from above."[19] At the elite level, those party leaders, officials, and experts who believed in maintaining markets, gradual growth, and the production of consumer goods were marginalized. As a process of policy formulation, the plan, much as the later Great Leap Forward in China, epitomized the political leadership's utter disregard for rational planning in production. Its first draft from 1927 "was already extraordinarily optimistic."[20] But the numbers were raised repeatedly to unrealistic levels due to pressure from the leadership, while basic contradictions, such as where the resources and skills for increased production would come from when many sectors were to grow together, were ignored. Industry was exhorted not only to fulfill but to "overfulfill" its targets. As Sheila Fitzpatrick has pointed out, the plan was not established "to allocate resources or balance demands but to drive the economy forward pell-mell."[21]

Because of prior organizational development and the campaign's own dynamics, the plan years (1929–32) saw an intense development of counter-bureaucracy that gravely undermined industrial efficiency and hence put the industrial sector even further away from meeting its targets. First of all, those years overlapped with an official and fierce attack on "bourgeois specialists," as the theme of class war, which had gained strength toward the end of the New Economic Policy, deepened after its decline. In heavy industry, the targets were factory experts and engineers from the Tsarist era. Not only was their professional authority curbed; many were arrested for what the government called "wrecking," that is, purposefully wasting or destroying state resources, delaying work, changing official plans, ignoring safety regulations, or abusing workers in order to undermine socialist development and Communist political rule. Some of the accused were tried and executed on charges of counterrevolution or treason. In some industries, half of the technical personnel were reportedly charged with criminal offenses.[22]

It is true that few experts or engineers within Soviet industry had been ardent Bolshevik supporters. But their arrests, trials, and convictions, which were based on false evidence, indicated not their machinations against the regime, but that the baiting of "bourgeois specialists" had deteriorated from individual acts by workers and factory officials to an all-out assault by the state for its own political purpose. On the one hand, these specialists were targeted for their criticism of or skepticism about the plan's fanciful goals—their punishment therefore helped the state stem any overt opposition against the industrialization drive. On the other hand, they were used as scapegoats for the inevitable production shortages, breakdowns, and failures resulting from the lack of rational planning by the higher authorities, which had become endemic by 1930.[23]

While the industrialization drive strengthened the control of industry by poorly educated red directors, the local authorities only incarcerated a small proportion of the indicted specialists because their expertise was needed for production purposes. Many of the arrested were punished with a demotion or salary reduction, and charges against others were dropped before or during trial.[24] As Nicholas Lampert has noted, the most likely outcome for arrested specialists was that they would "continue to work, either in prison, or in 'administrative exile,'" or within their own enterprises. The Soviet security police even hired out some of the imprisoned engineers and technicians "in its charge on particular projects, thereby stopping up some of the gaps created by the numerous arrests."[25] This kind of politically motivated but utilitarian-based punishment of "bourgeois specialists" resembles the counter-bureaucratic punishment of schoolteachers that we saw in Chapter 5. It turned the indicted into some sort of outcasts or political suspects within the industrial enterprise.

Thanks to rapid industrialization, the number of industrial managerial and technical staff was doubled during the plan period.[26] But many of the appointments were not based on professional credentials but a "good" class background or record of political service. Party, trade union, and government officials were transferred into industrial management; large numbers of workers without formal technical education were promoted to be engineers to cope with rising production targets. In 1929, early in the industrialization drive, almost half of the industrial engineers and technicians were so-called practicals (*praktiki*), that is, workers without any higher technical education. Other engineer posts were filled by technical institute graduates who, compared with their prerevolutionary predecessors, had completed "much shorter [training] courses."[27] The central government was aware of the decline in the professional level of the industrial staff. It thus set up "a system of industrial academies" aimed at providing "a fully fledged higher technical education" to the new staff, especially those in top positions. According to Lampert, however, "the great majority of students [who attended such academies] reached a much more modest level" than the government had expected. Nonetheless, many were appointed for the first time as "directors, chief engineers or shop managers" in factories.[28]

During the plan period, millions of additional workers were also brought onto the shop floor to cope with the industrial expansion. These were mainly "raw recruits" without any industrial training or experience.[29] Most were illiterate or barely literate peasants who had come to towns and cities to escape the misery of forced collectivization in the countryside. Their hiring resulted in "a rapid deterioration of the skill composition of the working class."[30] It harmed industrial efficiency in other ways. Unfamiliar with their new environment and occupation, as Peter Kenez has noted, these former peasants had a high turnover rate and "were not used to arriving on time, did not know how to take care of machinery, had very little interest in learning, and drank on the job."[31] But the local authorities really had no choice but to incorporate these peasant migrants into the industrial workforce, despite their inadequate backgrounds and poor attitude toward full-time industrial labor.

The above changes in the industrial enterprise possessed what Tucker has called a "Leninist pedigree"; they were traceable to Lenin's thinking on how a modern socialist society should be built.[32] The Stalinist regime, however, departed from Leninist organizational principles in one important respect—professional compensation. Though attacked by the regime, the "bourgeois specialists" by and large continued to receive their previous high salaries, much as happened under Mao in China. But rather than getting "ordinary workmen's wages" as Leninism prescribed, the new engineers and technical personnel in the Soviet Union, too, were handsomely rewarded by the state. By contrast, as the state diverted resources from housing, consumer products, and other areas to capital expenditure in heavy industry and construction projects, both old and new workers disproportionately suffered a general decline in living standards that included falling real wages, crammed housing, and shortages of consumer goods and even basic foodstuffs.[33]

As counter-bureaucratic development intensified in industry, so did friction and distrust among colleagues. Kendall Bailes has observed that under the New Economic Policy, relations between factory managers and technical specialists, though often hampered by differences in their training and class backgrounds, generally involved mutual cooperation. Managers depended on specialists for accurate production data and the fulfillment of official targets; specialists needed managers to negotiate viable targets and the timely supply of resources.[34] As the pressure to achieve inflated targets mounted under the plan, this alliance collapsed, with specialists suffering the consequences. Managers, especially red directors, tried to protect their jobs by using specialists as scapegoats for production breakdowns and failures. To meet the targets, they pressed quality-control personnel, in particular, to pass substandard products, to the extent that these people "were ignored and even persecuted" in factories.[35] Such self-interested reactions by managers resulted in even more defective goods, thus further fueling the state's suspicion that "wreckers" had penetrated industry.

Furthermore, "a severe generational and intraclass struggle" emerged in industry.[36] Since the mid-1920s, the red directors, though poorly educated, had risen to the top of industrial management, replacing "bourgeois specialists." Their positions, however, came under threat when a new generation of technical institute graduates arrived at the factories in the late 1920s. Thanks to Bolshevik reforms in education, many of these graduates "combined a working-class origin and party membership with higher technical knowledge."[37] Although they were less well trained than the senior technical personnel, their political and technical credentials were highly valued by the Stalinist leadership, just as the CCP leadership would later consider this kind of graduate an indispensable asset for improving China's socialist system.

To hold back the professional challenge presented by these graduates, the red directors found an ally in the "practicals" and potential "practicals," whose careers would be hurt if the state chose to promote the graduates en masse to engineer and other posts. By the early 1930s, schisms and mutual accusations between red directors and "practicals" on one side and technical institute graduates on the other side had appeared and would only grow worse. The young specialists complained that management deliberately underused or ignored them and that the "practicals" criticized and refused to help them at work. The red directors for their part noted that they preferred to work with the "practicals" and those workers who had gone to college and returned to the factories. Prefiguring what would happen some twenty years later in Shanghai secondary schools, these political appointees contended that the young specialists were not only incompetent but also arrogant.[38] Likewise, tensions intensified on the shop floor between old and new workers during the industrial expansion, much as they would develop between old and new teachers in the schools when the CCP rapidly expanded education after 1949. The old workers considered themselves to be the true working class that possessed the necessary skills and discipline for industrial work. The peasant-turned-workers were "subject to prejudice, discrimination, and harassment" by the senior workers and by foremen and management.[39]

The Impact of Counter-Bureaucracy on the Great Purges

Whereas the First Five-Year Plan deepened the reproduction of counter-bureaucracy in the Soviet industrial enterprise, the Great Purges of 1937–38 practically eliminated its senior staff, including the red directors. It thus further reduced the level of knowledge and skills available for production. Initiated by Stalin, a reign of terror descended upon the political, cultural, economic, and military elite, particularly against Communist Party members, at the end of the Second Five-Year Plan (1933–37). Approximately 1 million people were executed by the state, in addition to millions who were imprisoned, exiled, or demoted on false charges of wrecking, sabotage, and treason.[40] The reason for the mass murders and arrests will continue to puzzle historians, as well as whether the excesses should be traced to Lenin's political thinking or considered a uniquely Stalinist phenomenon.[41] The purges reinforced Stalin's personal dictatorship at the party's expense and strengthened the power of the security police. They resulted in "a constant renewal of elites," as officials were forced out of their posts and their replacements often did not last long either.[42]

Existing evidence suggests that in heavy industry, there was a direct connection between heretofore counter-bureaucratic industrialization and the Great Purges. Because regional governments had not been able to fulfill their production targets (even after such targets had been reduced under the Second Five-Year Plan), officials and industrial managers had been colluding to exaggerate production figures and conceal industrial problems. Their intent was to maintain "an image of aggressive loyalty" toward the central government, which was unwilling to accept delays or to discuss economic problems.[43] When production failures and industrial accidents had been exposed, as some inevitably would be due to their large numbers, regional governments would turn against specific individuals within the jurisdiction, who were then arrested, tried, and sentenced for sabotage or other crimes. As long as such tactics of deception and criminalization remained effective, regional leaders would continue to cooperate with one another, hiding the many problems that they encountered in the production process.

By the mid-1930s, however, it became increasingly difficult for regional governments to disguise their persistently poor industrial productivity, especially as Moscow demanded higher efficiency and returns from its massive investment. As James R. Harris has noted in his study of the Urals region, serious fractures began to emerge in the regional leadership in 1936, as members feared that they would become the next scapegoat used by their colleagues to placate the central government. When the latter hinted that saboteurs had infiltrated regional governments, "an avalanche of accusations, denunciations and incriminating information" appeared immediately within the regional political and industrial leadership.[44] The mutual attacks reinforced the center's belief that saboteurs had, indeed, penetrated regional governments, and thus intensified the center's effort to go after these people. This rapid unraveling of the local leadership under crisis foreshadowed what we have seen within schools and colleges during the Chinese Cultural Revolution. Their management personnel, too, turned against one another rapidly when Beijing turned against them.

Other aspects of counter-bureaucracy fueled the persecution of the Soviet elite during the Great Purges, just as they would accelerate the violence against the Chinese elite in the Cultural Revolution. The purges were strictly carried out by the state but received significant support from below, because the top-down attack, not unlike local uprisings in the Cultural Revolution, created plenty of career opportunities and allowed many to vent their pent-up resentment against the authorities with virtual impunity. In heavy industry, young technicians and engineers and "practicals," although not immune from attack themselves, were especially active in denouncing their superiors as wreckers, saboteurs, and foreign spies. They were best positioned to gain from their superiors' demise, given their political and professional credentials as well as the state's continuing stress on industrial growth. As Bailes pointed out, young specialists benefited most from the Great Purges. They rose to "dominate industrial management at the higher levels in the most important sectors of heavy industry," while "practicals" gained positions at the lower and middle levels.[45]

The state assault on industrial officials, factory directors, and technical personnel found support among the working class as well. As has been noted, income inequality in industry had been growing in the 1930s. In addition to receiving high salaries, factory managers and engineers had access to cars, chauffeurs, vacation homes, special shops and canteens, and luxury apartments. Party and state officials had become a group distinguishable by their privileged lifestyles and consumption patterns as well as access to housing, food items, and other state-controlled supplies.[46] By contrast, the living standards of workers had dropped, as real wages declined by almost half in the 1930s.[47] Moreover, the government had tightened labor discipline to raise industrial productivity. It curbed trade unions' role in the industrial process and deployed stiff penalties, including imprisonment and forced labor, for violations of work regulations. Amid such increasing social inequalities and state domination, the Great Purges, which mainly targeted the powerful, became a channel through which workers vented their frustration.[48]

If the Soviet participation in World War II checked the counter-bureaucratic upheaval in the workplace, political domination, administrative caprice, and violent punishment would reemerge afterward with full force until the end of the Stalin era. At the top level, constant personnel and policy change occurred in Stalin's inner circle. Within government, industry, and other institutions, politically motivated purges, including executions, took place throughout the late 1940s and early 1950s. Work was subject to severe political discipline that continued to devalue expertise. The case of Lysenkoism, in which scientifically groundless ideas came to dominate the discipline of biology, was a most blatant example of political ideology and control shaping scientific and technical work. At the lower reaches of society, life was no better than in the prewar years. As the state returned to its practice of "socialist primitive accumulation" to sustain industrial development, supplies of housing, consumer goods, and even basic food items dropped even further. The late Stalinist era was marred by intense repression and privations that militated against rational utilization of skills, management, compensation, and discipline.

Given the organizational history outlined above, it is hardly surprising that industrial efficiency in the Soviet economy remained low. As economists broadly agree, the impressive increase in gross industrial production during the Stalin era occurred because the economy "operated well off the cost curve: more industrial growth could have been achieved at the same cost, or the same growth could have been attained at lower cost."[49] Poor planning, coordination, and cooperation; lack of individual commitment to the labor process; workers' unfamiliarity with modern equipment; high personnel turnover and management inexperience; as well as fear and resentment were all hidden costs that undercut industrial efficiency. For the average wage earner, real per capita income was reduced by some 25 percent during the Stalin era, and for the rural population, about 40 percent.[50]

Stephen Kotkin's study of Magnitogorsk, the giant steel factory and city that the Stalinist regime established in the desolate Urals region during the 1930s, is perhaps the best evidence of the wastefulness and dysfunctions of Stalinist counter-bureaucratic industrialization. Throughout the decade, this steel plant, which was supposed to become at least an equal of the largest steel plant in the United States, was plagued by haphazard planning, faulty construction, and poor maintenance. As a result, production breakdowns, accidents, and crises; unexplained disappearance of funds, supplies, and equipment; as well as large amounts of defective and useless products were commonplace.[51] This gigantic "backyard" steel furnace would reincarnate in China during the Great Leap Forward as innumerable wasteful and literally backyard steel furnaces.

The above discussion of Soviet industry obviously does not do justice to the complexity of events that occurred at the policy, regional, or enterprise level over a thirty-five year period. My aim is merely to point out that at its height of expansion, this enterprise, despite receiving massive state investment, had few of the rational characteristics of modern bureaucracy or features that would have promoted technical efficiency, staff solidarity, or consent to authority. Instead, politically based appointment and decision making, shortages of expertise, as well as mass terror and arbitrary discipline penetrated the factories. Within the industrial enterprise, high Stalinism represented the high tide of counter-bureaucracy. Let us now turn to Chinese officialdom, another privileged institution among actually existing socialisms, and see how counter-bureaucracy developed there and affected Chinese socialism.

FORMATION OF COUNTER-BUREAUCRACY
IN CHINESE OFFICIALDOM

It is well recognized that as soon as the CCP seized power, it took over and reorganized the state.[52] From the party's perspective, the reconstruction of this institution was most critical for sustaining Communist political rule and turning China into a modern socialist polity. From high-level state agencies down to village governments, however, there rapidly appeared in varying degrees a nonrational division of labor, arbitrary punishment, income inequities, and a mismatch between qualifications and responsibilities. This transformation of government into a counter-bureaucracy took place despite the fact that the party set out to provide the institution with the best-qualified personnel and support.

One of the first tasks the party set itself after taking power was to cleanse the state of undesirable personnel. But because of fears that excessive layoffs would heighten popular resistance to the new regime, most officials were allowed to stay in their posts. The dismissed were normally heads of agencies or offices, ranking KMT members, and alleged wrongdoers. A mixture of Communist Party members made up of military personnel, political organizers, and former underground agents then moved into ranking posts at every level of government, much as what happened in schools, factories, and elsewhere, but at a quicker pace. For example, by the end of 1949, almost eight thousand CCP members had assumed posts in the Shanghai government and had formed party cells within bureaus and departments to supervise both routine operations and reform. After adding additional party members from elsewhere or by internal recruitment, the government boasted a total of fourteen thousand party members by 1953.[53] Meanwhile, it still contained roughly 70 to 80 percent of the officials carried over from the KMT era.[54] From then on, most of these officials and similar officials in other regions were reassigned to nongovernment jobs or replaced by people whom the party authorities considered politically more reliable.[55]

Because of the party's organizational history and ideology, a lack of professional expertise quickly appeared in higher-level governments, including those overseeing operations in major industrial cities. In the early 1950s, the still peasant-based party did not have a sufficiently large pool of technically trained cadres to meet its expanding requirements for planning, supervisory, and administrative staff in government. Thanks to the party's stress on political loyalty, large numbers of veteran revolutionaries with limited professional and managerial skills assumed ranking posts, becoming chief officials in highly technical areas of industry, finance, construction, and so on. Despite later shifts in the party's ideology, such loyalty would remain the main criterion guiding the assignment of official posts and, prior to the Cultural Revolution, was most commonly measured by one's party seniority. The veteran revolutionaries therefore normally kept their positions or were even promoted, as long as they did not commit major mistakes. As a result, higher-level governments were filled with technically ill-trained administrators.

It was precisely this lack of expertise among top officials that compelled the CCP regime, which wanted to transform China technologically and culturally, to furnish all levels of government with essential professional personnel. The latter were either carryovers from the KMT era or officially reappointed from elsewhere because of their technical training and skills. In theory, they would utilize their learning to help build factories, roads, and bridges; supervise public health and the reforms of education; redesign newspapers and radio programs; and direct other complex transformations of production and administration. In practice, however, they worked under the supervision and direction of the less-educated party members and had far fewer opportunities than the latter group of officials.

Ying-mao Kau's study of top officials in Wuhan, the largest and most industrialized city in central China, between 1949 and the Cultural Revolution is the best illustration of the impact of counter-bureaucratic appointment on staff composition and the division of labor in higher-level governments. Of some 150 officials whom he studied, almost 70 percent were CCP members and 60 percent were veteran revolutionaries. Although the officials were mostly from urban areas and relatively well educated, they were "poorly trained professionally and technically." Only 18 percent had college-level technical training. Moreover, "virtually all [the] professional skills" that were available resided in personnel who were *not* party members. These people were "clearly much better educated, specialized, and trained" than the party members, of whom nearly 70 percent had no higher education, specialized skills, or technical training. Nevertheless, the party members occupied the most powerful positions in political and social administration, while those who were not party members "were normally assigned to offices of lower political sensitivity and power." Promotion was another case in which the latter group suffered discrimination, as the party members had an overwhelming advantage despite their poorer technical qualifications. During the sixteen-year period covered by Kau's study, more than 80 percent of the party members were promoted, compared with only 14 percent of the officials who were not party members.[56]

Shanghai was the most industrialized city during this period. However, it is questionable whether the officials there were significantly better educated than those in Wuhan. Data on the educational qualifications of Shanghai officials are not available, but estimates are possible based on other information. In 1956, fewer than 26,300 of 193,600 CCP members in Shanghai had attended senior high school; by contrast, more than 50 percent had only a primary education due to the fact that recruitment into the party had been favoring workers and peasants. The entire government had a total of 40,400 party members.[57] Even a conservative estimate would suggest that at least half of these people at the forefront of the struggle to bring socialism to Shanghai had not attended senior high school, though it is unclear how these less-educated party members were distributed among offices.

By 1965 the educational level of Shanghai's party members had improved. Still, only 21 percent had attended senior high school or college, while almost 65 percent of all cadres in the municipality, a group that included party members and nonmembers in various types of establishments, had at least had some form of senior high education.[58] This implies that the educational qualifications of those who had authority in government and elsewhere may have decreased vis-à-vis that of their subordinates in the intervening years, which, as we saw in Chapter 3, was exactly what happened in secondary schools as teachers' academic qualifications improved faster than those of management's. On the whole, as Hong Yung Lee has noted, the CCP members who held power in urban areas were usually not much better educated than the general population, but many were expected to handle complex issues of governance that demanded specialized knowledge.[59] In short, the CCP adoption of the Leninist approach to socialist development equipped these people with authority but failed to furnish government with sufficient knowledge and skills.

Existing evidence suggests that counter-bureaucratic appointment penetrated even the military, otherwise arguably the most rationalized institution under Communist Party rule. Shortly after the revolution, the CCP began to convert its guerilla forces into a modern army with formal assignments, training, benefits, and conscription. With technical advice and aid from the Soviet Union, the effort was widely supported by veteran army commanders and newly trained officers. But the party also deployed a network of party committees, political departments, and political commissars in the military to control it directly. Here, too, this formal dichotomy between political and technical labor engendered tensions among colleagues. Because large numbers of military officers were themselves party members, their struggle against the political representatives seemed to have been rather overt compared with the resentment against this type of people in other places. According to one analysis, in the mid-1950s, army commanders and officers attacked "the system of political controls." Lauding their own professionalism, they considered "the party committees and the commissars an obstacle to [military] organizational efficiency" and criticized the political appointees for being too "incompetent to handle military affairs." Some officers ignored the political officers and even "took direct action" in abolishing the party committees.[60] But the official emphasis on political loyalty and party domination would hold sway in the military as in other institutions. By 1956 the party had launched "a full-scale rectification campaign" in the military. Its effort to control the armed force would intensify during the Anti-Rightist Campaign, as a "deluge of denunciations" descended on the officers opposing party control. Although the failure of the Great Leap Forward reinforced the importance of expertise in the military as elsewhere, the party did not make "any key concessions" to the view that involvement of party committees in the military should be curtailed.[61]

Michel Oksenberg's study of lower-level governments before the

Cultural Revolution shows that they, too, were afflicted with counter-bureaucratic appointments. After a decade of change, governments at the county, township, and village levels generally hosted a divided corps of officials. Groups of senior party members and demobilized soldiers, most of whom had been appointed for political reasons and were poorly educated, held important managerial and supervisory posts. By contrast, large numbers of secondary school graduates who were products of the educational expansion under CCP rule had technical responsibilities (such as soil improvement or pest control) or held staff positions in industry, communications, transportation, propaganda, or education. Although their skills were crucial for the local political economy, they had limited chances for promotion to management. Besides these two main groups, local officialdoms generally had other kinds of officeholders, party members and nonmembers, who had been recruited in different ways and were responsible for different types of work. Overall, Oksenberg indicated, local officials "tended to have different skills and expectations" and "somewhat dissimilar career patterns" that reinforced their own social identities at the expense of a shared professional identity.[62]

There were several reasons why lower-level governments commonly encountered shortages of professional skills, especially in the 1950s. First, the supply of college graduates, and even senior high school graduates, to the workplace was tight because education was still underdeveloped. Second, such governments went through rapid expansion despite the shortage of technically trained personnel, stretching what professional expertise there was even more thinly. Third, compared with higher-level agencies, these governments faced stronger competition from factories, universities, and other expanding establishments for well-trained personnel. The odds were therefore stacked against lower-level governments being able to assemble a professionally competent staff to carry out the reforms desired by Beijing.

Between 1950 and 1952 alone, the party and state recruited approximately 2.6 million officials, most of them to be stationed in lower-level governments. They were mostly young adults who supported political change or had completed one of the many short training courses organized by the CCP regime.[63] More than half of these people were former workers or peasants.[64] In the middle of conducting political and social reforms, the local authorities apparently "had not devoted enough attention to verifying political reliability or professional qualifications" of the recruits.[65] Issues of political trust and technical competence quickly surfaced as these people assumed their posts. For example, by 1952, tens of thousands of people had been recruited into party and state offices and other establishments to act as propagandists and reporters to help legitimize CCP rule. The government later discovered that among the recruits were "persons whose educational attainment [was] too low to enable them to meet the demands of their work," and that lax recruitment had even allowed "bandits and vagabonds" into the party.[66]

Through a series of cleansing campaigns, large numbers of people were removed from party membership because of poor political qualifications. But the even larger number of newly recruited officials who had inadequate skills could not be purged from local governments as easily. Their dismissal would have paralyzed the party's ambitious reforms or even led to social unrest due to a sudden rise in unemployment. By 1955 Chinese officialdom was still filled with people of dubious technical qualification. It was reported that 2 million out of 5.3 million cadres nationwide had only a primary education or less, while 3 million had a junior or senior high education.[67] Most of these people had jobs in the sprawling layers of lower and middle management in government and other sectors. They were situated on the frontline of the CCP's effort to transform China into a modern socialist society.

The lack of professional skill in lower-level governments was also a perverse result of the downward transfers of officials aimed at rectifying what Beijing considered a top-heavy state apparatus. Before the Cultural Revolution, these transfers peaked in 1955, the late 1950s, and just before the mass movement.[68] Although some of the "sent-down" cadres would later return to their previous positions, most stayed at the lower levels. In 1955 no fewer than 2,200 "offices and sections" controlled by central ministries were abolished, with some ministries cutting more than half of their staff.[69] In 1957 the Wuhan government alone reassigned 32,000 cadres to local governments and other establishments, while 30 to 50 percent of the officials in other major cities were sent down.[70] In Shanghai, at least 25,000 officials and other personnel were transferred to lower-level governments, schools, and other establishments between 1958 and 1965.[71]

Beijing's instructions were that the establishments involved in the transfers should take care to match skill to post, such as matching technicians to technical jobs and midlevel officials to administrative positions. In practice, this entailed complex coordination among large numbers of workplaces. Even if all of them had fully cooperated with one another, many transferees might still have received assignments that ill fitted their academic or occupational training. More seriously, as we saw with teacher recruitment throughout the 1950s, higher-level establishments normally decided which staff members to release. They acted in their own best interests, keeping the most qualified personnel and selecting those to be transferred from the rest. This suggests that although the downward transfer of officials offered local governments some technical benefits, such governments were forced to absorb personnel whose skill levels were relatively low or did not match positions open. In particular, the CCP emphasis on individual political reliability in officialdom provided higher-level agencies an incentive to release people with flawed records, which meant that lower-level governments would tend to have larger proportions of officials who had been guilty of wrongdoing or bad performance, who had "poor" class backgrounds, or whose relations with management had been problematic. Nevertheless, the proportion of such "dubious" personnel in local governments should be smaller than in local factories, schools, or other establishments located further down on the institutional hierarchy under CCP rule.

Compared with industry, education, and other sectors, the government had fewer people with salary retention supplements or a more rational salary structure. With their desire to pursue economic growth as well as social equality, Mao and other CCP leaders constantly struggled with the use of salary retention supplements. On one hand, such supplements could help motivate "bourgeois intellectuals" to cooperate with the regime; on the other hand, they produced obvious income inequalities favoring people with dubious political loyalty and "poor" class backgrounds and provoking resentment from the rest of the workforce. From early on, Beijing had been devising plans to maintain, reduce, or even eliminate salary retention supplements to deal with issues of productivity, fairness, and morale in the workplace. Depending on sectors, some supplements were terminated or cut in the 1950s. Others, such as those within Shanghai secondary education, were fully preserved.

In the mid-1950s, however, Beijing canceled the payment of salary retention supplements in government. Housing, transport, and other subsidies were offered, instead, to officials who needed economic assistance.[72] A main reason why only the government was targeted for the cancellation was that officials were much less likely than professors, engineers, or other professionals to protest it. Most CCP members in government did not have retained salaries to begin with. By the mid-1950s, large numbers of high-paid officials who had served the KMT regime had already been transferred out of officialdom. Equally important, the cancellation would boost the image of government by making all officials remunerate by postrevolutionary and leaner standards. However, retained salaries were not therefore eliminated completely from Chinese officialdom. Because governments constantly used their privileged institutional positions to upgrade their staff, various kinds of political and technical personnel from other sectors were frequently recruited into officialdom. Since some of these people had had salaries higher than the official standards for their new posts, government offices were permitted to compensate them by paying their original salaries or letting them keep a salary retention supplement to assuage any dissatisfaction due to the transfers. By the late 1950s, this policy had produced in the Shanghai government what was called "new salary retention supplements" (*xin baoliu gongzi*).

On the eve of the Cultural Revolution, what was most contentious about remuneration in officialdom was not the reemergence of salary supplements but income stagnation. Like schoolteachers, most officials had seen little or no salary increase for years due to the failure of the Great Leap Forward as a production campaign. The college and secondary school graduates who had entered government after the mid-1950s were stuck at the lowest income levels even as these people gained work experience and responsibility. Since the state provided its staff with superior medical, housing, and other subsidies, the displeasure of low-income officials was partly alleviated by the availability of such benefits. But the lack of a comfortable salary still meant that these people, compared with their better-paid colleagues, had limited money to purchase food and consumer goods on top of regularly rationed items.[73] As in other institutions, such experience was especially hard on those who had recently started their careers and had expectations of marrying and raising a young family.

The state was arguably the most privileged institution under CCP rule. However, political domination, shortages of expertise, and other nonrational features appeared at every level of this institution after 1949. As we shall see below, this development of counter-bureaucracy in government was a major cause of the economic collapse and mass famine of the Great Leap Forward. More broadly, the reproduction of counter-bureaucracy contributed to the breakdown of social order during the Cultural Revolution, as well as the poor performance of the Chinese economy during the Mao era.

COUNTER-BUREAUCRATIC TRAUMAS
IN SOCIALIST CHINA

By any standards, the Great Leap Forward (1958–60) represented a monumental failure in the history of governance. Because of gross official mismanagement in this three-year production campaign, an estimated 15 to 46 million people starved to death, while scarce and valuable resources were squandered.[74] Virtually the entire population labored for industrial or agricultural growth only to see their quality of life decline dramatically. Recent research confirms that Mao, with his millennial vision of socialist development in China, played an unparalleled role in this tragic outcome. Had he not held delusional expectations for growth rates and a rapid transition to communism, or for how they could be achieved by a relatively undereducated population, the mass famine would not have occurred. Had he promoted a genuine retreat from the Great Leap Forward—instead of further accelerating it—as soon as signs of human suffering appeared, fewer people would have perished.[75]

The Great Leap disaster, however, would not have occurred at all had the state not been constituted as a counter-bureaucracy after 1949. The emphasis on political loyalty, denigration of expertise, and arbitrary deployment of punishment within officialdom were *essential* conditions that enabled Mao to translate his personal fantasies into immensely destructive state policies and production practices. Like the Soviet industrialization drive, the Great Leap Forward thus revealed that counter-bureaucracy was a powerful instrument of political domination. But because counter-bureaucracy had already vitiated the technical capacity of the Chinese state, the latter could not have generated stellar economic growth as Mao or others imagined. In fact, through his reckless measures, Mao deepened counter-bureaucratic development in the state apparatus, thereby exacerbating the very political and technical problems it needed to correct to improve as an instrument of rule. Small wonder the campaign's outcome was exactly the opposite of what he intended—rapid economic collapse instead of rapid economic growth.

As early as mid-1955, Mao began to muscle his own ideas of eco-nomic expansion onto the state plan. With support at various levels of the government, he had sidelined the personnel and institutions re-sponsible for industrial and agricultural planning in Beijing by late 1957 and had taken over policy making.[76] Mao sanctified decentralization and mass mobilization as *the* means for achieving leaps and bounds in production. Under his direction, the 1958 Sixty Articles on Work Meth-ods announced national production targets for grain, cotton, steel, and coal, as well as other reforms that would have been unachievable even in the best circumstances given the resources available to the country. Provincial governments were compelled to set up their own equally, if not more, fanciful targets based on such figures, whose fulfillment was mandatory and overfulfillment virtually required, as had been the case in the industrial sector during the Soviet industrialization drive.[77]

Mao's success in turning the initiatives of the Great Leap Forward into state policies was a testimony to his political stature and prow-ess. He browbeat, outmaneuvered, or gained the support of other par-ty leaders, attacked those who questioned his belief in rapid growth, and subjected even some of his close colleagues, most notably Marshal Peng Dehuai, to dismissal and other penalties.[78] But with the demand for loyalty and punishment for opposition well institutionalized within officialdom, he was able to extend his domination over policy making to lower levels of government. Many officials willingly heeded Mao's escalating calls for expanding production; the rest were skeptical of his initiatives on technical grounds. In particular, the Anti-Rightist Cam-paign, which began in mid-1957 and was resuscitated in 1959, had been a main vehicle through which Mao secured compliance at the lo-cal level.[79] Because the party had no clearly stated or legally binding rules on the punishment of rightists, no officials were certain what their sentence might be if indicted for sabotage, which only reinforced their tendency to follow higher-level decisions.

In this oppressive political climate, local officials fell in line rapidly. They set up wildly unrealistic industrial and agricultural production targets; implemented technically dubious and wasteful practices laud-ed by central government; and mobilized and pressured the local pop-ulation into unceasing labor. It did not matter whether they believed that China could develop as rapidly as Mao predicted. The alternative to displaying effusive support for his initiatives was to risk punish-ment, as any hesitation or vacillation might be interpreted as sabotage by one's colleagues or higher authorities. Among the Great Leap Forward's projects, the mass establishment of local blast furnaces during the autumn of 1958 best exemplified the extreme disregard for technical expertise. The campaign lacked any technical merits but became a national movement for raising iron and steel production. It disrupted regular production, wasted tremendous amounts of resources, and diverted much-needed labor supply from agricultural production, which had, too, been plunged into chaos by the Great Leap Forward.[80]

As political pressure mounted, local officials further raised the production targets and compressed the timetables in obedience to Mao's changing and grander visions of development. They intensified pressure on the local population and even knowingly competed with one another to set ever more unachievable goals.[81] When both industrial and agricultural production failed to meet the targets, as it inevitably would, they reported false or inflated figures to indicate their conformity to and enthusiasm for the Great Leap Forwards's objectives, as Soviet officials had done in the 1930s industrialization drive.[82] The higher authorities, in turn, did the same in relation to their superiors. In the countryside, this resulted in rising requisitioning of grain based on false production data, all the while when harvesting was being neglected.

Through a counter-bureaucratic state apparatus, Mao imposed his political will on the entire country. His Great Leap approaches to development were carried through the many levels of officialdom and converted into daily production practices and the mobilization of the populace. Because the elevation of political loyalty contributed to an extreme disdain for expertise and constant threat of punishment, the Great Leap Forward engendered an unprecedented level of ritualistic conformity within officialdom that feigned a semblance of success, even when disaster was looming. This gigantic antirational machine of political domination that was the Chinese Communist state could not but guarantee the supreme leader a rude awakening. In three short years, the Great Leap Forward killed millions of people and produced a major setback in the economy.[83]

As a form of workplace administration, counter-bureaucracy had widely penetrated China's political economy by the mid-1950s. The outpouring of complaints by different occupational groups against the ruling regime, party officials, activists, and salary inequities during the Hundred Flowers Campaign indicated that state-society relations and social relations inside work establishments were already quite strained.[84] The Anti-Rightist Campaign that followed and the failure of the Great Leap Forward only intensified such tensions. What came after the Great Leap debacle, however, was not any organizational rationalization in the Weberian sense that would have directly or indirectly improved popular support for the CCP regime or workplace solidarity. Rather, with Mao retreating from policy making, the party reverted to its Leninist approaches to developing socialism. The organizational features of the workplace before the Great Leap Forward—emphasis on political loyalty, distrust of nonparty professionals, punishment of dissenters, retention of wrongdoers, and income inequities—remained as defining workplace features for the last few years before the Cultural Revolution descended upon China.

Compared to the mass political conformity of the Great Leap Forward, the Cultural Revolution presented the apparent contradiction of mass political upheavals. But this state-sponsored popular movement, too, was deeply entwined with the development of counter-bureaucracy under CCP rule. If the Great Leap Forward exemplified the tremendous economic destruction the counter-bureaucratic state inflicted upon society, the Cultural Revolution was evidence par excellence of the damage that the normalization of counter-bureaucracy had done to the social fabric.

In mid-1966 Mao once again exploited his supreme stature to pursue radical change. His aim was to rectify the structure of political authority, which he believed had become an obstacle to socialist development. Supported by a small group within the party elite, he launched the Cultural Revolution to attack what he called "capitalist restoration" within state and society. By the end of the year, party members of all generations, professional personnel, young and old activists, and factory workers and laborers were embroiled in a widening struggle against one another and against party and state officials. Much as what we saw in schools and colleges in Chapter 6, these people's activism mingled with and fueled the Red Guard movement, which Mao had initiated and manipulated to promote his political objectives. Large numbers of management personnel had already engaged in struggle with their subordinates and Red Guards and had been removed from office and physically attacked. Under internal and external pressure, the hierarchical structures within party and state agencies unraveled shortly after as senior party officials lost control of management or were forced to share decision making with others.

There is no question that Mao and his high-level supporters played the critical role in launching the mass movement. But the upheaval and struggle that quickly spread across work establishments must be understood within the context of their own counter-bureaucratic constitutions.[85] For almost two decades of rule, the CCP regime failed to instill in the workplace any shared understanding or interest that would have promoted staff solidarity, let alone collective commitment to the socialist project. To the contrary, the institutionalization of Leninist practices engendered multidimensional conflict among colleagues as well as resentment against the state and management. Tensions between party members and the ordinary staff, activists and nonactivists, the young and the old, as well as lawbreakers and their supervisors were widespread and kept in check only by the threat of punishment for anyone who violated official policies. As the previous chapters on the Shanghai secondary school teachers suggest, people who had been dissatisfied with their lot had been reacting with public and private complaints, halfhearted cooperation in the workplace, and even open protest.

Once Mao withdrew his approval for and, in fact, promoted assault on the existing counter-bureaucratic order, particularly after the "Sixteen Articles" in August 1966, those who were frustrated in their careers began to attack their colleagues and superiors as well as party and state officials for "taking the capitalist road" or thwarting socialist development. Individuals who had been officially disciplined, including rightists and "bad elements," and who had been alienated by management due to their social background (class or otherwise) were very active in fomenting attack.[86] Young party members and activists, who had more to gain than to lose from the demise of the Leninist-based order, actively participated in the struggle, too. Others condemned their colleagues and higher authorities in order to protect their own safety. Responding to the dynamics and opportunities created by the mass movement, factions emerged in the workplace, including governments, to compete for control, all claiming allegiance to Mao. Some grew into much larger organizations that worked with student Red Guards to vie for political power.[87]

The Cultural Revolution showed that after nearly two decades of building socialism, the CCP had produced not a stable political order, but a fragile system of rule. The absence of social solidarity in the workplace was a condition of this counter-bureaucratic system that enabled Mao to divide the workforce and turn its members against one another. But he underestimated the extent of resentment in the workplace as well as the dissatisfaction against the state. Like the Great Leap Forward, the Cultural Revolution, too, slipped out of his control. A week after Nie Yuanzi's poster attacking the Beijing municipal government and Peking University was published nationally, Mao indicated that the mass movement would last for about three months.[88] He failed to apprehend the deep sense of frustration, mutual enmity, and resentment within the socialist system that the party had built after 1949, and that he had unleashed with his call to rebellion. It would take the regime three years to return social order to China.

In many cases workplaces disrupted by the Cultural Revolution began to return to normal productivity levels by the late 1960s. By then, what the state called revolutionary committees, which contained various mixes of party cadres, military personnel, workers, and peasants had been widely established to effect popular participation in management. Between August 1968 and September 1969, for example, some ninety thousand members belonging to worker propaganda teams moved into two thousand work establishments in Shanghai, including the municipal, district, and county governments.[89] The institutionalization of such committees displaced large numbers of management personnel from their jobs, if they had not already been removed by popular uprisings. Many administrators were reappointed to positions with little relation to their technical training.[90] But popular management really existed in name only. As political struggle persisted at the elite level, different factions below tried to gain control of the workplace with different organizational measures.[91] Although such competitions were less transparent and violent than those that had occurred during the mass movement, the mutual distrust among colleagues had been exacerbated by the previous attacks and abuse these personnel had endured or witnessed. Andrew Walder was right when he noted that workplace reorganization after the Cultural Revolution was not only based on "half-formed ideas" and "vague principles" at the elite level; it was "implemented piecemeal in rapid, unplanned bursts" locally.[92] Such an inauspicious denouement of the mass movement symbolized the continuation of power struggle within state and society.

At the rank-and-file level of the workplace, what emerged was anything but a collective effort to raise production or quality of work. The normalization of revolutionary committees, much as the previous use of CCP management, discouraged cooperation from the educated or professionally experienced. Worse, for fear that their professional opin-

ions might be interpreted as criticism of Maoist anti-intellectual development strategies, many of the professionally skilled refrained from using their expertise to engage in production or reproduction genuinely.
Other than abolishing individual bonuses in the industrial enterprise as
being a bourgeois practice, as Christopher Howe has pointed out, the
party maintained a "conservative policy" on salaries after the Cultural
Revolution, making little change to the previously standardized schedules.[93] In most workplaces, this virtually meant a freeze on wages and
salaries and a reduction in subsidies that reinforced existing patterns
of income inequality. With little to reward subordinates materially,
management encountered serious problems of labor morale and cooperation. The outcome was increased indifference, absenteeism, loafing,
and other discipline problems in the workplace.[94]

The rise of Maoist organizational practices therefore hardly improved any collective commitment to the socialist project as Mao had
wished. As an ideology, Maoism promoted popular participation in
management and personal devotion to work as a means of protecting
and furthering the development of socialism in China. It was a reaction
to the Leninist tactics that insist on strict party control and the deployment of professional knowledge. Mao believed that such tactics had
re-created social inequities and corrupted Chinese socialism. From a
Weberian perspective, however, Maoism and Leninism were similar
with respect to organizational rationalization and the socialist project—they both engendered counter-bureaucratic administrations that
undermined the official effort of building a sustainable socialist society.
After the Cultural Revolution, the workplace saw a further erosion of
technical efficiency, staff morale, and social solidarity.

There is no doubt that the CCP made great strides in modernizing
China after 1949, just as it is clear that the Bolsheviks played a primary
role in industrializing the Soviet Union. Within a short time, the institutions of state, industry, education, communication, and welfare
were much larger and more sophisticated than they had ever been, and
industrial as well as agricultural outputs increased substantially.[95] On
the whole, however, China saw only an unenviable rate of economic
growth during the Mao era as compared to neighboring Japan, Taiwan,
or South Korea, all of which experienced an economic takeoff sometime
during this period, thanks in part to their conscious rationalization of
government. In fact, in the wake of the Mao era, critical economic measures indicated that after three decades of socialism, the overall living

standard in Mainland China had not risen much at all. In urban areas, real wages and per capita housing space (not counting the impact of deterioration) had declined by almost 20 percent since the mid-1950s. Like their counterparts in other Soviet-type societies, China's urbanites endured "an extreme shortage" of fruit, vegetables, and meat as well as consumer goods and basic services. In the countryside, the quality of diet was even worse, comparable to the poverty-stricken countries of Ethiopia and Bangladesh. The grain consumption of 20 percent of the rural population "did not meet official Chinese subsistence standards."[96] Perhaps more disturbing to the Chinese leadership, who had once proclaimed confidently rapid industrialization, was that industrial output per unit of capital invested had declined by 25 percent since the early 1950s, while the industrial growth that did occur was accounted for "by the shifting of resources from other sectors into industry."[97] In other words, the reproduction of counter-bureaucracy, Leninist- or Maoist-style, had restricted China's industrial growth despite the fact that the CCP regime had been squeezing the peasantry and the working class by limiting individual and household consumption.

UNSUSTAINABLE SYSTEMS OF RULE

No organization perfectly matches the rational bureaucracy described by Weber. He would have been first to admit, as his ideal-type construct implies, that even the most modern of modern organizations deviate from the rational bureaucracy in various ways. Compliance with informal rather than formally stated rules; non-merit-based remuneration; nepotism in discipline, appointment, and promotion; as well as other nonrational features can be commonly found in modern organizations. But, for Weber, what makes these organizations historically and analytically distinct—and superior to other forms of administration—is their systematic use of formally rational norms to regulate organizational structure and the actions of officeholders. In his view, such rationality was rarely found in the past.

In this chapter I have shown that two of the most powerful and privileged institutions within actually existing socialisms—Chinese officialdom and Soviet industry—were not modern bureaucratic administrations and should be not taken as such. For three decades or more, the structure of one institution was strongly influenced by Leninist thinking, and the other institution had been Leninist-based before being reconfigured on the basis of Maoist ideas. Although the two institutions possessed many features that are identical to those of modern bureaucratic administrations (such as distinct offices, long-term careers, regular compensation, and the stress on written records), they had other basic arrangements that make their comparison with modern bureaucracy inappropriate and misleading. For one thing, no modern noncommunist political regime has as deliberately and systematically disregarded professional knowledge and skills in government or industry as the Soviet or Chinese Communist leadership. Second, certainly no such regime has ignored rational planning and pursued rapid economic growth simultaneously. Third, within both Chinese officialdom and Soviet industry, intrusive and arbitrary punishment, including imprisonment and capital sentence, was a fact of life. Fourth, a group of pariahs susceptible to abuse by management and colleagues was always present in the workplace. These were basic organizational features of the two institutions that made them counter-bureaucratic rather than modern bureaucratic.

The Stalin era and the Mao era represented the high tide of counter-bureaucracy in the Soviet Union and China respectively. Behind the reproduction of communist political rule and apparent economic growth, the ruling regimes, in fact, failed to transform China or Russia into sustainable socialist societies. Economically, poor productivity, excessive waste, inferior products, declining real wages, and low per capita income and living standards were characteristics of these socialist systems, whether they should be labeled Leninist, Maoist, or Stalinist.[98] Politically, mutual distrust, political disaffection, silent discontent, fear, and resentment were major emotional responses to Communist Party rule. Such development could not but undermine both elite and popular confidence in the socialist systems.

To put this differently, the Soviet and the Chinese counter-bureaucracies contained self-reforming potential from the beginning, because of the inescapable problems of political disaffection and technical inefficiency the systems posed for their rulers and the constant pressure for institutional improvement from lower levels. Here lies another major difference between counter-bureaucracy and modern bureaucracy— that is, organizational stability. Weber contended that one of the primary benefits modern bureaucratic administrations offer to management is predictability and stability of work operations. The more rationalized a workplace is, the more its labor force would defend its constitution for its own good. That is why he suggests that highly matured modern bureaucratic systems are virtually indestructible. By contrast, the types of social inequality and uncertainty, not to mention the violent social upheavals, the Soviet and Chinese Communist regimes forced upon state and society through the normalization of counter-bureaucracy engendered enormous desire for reform. Change rather than stability had been a feature of both Stalin's Russia and Mao's China. The most significant reforms of the Soviet and Chinese counter-bureaucratic systems of rule, however, came only after Stalin and Mao were gone. How the changes reshaped these systems of rule and the relations of these changes to the decline of the socialist systems are topics of Chapter 8.

8

Rethinking Socialism

One of the most profound changes during the transition to socialism in China and Russia was the normalization of counter-bureaucracy. This type of workplace organization penetrated government, industry, education, and other institutions. In the previous chapters I have drawn on different cases and events to elucidate the major features of such administration—politically based authority, shortages of expertise, nonrational compensation, and intrusive and arbitrary discipline. The discussion has revealed a pattern of organization that diverged substantively from modern bureaucratic administration. But the resulting administration was not a modern instance of patrimonial or traditional bureaucracy. The Chinese and Soviet Communist leaderships were self-conscious modernizers who understood the need for controlling the workplace through *persistent* intervention. It is hard to imagine any transition to socialism had they not deployed distinct offices and careers, stable compensation, regular supervision, thorough documentation, and other modern techniques of workplace control appearing only irregularly in traditional economies. Counter-bureaucracy had the shell but not the content of modern bureaucracy.

Besides tracing the ideological origins of counter-bureaucracy and its evolution in specific institutions, the preceding chapters have explored the impact of such administration on the historical transition to socialism. For more than a quarter century in China and almost four decades in Russia, workplace shortages of expertise and competence were commonplace. Serious conflict and distrust marred the relations among colleagues. The workforce, especially the educated and professionally experienced, was subject to episodic struggle and violence. Such developments undermined social solidarity in the workplace, labor productivity, as well as popular commitment to communist political rule and socialist projects. To be sure, the Chinese and Soviet economies grew significantly, but they were characterized by severe squandering of resources, unenviable living standards, and mediocre growth rates compared to the developing countries that "took off" in the mid-twentieth century. The Communist regimes did not deliberately bring about these economic consequences, but in retrospect, the latter were inevitable given the deployment of counter-bureaucratic administration in the workplace.

In this closing chapter, I address three questions related to the decline of actually existing socialisms. What role did counter-bureaucracy play in their decline during the late 1980s and early 1990s? Why did major intellectual perspectives on such societies at the time or prior to their decline fail to anticipate this momentous event? And what is the implication of the decline of actually existing socialisms for future theories of socialism? In other words, I explore the theoretical interpretations of this historic process at different levels based on my argument that actually existing socialisms were counter-bureaucratic. In so doing, I seek to demonstrate that Weber's thinking provides excellent insight into each of the issues. His work is essential for understanding what went wrong, not only with Soviet-type societies, but with research on such societies as well. It is also critical for rethinking the viability of the socialist alternative to capitalism.

COUNTER-BUREAUCRATIC EVOLUTIONS: NEOTRADITIONAL CORRUPTION AND CONDITIONAL TOLERANCE

In China, the high tide of counter-bureaucracy had ended by the late 1970s in the wake of the Mao era. In the Soviet Union, the ascent of Khrushchev in the mid-1950s was a watershed in socialist organization. But the Chinese and Soviet workplaces did not evolve into modern bureaucratic administrations that would strengthen rational interest in subordination. Rather, their counter-bureaucratic characteristics fueled the growth of what Ken Jowitt has described as "neotraditional" patterns of official corruption. At the societal level, distrust and resentment toward political authority evolved into what Jan Pakulski has called "conditional tolerance" toward the state. These systemic outcomes further weakened public support for the Communist regimes.

Before we examine the evolution toward neotraditional corruption and conditional tolerance in Soviet-type societies, it is necessary to summarize other specific changes that happened to these societies after the high tide of counter-bureaucracy, for these changes have been taken wrongly as evidence of the societies going through Weberian-style organizational rationalization. In particular, the misunderstanding engendered the notable thesis of *institutional convergence* three decades ago that highlights functional specification, technical specialization, and hierarchical and procedural formalization in Soviet-type societies, and therefore their supposed tendency to resemble Western societies.[1] The thesis precisely reinforces the notion that Soviet-type societies represent domination by bureaucracy and underestimates their continuing disorganization at workplace level.

In the Soviet Union and China, state terror and state-sponsored persecutions declined rapidly after the death of Stalin and of Mao. Under Khrushchev and Brezhnev, Soviet rule was purged of extreme concentration of power and approaches to social change. Under Deng Xiaopeng, the Chinese Communist Party (CCP) abandoned tactics of mass mobilization and repudiated the Cultural Revolution and the Anti-Rightist Campaign as mistakes. The upheaval of "building socialism" was finally over. In the Soviet Union, a new era officially referred to as "real, existing socialism" was announced. In China, the "four modernizations" of agriculture, industry, defense, and science and technology became primary state objectives.

Following a Stalinist trend, the Soviet authorities inserted large numbers of college and technical college graduates into official and management posts. By the early 1970s, "nearly all significant Soviet officials [were] college graduates, generally with specialized training appropriate for the post they hold," an impressive achievement by any standard of modernization. Although being a party member was still important for getting ahead, "party membership [became] less an independent requirement for promotion than a sign that the person [was] seen as having the technocratic criteria for it."[2] In China, technical qualification gained unprecedented importance in job assignment after Mao. A new corps of "bureaucratic technocrats" who were selected from the best educated and best trained started to dominate officialdom.[3] Languishing scientists, academics, and experts were reappointed to professional posts.

Class struggle was downplayed in both countries as a principle of organizing society. Class background no longer had the same fateful influence on job appointment, college enrollment, overseas travel, or other career opportunities. Professors, writers, and artists began to explore previously prohibited political, intellectual, and creative themes. Large numbers of former dissidents and "wrongdoers" were released from confinement and returned to work. The ruling regimes focused on improving consumer goods production, household income, and general living standards over those of the Stalin and Mao eras. For the first time, the Soviet government subsidized agriculture rather than squeezing it for industrial development. The CCP took the even more radical approach of abolishing collective farming and successfully raised agricultural production and peasant income.

Did these changes indicate that organizational rationalization dominated after Stalin and after Mao? How credible was the 1970s contention of institutional convergence between Soviet-type and Western societies? In an incisive critique of scholarship on the post-Stalin Soviet Union and Eastern Europe (written before the demise of socialism), Pakulski suggests that it is "conceptual stretching" to consider workplace organization in these societies a variant of the rational bureaucracy. Although reforms had been instituted, workplaces still lacked the *legal-rational* character that underlies what Weber called modern bureaucratic administration. Official action was still not based on a consistent system of legal, rational, and impersonal norms. Among the many workplace features that Pakulski has enumerated as "nonbureaucratic" are the major characteristics of counter-bureaucracy discussed in this book—political domination, nonmeritocratic appointment, arbitrary discipline, and nonrational compensation.[4] They had survived the Stalin years. His argument should be extended to organizational change in post-Mao China.

Although official appointment in Soviet-type societies increasingly favored technically qualified personnel, it was far from merit-based or bound by rational rules or procedures. At the elite level, the selection of top officials in such societies might not differ from that in other societies, as political and personal loyalty was essential. Beneath this level, however, the party continued to allocate jobs on the basis of political loyalty, but with an added emphasis on professional qualification. As a result, party members still dominated middle and senior management inside and outside of government. Technical expertise alone did not guarantee work authority. Evidence on post-Mao China indicates that professionals who were not party members were consistently steered to technical positions with little management authority.[5]

The relaxation of state control and discipline in the post-Stalin and post-Mao eras did not mean that the exercise of official authority was less arbitrary. "The means of compulsion" and "the conditions of their use" were still "neither sharply defined, nor strictly enforced."[6] Professors, writers, and others whose work was vulnerable to political attack continued to tread between shifting ideological limits. An excellent example is the 1983 Chinese Campaign Against Spiritual Pollution that targeted things as different as pornography, individualism, stylish clothing, corruption, superstition, and philosophical and artistic works. Its initiation, implementation, and denouement were all consequences of political struggle within different levels of government rather than based on clearly defined legal regulations.[7]

Moreover, Communist Party leaders and cadres continued to exercise disproportionate influence on criminal sentencing. There was no independent judiciary free of party interference in China or in the Soviet Union, but rather plenty of "informal mechanisms" that shaped the penal process.[8] Although the two governments raised gross household income and remunerated the workforce based on standardized salary schedules, party and state officials still controlled nonmonetary benefits such as housing and access to vacation homes, bicycles, and watches, and doled out such benefits "arbitrarily in exchange for political favors."[9]

The persistence of the nonrational features above in Soviet-type societies undermined the thesis of institutional convergence. Furthermore, other studies reported that party cadres widely exploited their appointment or authority for personal gain. They misappropriated state properties, embezzled state funds, sold state offices, engaged in smuggling, and took bribes for almost everything. Reliance on personal or patron-client relationships had become a critical means for average citizens to acquire housing, jobs, pay raises, promotion, travel visas, college admission, and so on.[10] The spread of official corruption and particularist ties demonstrated further that workplaces in Soviet-type societies were not founded on legal, impersonal, and rational norms and were hardly comparable to modern bureaucratic administration in Western societies.

What then happened to the Soviet Union or China after the high tide of counter-bureaucracy, if organizational rationalization is an inappropriate characterization? It is here that Jowitt's analysis of official corruption helps illuminate a long-term consequence of counter-bureaucracy in Soviet-type societies. Jowitt contends that after the Stalin years, Soviet and Eastern European regimes descended into "a neotraditional status organization of cadres primarily oriented to personal, familial, and material concerns."[11] This degeneration into widespread corruption had less to do with any traditions of official abuse than with the party's unparalleled intervention in state and society. Jowitt notes that the party had been constituted as "a corporate, privileged status group" that asserted its interests and identity "in opposition to the rest of society,"[12] but party members had no *legitimate* means to improve their livelihoods except through official promotion or by securing extra benefits from the state.

Jowitt contends that for some time the party kept "a persistent tendency to organizational corruption" under control, especially through the deployment of *all-consuming* "social combat tasks" such as the Soviet industrialization drive and the Chinese Great Leap Forward.[13] Once the party discarded such combat tasks, its members started to use their power and positions to pursue their own interests en masse. Moreover, he suggests that the party's quest for rapid development without rational planning had normalized informal practices and reliance on "covert, personalized, hierarchical relationships" in the workplace. Such means of interaction became important mechanisms supporting corruption.[14]

The preceding chapters show that what Jowitt identified at the regime level before the spread of official corruption—that is, the party as a status organization, tight control on individual income, lack of rational planning, and use of coercion—was articulated within the workplace as counter-bureaucracy. This distinction between regime structure and workplace constitution is important for two reasons. A focus on the workplace would further clarify the institutional conditions leading to rampant corruption in Soviet-type societies. What seems most pertinent here is that despite their everyday domination, large numbers of party cadres had been alienated from their work, from their colleagues, and even from the state during the high tide of counter-bureaucracy. These relations of theirs would seem to militate against their commitment to official goals and values afterward. More important, Jowitt's account of regime structure barely touches upon popular reactions toward the party after its retreat from social combat tasks, mass terror, and class struggle. Did ordinary members of the workforce become more supportive of the government when their pain and suffering were lessened by significant policy change? Or, were they less supportive of Communist political rule and the socialist project? In other words, what was the legacy of the high tide of counter-bureaucracy among the general population?

As we have seen, the workplace was rife with tensions during the Stalin and Mao years, due to the reproduction of counter-bureaucracy. In general, ordinary staff members and workers had poorer access to authority, benefits, and comfort than did party members. If the latter's rampant corruption afterward confirmed that they had developed little genuine commitment toward the party—despite their privileged status—the experience of subjugation shared by the rest of the work-force was a formidable obstacle the government had to overcome to gain their support.[15] To be sure, with new approaches to appointment and promotion, the Soviet and Chinese regimes created new groups of beneficiaries in the workplace and hence new sources of political support. The general rise in living standards helped the regimes, too, before economic stagnation or crises hit the socialist systems again. Nonetheless, as Pakulski has made it clear, the systemic domination by party members, arbitrary deployment of official discipline, and tightly state-controlled distribution of goods, services, and benefits persisted in Soviet-type societies. The general population was still subjected to "conditions of threats, rewards for conformism, restricted alternatives, disciplinarian pressures, and the absorbing struggle for economic sur-vival" in the post-Stalin era and the post-Mao era.[16] In other words, state-society relations might have been less tense than before, but they were marred by both the legacy of counter-bureaucracy and the per-petuation of counter-bureaucratic features in the workplace.[17]

Pakulski is correct when he notes in his own Weberian analyses that mass political consent never really existed in Soviet-type societies. If mass compliance had been a function of state coercion, ideological ma-nipulation, and promises for a bright socialist future during the mo-bilization phase of such societies (or what I have called the high tide of counter-bureaucracy), *conditional tolerance* was the popular response toward the government afterward. That is, in the absence of any real regime change at the political level or organizational rationalization at the workplace level, most people responded to the state according to their understanding of "which types of behavior are likely to be re-warded and which increase the risks of punishment" in order to pro-tect their own welfare.[18] Even though the ruling regimes had changed the rule of the game, "the overall costs of non-compliance" remained

high, including job loss and imprisonment, but "rewards for conformity were considerable." In such circumstances, mass conformity was
"the natural outcome."[19] There was little genuine acceptance of official
values, goals, and norms in the general population in the post-Stalin
and post-Mao years, while the socialist economies metastasized into
widespread official corruption that further damaged the legitimacy of
Communist Party rule.

Like the distinction between modern bureaucracy and counter-bureaucracy at the organizational level, this distinction between political consent and conditional tolerance at the individual level is critical
for understanding the decline of Soviet-type societies. Political consent
indicates voluntary subordination to the state; conditional tolerance is
based on calculation of short-term cost and benefits. Pakulski argues
that so long as the price for political resistance was generally perceived
to be high in such societies, conditional tolerance reproduced social
stability by discouraging political protest or action against the ruling
regimes. Mass political dissatisfaction was, instead, expressed through
various forms of passive resistance such as rule evasion, absenteeism,
ritualism, corruption, religious activities, and pilfering that undermined
Communist political rule in a less public but no less serious manner.[20]
Some of these forms, such as ritualism and rule evasion, had been common during the high tide of counter-bureaucratic development; others
appeared widely after the state had retreated from social combat tasks.
The spread of conditional tolerance explains why there had not been
organized mass protest against the Soviet or Eastern European regimes
shortly before their demise and why their collapses were instantly embraced by the general population.[21] It helps clarify why a protest movement pressuring for political change quickly snowballed in China and
threatened the CCP's survival in the spring of 1989.

The 1989–91 revolutions ended Communist political rule in the Soviet Union and Eastern Europe. By contrast, the CCP survived the 1989
nationwide political movement. Since then, it has dismantled the socialist system it had erected to maintain its hold on power. Many factors led to the unraveling of the socialist systems in the Soviet Union,
China, and Eastern Europe. Among the most important were the unsuccessful political or economic reforms conducted by the regimes in
the 1980s, international political pressure, ethnic tension within Communist countries and, quite importantly, the Soviet decision not to interfere militarily in faltering Eastern Europe in the late 1980s, which

set off a chain of irreversible events. This study of counter-bureaucracy does not pinpoint the precise reasons for the collapse or survival of the Communist regimes, an analysis of which will require detailed delineation of political struggles and structural as well as contingent factors on the eve of the critical moments.[22] I have highlighted, instead, the types of destabilizing tensions Soviet-type societies long endured due to their rejection of modern bureaucracy for counter-bureaucracy.

Founded on anti-Weberian ideologies, Soviet-type societies had not been able to establish organizational features that would have promoted rational subordination in the workforce. The workplace was rife with social friction, political dissatisfaction, and problems of inefficiency. Despite systemic reforms after Stalin and after Mao, the structural and psychological consequences of the high tide of counter-bureaucracy persisted in the form of widespread official corruption and general conditional tolerance that further harmed the Communist regimes. In the end, dramatic change came in one form or another. We shall see below that even though this history of workplace disorganization proved to be detrimental to Soviet-type societies, it has not been well documented or understood, which is a main reason why major theoretical perspectives on such societies failed to anticipate their decline in the 1980s.

BRINGING WEBER BACK IN

Weber's sociology has long influenced the study of actually existing socialisms. From the totalitarian model of Communism that dominated early research to latest analyses, his ideas have been cited, applied, and reconceptualized for understanding such societies. But the 1989–91 collapse of the Soviet and Eastern European regimes betrayed how poorly research fared in foreseeing their demise. Social scientists were clearly no better than politicians, historians, and journalists in anticipating this historic turn of events.[23] Should Weber share the blame for the shortcomings of past research? This book, too, has relied on his ideas to reexamine Soviet-type societies. It is time to take advantage of hindsight and revisit past research. Briefly, Weber's concept of modern bureaucracy has been misinterpreted or ignored by major intellectual perspectives on the organization of Soviet-type societies, leading to the misunderstanding that they were relatively well organized rather than poorly rationalized. Nevertheless, his sociology is still a powerful tool for studying Soviet-type societies and, particularly, the administrative origin of their decline.

The mistaken idea that Soviet-type societies contained modern bureaucratic rather than counter-bureaucratic administration first appeared in the totalitarian model of Communism, though not in Hannah Arendt's famous work *Origins of Totalitarianism*.[24] Arendt was "extremely critical of attempts" to apply Weber's ideal-type concept of bureaucracy to the Bolshevik or Nazi regimes. For her, both regimes permitted "no room for positive law, stability, or predictability, but instead unleashe[d] unceasing, turbulent movement."[25] They lacked the legal-rational character that Weber attributed to modern bureaucracy. Later works on totalitarianism in Soviet-type societies lacked the theoretical astuteness to distinguish their debilitating patterns of organization from Weber's original arguments that "a higher degree of formal bureaucratization" would occur *if* an evolution toward socialism should take place in industrialized Europe.[26] In fact, the reverse happened intellectually: Weber's thinking on modern bureaucracy was invoked to explain the nature of Communist regimes and their means of political domination. As a result, actually existing socialisms seemed more coherent or viable organizationally than they really were. Weber's theory of modern bureaucracy became an apologia for Communist political domination rather than its critique.

Studies of totalitarianism in Soviet-type societies do not have any uniform, let alone rigorously Weberian, definition of bureaucracy. However, they coined phrases such as *totalitarian bureaucratization, rationalist totalitarianism,* and *bureaucratic absolutism* that imply that such societies were highly bureaucratized, even more so than Western capitalist societies.[27] In these studies, bureaucratic development refers to various aspects of organizational rationalization characteristic of modernity, namely, institutionalization of hierarchical control, functional differentiation, technical specialization, and concentration of the means of coercion in the state apparatus. This conception of bureaucratization is traced to Weber's understanding of history but not his works on social administration. To be sure, these studies note that this Weberian notion of bureaucratic evolution is not completely applicable to Soviet-type societies, because of their anomalous stress on ideology, political loyalty, and party control, as well as the fact of widespread coercion. Nonetheless, the notion of bureaucratic evolution is firmly assimilated into the totalitarian model of Communism to depict organizational development in such societies as part of a world-historical process of "bureaucratization." Hence Carl Friedrich and Zbigniew Brzezinski have noted that the expansion of the party and state in the Soviet Union

"may be compared to the dual development of bureaucracy in democratic capitalist countries, where we can observe a steady expansion of
bureaucracy in both the government and nongovernmental spheres of
group life, especially business and trade unions."[28] For the two scholars, the difference in bureaucratic development between socialist and
capitalist societies was not regarded as substantive, but rather they pos-
ited that bureaucratization was completely controlled by the political
power under Communist Party rule.

Weber's concept of modern bureaucracy is further reinterpreted by
such studies for explaining Communist political domination. In this regard, bureaucratization in Soviet-type societies does not only mean a
centralization of power, the expansion of the party and state, and the
proliferation of agencies directing political, economic, and social life; it
incorporates Weber's understanding of the impersonality, goal-driven
orientation, and technical efficiency of modern bureaucracy. The contention offered by such research is not that Soviet-type societies had
become fully rationalized in the Weberian sense, but that his concept
of modern bureaucracy helps explain the nature of Communist rule.
Besides deploying terror, coercion, and ideology, the regimes were said
to have built a powerful bureaucratic machine with the ability to penetrate society at every level.

As we have seen, behind the formal hierarchies, long-term careers,
distinct offices, regular compensation, and constant supervision established by the Chinese and Soviet regimes, little within the workplace
was comparable to the rational constitution of the Weberian bureaucracy. The above totalitarian image of Communism has thus conflated
the shell of modern bureaucracy with its content. Communist regimes
did not achieve powerful political domination because they adopted
modern bureaucratic measures, but because they deployed counter-bureaucratic measures. Precisely because they did so, their socialist systems suffered from pervasive staff conflict, discontent, ritualism, and
power struggle that undermined economic performance and political
support for the ruling regimes.

With the "bureaucratic" models of socialism that appeared in the
1960s and 1970s, the misidentification of organizations in Soviet-type
societies with modern bureaucratic administration reached a new
height. These models emerged as an intellectual response to the decline
of state terror, political campaigns, and the Stalin cult in the post-Stalin
Soviet Union and Eastern Europe, which demanded new understand-

ing of the nature of Communist political rule. The already *reinterpreted* Weberian notion of bureaucratization, which downplayed the legal-rational foundation of modern bureaucracy, was turned into a theoretical underpinning of research, and the organization of governments, factories, and other workplaces became a major object of study. A diversity of empirical findings emerged to be sure, but terms such as *monohierarchical bureaucracy, administered society,* and *organizational society* entered the mainstream research lexicon on Soviet-type societies.[29] They further imply that such societies must be understood in terms of bureaucratic domination.

In other words, such "bureaucratic" models of socialism focused and elaborated on one of the principal elements of the totalitarian theory of Communism. If Communist regimes were no longer totalitarian by the post-Stalin era, the logic goes, their rule had become more bureaucratic, that is, more rational, more orderly, and with more controls at the local level. This perception was used to explain the reproduction of Communist Party rule in large parts of the world despite the ruling regimes' intolerance for democratic political participation and individual freedoms. Sharing such an intellectual spirit, Samuel Huntington has noted that the most remarkable achievement of Marxist-Leninist regimes, compared to other forms of authoritarian rule, was not their use of ideological persuasion or coercion, but their superior effort in building organizations such as governments, party cells, and labor federations that harnessed otherwise volatile social forces. He has concluded that Communist regimes had been able to erect well-organized, broad-based systems of rule.[30] Taking the "bureaucratic" argument even further, one observer has suggested that bureaucratic development had been "completely carried through" in the post-Stalin Soviet Union and even paraphrased Weber to contend that the Soviet regime had "a seemingly 'unshatterable' bureaucracy."[31]

At the organizational level, these "bureaucratic" models of socialism misread the evolution of controls in post-Stalin Soviet-type societies as a higher stage of their bureaucratic development. They continue the overestimation of the organizational coherence of such societies. The thesis of institutional convergence between Soviet-type and Western societies is a corollary of this mistake. We have seen that there was only superficial organizational rationalization in Soviet-type societies after Stalin and after Mao. More significant, however, was the growth of official corruption, patron-client relations, and passive resistance in the workplace. Such behavior, which permeated state and society, was incompatible with any effective administration by modern bureaucracy. It betrayed that organizations in Soviet-type societies were poorly rationalized.

At the individual level, these "bureaucratic" models failed to distinguish political consent from conditional tolerance.[32] They thus overestimated popular support for Communist political rule. When Weber suggests that modern bureaucracy is a power instrument of the first order—"practically indestructible when fully developed"—he has in mind that the officeholders morally accept their subordination because they identify with the legal-rational foundation of the administration. By contrast, important reasons why large numbers of officials and ordinary staff members in Soviet-type societies followed orders daily, when they were not undercutting those orders in one way or another, are their fear of punishment, desire for personal gain, or lack of alternatives. The 1989–91 political turmoil in such societies demonstrated the dearth of popular commitment to Communist political rule. Far from being "seemingly unshatterable," socialist counter-bureaucracy was its own gravedigger.

There are two other influential intellectual perspectives on actually existing socialisms that overestimate their organizational coherence and sustainability, and therefore contributed to social science's failure to anticipate their decline. The shortcomings of these perspectives, however, did not stem from their misinterpretation of Weber as much as it did from ignoring him. In other words, they lack an in-depth analysis of the organization of the workplace within socialist systems.

Most notably associated with George Konrád's and Ivan Szelényi's research on Eastern Europe, the New Class theory of socialism became popular in the late 1970s. It contends that the historical transition to socialism produced conditions for class domination by intellectuals. The rise of socialism, as Alvin Gouldner averred, represented "the final removal" of the old-moneyed class that had long thwarted intellectuals' ascent to class power.[33] The New Class theory is based on a Marxian analysis of the institution of redistribution in Soviet-type societies. Unlike Trotsky, Djilas, and others, who had argued that party officials had become a class of exploiters, Konrád and Szelényi did not see a "class dichotomy" between such officials, who had power to expropriate and redistribute economic surplus, and workers and peasants, who produced such surplus. Rather, they maintained that the real fissure was between intellectuals and direct producers.

In these societies, Konrád and Szelényi noted, the state not only claimed "a monopoly of technical knowledge" to determine production, distribution, and consumption, but also employed large numbers of people placed outside officialdom to legitimize Communist political rule.[34] Socialist redistribution engendered "a whole model of civilization" with "three partners of equal importance": "The stratum of economists and technocrats, which actually carries out the work of central redistribution; the administrative and political bureaucracy, which guarantees the undisturbed functioning of the redistributive process, by police measures if necessary; and finally the ideological, scientific, and artistic intelligentsia, which produces, perpetuates, and disseminates the culture and ethos of rational distribution." The intelligentsia, especially during the post-Stalin years when state terror and concentration of power had been reduced, was "the class par excellence of a social order based on technical expertise."[35] As long as the professionally trained and college-educated cooperated with the regime, they would participate in the planning, execution, and legitimation of central redistribution and partake in privileged lifestyles unavailable to direct producers. In China, Konrád and Szelényi stated, this transition to class domination by intellectuals was delayed by Mao's distrust of intellectuals and higher learning.

There are three dubious assumptions in the New Class theory of socialism. First, most intellectuals apparently supported Communist political rule. Second, intellectuals seem to have worked well together, putting themselves "on the road to class power." Third, Soviet and Eastern European societies seem to have been evolving toward greater technical rationality as intellectuals assumed authority positions. This image of Soviet-type societies fits poorly with the description of rampant corruption, political disaffection, and quasi coercion in the works of Jowitt, Pakulski, and others. Even Konrád's and Szelényi's own depiction of workplace conditions casts doubts on the above assumptions.

An engineer from a small factory could advance to a position where he might supervise the investment of billions. An architect accustomed to designing private villas could go on to draw the plans for giant industrial complexes or whole sections of cities. An economist who once had to be content with a well-paid but not very influential consular post, or at best a university professorship, could now be the head of a planning office with a budget in the billions. A poet who once paid for the publication of his verses out of the proceeds of a clerical job could now live in a one-time chocolate manufacturer's villa, and see his poem published in editions of tens of thousands and recited on revolutionary holidays in hundreds of factory and village houses of culture. . . . Who wound up where was in many cases a matter of sheer luck, the work of a sometimes comically absurd combination of circumstance . . . [which] made it possible to suppose that they [that is, intellectuals] were not unwaveringly committed to the interests of the [political] elite.[36]

Put differently, Konrád and Szelényi realized that compared to that of the West, the socialist workplace was poorly rationalized. Political appointment and control persisted at the expense of technical and rational norms and engendered widespread dissatisfaction. But the two researchers failed to integrate these critical observations into their own Marxian account of Soviet-type societies. What their New Class thesis missed is precisely a Weberian analysis of administrative disorganization at the workplace level. As a result, they mistakenly saw "an evermore united intelligentsia" standing on "the threshold of class power" when these people, whose knowledge and skills were essential to any modern political rule, perpetually labored under an intense degree of disorganization.[37]

In the 1980s research on informal practices in Soviet-type societies focused on the institution of redistribution, too. Unlike the New Class proponents, its main concern was not the evolution of class domination but the economic behavior engendered by central planning. Studies show that insufficient supply of goods and services through central redistribution, and the latter's inefficiency and rigidity, fostered a "second economy" everywhere. Widespread transactions of goods and services took place outside the state plan based on private sale, gift exchange, moonlighting, pilfering, official corruption, bribery, clientelism, and other informal or illegal practices.[38] Such transactions redistributed what had been centrally allocated by the government. Zygmunt Bauman has noted that clientelism and informal connections formed "a functional equivalent of law and/or the impersonal marketplace" found in developed capitalist societies.[39] Studies of informal practices thus lent support to the "neotraditional" image of widespread official corruption and rule-evading behavior in Soviet-type societies. Unlike the "bureaucratic" or New Class models of socialism, they were more critical of the organization of such societies, and they highlighted the notion that official decisions, authority, and actions were often undermined by informal practices.[40]

As an intellectual perspective, research on informal practices recognizes that the formal structure of Soviet-type societies was poorly rationalized for meeting social needs. But it fails to address the fragility of such societies or the vulnerability of the ruling regimes. Although informal practices and the second economy were regarded as subversive of state power, they were also treated as corrective mechanisms for central planning. For example, it has been noted that such practices helped ease production problems such as late deliveries of raw materials, bottlenecks, and idle labor time, and that they assisted individuals in meeting unsatisfied needs. In other words, the spread of informalism reduced popular demands on the state for goods and services by making them available from other sources, as well as acting as a safety valve for Communist political rule by channelling social dissatisfaction with work, income, and opportunities into more or less individualized solutions.[41]

In focusing on how people and enterprises coped with central planning, studies of informal practices are not sufficiently attentive to the depth of social dissatisfaction in Soviet-type societies and its relations to workplace organization. Most people who took part in the second economy or engaged in informal practices did so because formal channels, tightly controlled by the state, failed to address their needs. Poor official planning, widespread corruption, and technical inefficiency harmed the institution of redistribution. To get what they wanted, enterprises and individuals had no alternative but to resort to clientelist ties or even illegal actions. Some were forced to submit to what Bauman called "whimsical agents of social power" to get the goods, services, or positions they wanted.[42]

In other words, studies of informal practices tend to concentrate on one side of their double-edged politics vis-à-vis the state. As much as "black-market" activities and informal practices helped the Communist regimes maintain social stability despite their failure to provide sufficient goods and services, these actions were accompanied, to a large extent, by feelings of dissatisfaction and resentment that the state had not been able to deliver goods and services satisfactorily. Depending on their cost, the taking of such actions itself may have led to further dissatisfaction with the state. Informal practices were not a cure for, but a consequence of, the lack of rational bureaucratic arrangements in Soviet-type societies. Their proliferation suggested that there was widespread dissatisfaction with the political authority.

There has been no shortage of studies of Soviet-type societies that refer to Weber's ideas. What is lacking is research that takes them seri-

ously. In particular, his concept of modern bureaucracy is more struc-
turally and historically specific than has generally been assumed. Existing studies have not only misinterpreted organizations in Soviet-type
societies as a variant of modern bureaucracy; they have ignored a care-
ful analysis of workplace administration and its social and political
implications. None of above-mentioned intellectual perspectives that
dominated research on Soviet-type societies from the 1950s to the 1980s
included a sufficient picture of the extent of workplace disorganization.
Without such a picture, they overestimated the strength and legitimacy
of Communist political rule.

In this book, I have returned to Weber to demonstrate that his concept of modern bureaucracy is profoundly important for studying Soviet-type societies. I have offered an account of administrative disorganization in such societies, starting with political ideology, through
workplace constitution, and to the erosion of support for Communist
Party rule. In the end, the failure of Soviet-type societies was a failure of
the ruling regimes to establish legitimate authority to protect their own
rule. This book has argued that the reproduction of counter-bureaucratic features in the workplace was central to this failure and therefore
to the decline of such societies.

For most of the twentieth century, Weber was seemingly proved
wrong by Lenin and his vision that modern societies and modern bureaucracy need not be coextensive. The antibureaucratic model of the
Paris Commune that Lenin described in *The State and Revolution* was
merely a theoretical alternative to modern bureaucratic administration.
Built on counter-bureaucratic administration, Soviet-type societies represented, materially, another way of organizing modern societies. The
fin de siècle decline of actually existing socialisms, however, has vin-
dicated Weber. Though actually existing socialisms were modern, they
were also unsustainable. The decline of Soviet-type societies raises a
critical question for the theory of socialism: what should be the relation between socialism and modern bureaucracy? This is obviously a
complicated question, but the failure of Soviet-type societies makes addressing it more necessary than ever.

WHITHER SOCIALISM AND MODERN BUREAUCRACY

The decline of Soviet-type societies since the late 1980s has strengthened capitalism worldwide and turned socialism into a fringe political
idea. Privatization, deregulation, "free" trade, and "open" markets are

nowadays dominant economic trends in Europe, Asia, and the Americas. The analytical lesson to be learned from the failure of Soviet-type societies, however, is not that humankind has reached "the end of history" as Francis Fukuyama has claimed,[43] but that the institution of modern bureaucracy must be theorized back into socialism for the latter to become a credible alternative to capitalism again.

To recapitulate the theoretical argument of this book, the central problem of actually existing socialisms was that Marxist-Leninist regimes rejected rational administration. Leninism and Maoism are anti-Weberian ideologies that engendered technically inefficient, socially divisive, and politically unsustainable socialist systems. They are deeply flawed as both theory and practice of government, modernization, and socialism. This is not to say that Soviet-type societies would have survived for sure had the regimes deployed modern bureaucracy instead of counter-bureaucracy. Rational administration can encompass different styles and substances of governance and can create political difficulties for ruling regimes, too. It would be futile to speculate whether Soviet-type societies would have persisted had they embraced modern bureaucracy. However, it is clear that the lack of such administration in these societies contributed to their decline.

To put this in a different way, the failure of Soviet-type societies hardly proves that "big government," or too much state intervention in social life, is doomed to failure. The *proper* analytical conclusion is that no modern state can do without modern bureaucracy. This distinction has important theoretical implications. It undermines the argument, in economics in particular, that it was excessive bureaucratic or state coordination of production and reproduction that led to the failure of Soviet-type societies.[44] This argument does not distinguish official administration in such societies from rational administration. It thus disguises the central problem of their governance, that is, the fact that decisions and work at every level were conducted within debilitating counter-bureaucratic environments. Without sufficiently investigating how workplace disorganization led to systemic tensions, it implies, wrongly, that central planning per se undermined Soviet-type societies.

The failure of Soviet-type societies is therefore not an analytical justification for denying the state a strong role in social life. But the Right in the United States and Europe, building on Ronald Reagan's and Margaret Thatcher's legacies, has exploited the failure of actually existing socialisms to further restrain government intervention in the market as well as to promote privatization of previously state-controlled social services and investments. In spite of well-documented successes in the building of public education, telecommunication, transportation, health care, housing, and pensions systems in a relatively short stretch of the twentieth century, the Right argues that state intervention is "inherently inefficient and unnecessarily intrusive in people's lives."[45] Francis Fukuyama's now-famous thesis of "the end of history," which indicates that capitalist democracy may constitute the "final form of human government," provides ideological support for extending the commodification of human labor to every corner of the world. Using the demise of Soviet-type societies, Fukuyama has represented the particular interest of the bourgeoisie as *truly* the interest of all—that is, the entire future of humanity.

If there is an analytical lesson to be learned from the demise of Soviet-type societies, it is not about capitalism's future as much as it is about the socialist alternative itself. Specifically, it is about the role of modern bureaucracy during the transition to socialism.[46] The place of such administration is quite unclear in Marx's and Engels's famous but terse exposition of the transition to socialism. With Lenin and Mao, modern bureaucracy became an object of opprobrium. But socialism, like capitalism, is a system of division of labor. Its long-term feasibility has to be based on members of the workforce consenting to their assignments and subordination within the workplace, which is precisely what did not occur in Soviet-type societies. But if Weber is correct in arguing that modern bureaucracy is the best means of fostering rational subordination in modern societies—and, indeed, the only means in the long run—it would be difficult to imagine a credible transition to socialism that does not require the service of modern bureaucracy, whether the transition takes place by evolution or by revolution. The mere need for the society to maintain an efficient system of production and reproduction, and therefore a cooperative workforce, suggests that modern bureaucracy would be indispensable. Otherwise, an alternative form of administration, different from counter-bureaucracy and capable of accomplishing the technical and social functions of modern bureaucracy, would have to be invented for the transition to socialism.

However, any explication of the role of modern bureaucracy during the transition to socialism must also address Weber's pessimism about the liberating potential of socialism based on rational administration. In his 1922 musing on a possible evolution toward socialism in Western

Europe, Weber did not doubt whether socialism could be achievable in these developed societies. The evolution seemed entirely possible because it would be determined by political struggle. What worried him was that the socialist societies that emerged might inflict more pain and suffering on the working class than the displaced capitalist systems had done. As the state became the sovereign organizer of the workplace, the checks and balances of power that had existed between government and the bourgeoisie under capitalism would diminish. Meanwhile, the complexity of operating the process of production and reproduction would tend to concentrate power in a corps of officials. What would then deter the state from prolonging the work week, reducing wages and benefits, limiting job choices, and outlawing strikes altogether after the bourgeoisie has disappeared? As Weber points out, socialism may bring about "the dictatorship of the official" rather than of the working class.[47]

To be sure, the kinds of workplace abuse that Weber implies may occur under rational socialism are rather different from those that happened under actually existing socialisms. Based on counter-bureaucratic administrations that disregarded technical, impersonal, and rational norms, actually existing socialisms, as we have seen, engendered not only episodic upheavals, struggles, and suppression in the workplace, but also irregularly lax punishment and unpredictable benefits and career opportunities for individuals. Fear and doubt, as well as ritualism and clientelism, were thus common responses to life under counter-bureaucratic administration. By contrast, rational socialism would be based on the use of technical, impersonal, and rational norms. If it turns out to be less violent, murderous, and cataclysmic than actually existing socialisms, it may also eliminate the gentle interludes, the episodes of unexpected leniency and rapid upward mobility and, more generally, the social space and informal practices with which individuals negotiated their welfare under actually existing socialisms. Without an effective check on state power, rational socialism may invite, truly for the first time in history, a "complete and nightmarish bureaucratic domination."[48] Theories of possible future socialisms thus need to address not only the role of modern bureaucracy but also its political implications during and after the transition to socialism. They must not disregard Weber as previous theories and practice of socialism did.

Reference Matter

Appendix: Backgrounds of Informants

Five pieces of data are listed below for each informant: (1) occupation before becoming a schoolteacher under CCP rule; (2) gender; (3) highest faculty position attained before the Cultural Revolution; (4) age in 1966 when the Cultural Revolution began; and (5) membership in the Chinese Communist Party (CCP).

1. CCP government official, female, politics teacher, 36
2. Primary school teacher, female, politics teacher, 31 (CCP member)
3. KMT-era schoolteacher, female, head of instruction, 41 (CCP member)
4. CCP government official, male, head of instruction, 40
5. KMT-era schoolteacher, female, mathematics teacher, 38
6. KMT-era schoolteacher, male, literature teacher, 36 (CCP member)
7. Factory worker, female, politics teacher, 31 (CCP member)
8. Bank employee, male, physics teacher, 46
9. Unemployed intellectual, male, biology teacher, 37
10. KMT-era schoolteacher, male, head of instruction, 40 (CCP member)
11. KMT-era schoolteacher, female, mathematics teacher, 47
12. CCP-era college graduate, male, assistant head of instruction, 30
13. Factory worker/college graduate, male, head of politics teachers, 31 (CCP member)
14. Underground CCP agent, male, school principal-cum-party-secretary, 48 (CCP member)
15. Demobilized soldier, male, head of literature teachers, 35
16. CCP government official, male, assistant head of instruction, 36 (CCP member)
17. Homemaker, female, head of Russian-language teachers, 43 (CCP member)
18. Part-time schoolteacher, male, head of mathematics teachers, 39
19. Laborer/college graduate, male, assistant head of literature teachers, 37 (CCP member)

20. KMT-era head of instruction, female, head of general affairs, 62
21. Unemployed intellectual, male, geography teacher, 43
22. Bank employee, male, biology teacher, 37
23. Homemaker, female, mathematics teacher, 46
24. High school student, male, acting school party secretary, 32 (CCP member)
25. Primary school teacher, female, head of politics teachers, 32
26. Demobilized soldier, male, head of Russian-language teachers, 41
27. KMT-era schoolteacher, female, head of mathematics teacher, 50
28. KMT-era schoolteacher, male, head of literature teacher, 51
29. Office assistant/college graduate, female, literature teacher, 38
30. CCP-era college graduate, male, assistant head of instruction, 28
31. Underground CCP agent, female, school principal-cum-party-secretary, 42 (CCP member)
32. Demobilized soldier, male, literature teacher, 35
33. CCP-era college graduate, male, biology teacher, 29
34. KMT-era schoolteacher, male, head of instruction, 43
35. Underground CCP agent, male, deputy principal-cum-party-secretary, 41 (CCP member)
36. CCP-era college graduate, male, head of physical education teachers, 24
37. CCP-era college graduate, male, head of physical education teachers, 26
38. Homemaker, female, head of Russian-language teachers, 40
39. CCP government official, female, assistant head of politics teachers, 35
40. Unemployed intellectual, female, head of English teachers, 50
41. Insurance company employee, female, mathematics teacher, 36
42. Underground CCP agent, female, deputy principal-cum-party-secretary, 46 (CCP member)
43. CCP government official, female, school principal-cum-party-secretary, 40 (CCP member)
44. CCP-era college graduate, male, assistant head of literature teachers, 24
45. Factory worker, male, politics teacher, 33 (CCP member)
46. Homemaker, female, biology teacher, 46
47. CCP-era college graduate, male, assistant head of literature teachers, 29 (CCP member)
48. CCP government official, female, history teacher, 38
49. CCP government official, female, assistant head of politics teachers, 37
50. Primary school teacher, female, literature teacher, 31
51. Unemployed intellectual, male, physics teacher, 44
52. KMT-era head of general affairs, male, head of general affairs, 52
53. Part-time schoolteacher, female, history teacher, 38
54. Bank employee, male, mathematics teacher, 46
55. Demobilized soldier, male, head of physical education teachers, 41
56. Teachers school instructor, female, literature teacher, 30
57. CCP-era college graduate, male, assistant head of politics teachers, 31
58. KMT-era schoolteacher, male, assistant head of instruction, 41 (CCP member)

59. CCP government officials, female, assistant head of geography teachers, 37
60. Homemaker, female, biology teacher, 42
61. Factory worker, male, deputy principal-cum-party-secretary, 38 (CCP member)
62. CCP-era college graduate, female, head of literature teachers, 31

Summary

1. Males, 34
   Females, 28

2. Communist Party members, 19
   Nonparty members, 43

3. KMT-era faculty, 11   Demobilized soldiers, 4
   CCP-era college graduates, 9   Bank/insurance employees, 4
   CCP government officials, 8   Unemployed intellectuals, 4
   Homemakers, 5   Underground CCP agents, 4
   Workers/laborers, 5   Others, 8

Notes

1. Lipset and Bence (1994) summarize the intellectual reactions to the demise of Soviet-type societies.
2. Kirby (2006).
3. Hough (1977, 49).
4. Pakulski (1986a).
5. For example, Whyte (1973), Jowitt (1992), and Lü (2000).
6. McNeal (1959) and Lewin (1969).
7. Trotsky ([1937] 1967, 249) and Djilas (1957, 38).
8. Whyte (1973; 1989).
9. Hodges (1981, xii) and Lefort (1986, 92–93).
10. Weber (1978a, 225).
11. Moore (1954, 188–90).
12. Meyer (1970, 48).
13. For example, Friedrich and Brzezinski (1965) and Aron (1965, 235). A summary of these concepts appears in Hough (1977, 50–51).
14. Harding (1981, 329–30).
15. For example, Meisner (1986, 262) states that bureaucratization "marked and molded virtually all facets of Chinese economic, social, and political life in the early 1960s." Schurmann (1968), Kau (1971), and Pepper (1996) share similar views.
16. Pakulski (1986a, 6).
17. Both past and recent research on socialist China demonstrates that the mentioned features were regularly found in organizations. For example, Walder (1986), Yang (1994), Zhou et al. (1996), Walder et al. (2000), Bian et al. (2001), and Zhou (2001).
18. Pakulski (1986a, 11).
19. This view is expressed most clearly by Kornai (1992), Pei (1994), and Verdery (1996).
20. Kornai (1992, 40, 98).

21. Weber (1978a, 1041).

22. Parkin (1982, 81).

23. Antonio (1979, 896).

24. Antonio (1979, 896) and (1984, 157).

25. Weber (1978a, 223, 987–88).

26. A long list of works exists in these regards; for example, Gouldner (1954), Barnard (1962), Burawoy (1979), Parkin (1982), Hochschild (1983), and Perrow (1993).

27. A long list of works can also be found; for example, Johnson (1982), Callaghy (1984), Gold (1986), Schneider (1991), Evans (1995), and Evans and Rauch (1999).

28. Weber (1978a, 225, 975).

29. Antonio (1979, 897).

30. Antonio (1986, 20–23).

31. Laird (1970, 122) and Whyte (1989, 252).

32. To be sure, Weber thought highly of Marx's works as scholarship because they provide concrete models for understanding history and society that further research and analysis. See Mommsen (1984, 234–61) for an excellent explanation of Weber's work in relation to Marx's.

33. Weber (1978b, 257, 262) (my emphasis).

34. Weber (1978a, 225).

35. Weber (1978b, 255).

36. Weber (1978a, 1402).

37. Mommsen (1985, 241).

38. Weber (1978a, 284).

39. Mommsen (1984, 274–80).

40. Pakulski (1986a, 13).

41. Weiss (1985, 117).

42. Wright (1974, 83–85).

43. Lenin ([1918] 1965, vol. 25, 480–81).

44. Wright (1974) and Polan (1984) are excellent comparisons of Lenin's and Weber's views on modern bureaucracy.

45. Lenin ([1918] 1965, vol. 25, 426–27).

46. Lewin (1969) and Anderson (1995).

47. Lenin ([1919] 1965, vol. 27, 345, 349; vol. 28, 215, 380–81; vol. 29, 69–70).

48. Lenin ([1965] 1965, vol. 29, 72).

49. Lenin ([1919] 1965, vol. 30, 248).

50. Lenin ([1918–19] 1965, vol. 25, pp. 426–27, vol. 27, 246; vol. 29, 114, 154).

51. Mao ([1950] 1977, vol. 5, 35).

52. Quoted in Schram (1989, 114).

53. Mao ([1950] 1977, vol. 5, 357).

54. Schram (1989, 125–26, 162–63).

55. Ibid., pp. 163–69.

56. Weber (1978a, 956–58).

57. For example, Walder (1986, 250–51), Jowitt (1992, 13–17, 62–87), and Lü (2000, 249–52).

58. Bendix (1960, 334–41).
59. Weber (1978a, 987).
60. Weber (1978b, 255).
61. Kahlberg (1985).
62. For example, Erlich (1960), Cohen (1977), Polan (1984), and MacFarquhar (1974–97).

CHAPTER 2

1. Shanghai Municipal Archives (SMA) B105-2-393 (1961, 1–2) (SMA material refers to documents catalogued at the archives. Catalogue B105 consists of documents compiled by the post-1949 Shanghai Education Bureau). See *Shanghaishi dang'anguan zhinan* (1999) for further information on the catalogues from which I have drawn material for this book.
2. Kirby (2000, 152).
3. Xu (2001, 16).
4. Kirby (1984, 95–99), Pepper (1996, 110), and Xu (2001, 272).
5. Yeh (1996, 118–46), Xu (2001), and Ye (2001, 67–72).
6. Strauss (1998).
7. Ibid., p. 185.
8. Xu (2001, 98–100).
9. *Shanghaishi jiaoyuju yewu baogao* (1930, 18), and SMA Q1-18-250 (1947, 36). SMA catalogue Q1 consists of documents produced under the pre-1949 Shanghai Municipal Government.
10. *Jing'an difangzhi* (1996, 895).
11. *Jinshan xianzhi* (1985, 769).
12. *Jing'an difangzhi* (1996, 100, 895).
13. SMA Q235-2-597 (1948, 176–82) and Q235-2-621 (1948, 77–81). SMA catalogue Q235 contains documents from the pre-1949 Shanghai Education Bureau.
14. Although primary education was more common in Shanghai, 58 and 41 percent of the children living outside the French and the International Concession did not receive any form of schooling in 1929 and 1935 respectively; Henriot (1993, 189).
15. *Shanghaishi zhongdeng jiaoyu gaikuang* (1948) provides an overview of individual campuses. Information on secondary schools is also available in Xu Zhong'an (1991), Yao Zhuangxing and Yuan Cai (1992), Li Huaxing (1997), Wang Bingzhao (1997), *Jing'an wenshi* (1991–95), and Henriot (1993, 185–201).
16. Li Huaxing (1997, 518).
17. Gold (1986), Evans (1995), and Evans and Rauch (1999).
18. In the fall of 1936, Shanghai had 120 private regular and vocational secondary schools, 34,500 students, and 3,470 faculty and staff. In 1945 there were 133 schools, 53,200 students, and 3,580 faculty and staff; SMA Q1-18-250 (1947, 19).
19. The Japanese occupation triggered complicated movements of schools, teachers, and students into and out of the city. If the postwar reconstruction

of the schools hinted at the extent of their damage, it was their physical rather than personnel aspect that was devastated. After the KMT regained control, it stressed the rebuilding and reequipping of schoolhouses but mentioned little about faculty quality; *Shanghaishi zhongdeng jiaoyu gaikua*ng (1948).

20. Li Huaxing (1997, 530, fn. 1) and Xing Ping (1996, 320).

21. Li Huaxing (1997, 517–24).

22. Ibid., p. 525.

23. Chen Xuexun (1994, 224–36, 309).

24. Ibid., p. 343.

25. Led by Chen Guofu and Chen Lifu, the C.C. Clique, a dominant faction within the KMT, exerted powerful influence over party organizations and the state administration, including cultural and educational agencies. It controlled some newspapers and the secret police agency, the Central Bureau of Statistics and Investigation (*Zhongtong*). With a staunchly anti-Communist orientation, it "favored the revival of traditional moral values and ideals"; Leung (1992, 27–28) and Xiang Bolong (1996).

26. Deng Yuchang (1989, 151).

27. At a school in the Subei area outside of Shanghai, the Japanese teacher earned 264 yuan per month while the Chinese principal earned 100 yuan; Mao Lirui and Shen Guanqun (1987, 420–30). Unclear, however, were the roles Chinese and Japanese faculty members played in schools during the Japanese occupation. Through a collaborationist regime, the Japanese apparently continued many student organizations, such as the Boy Scouts, and modified them to fit the new ruling ideas; Wasserstrom (1991, 167) and Chen Xuexun (1994, 341–48).

28. Fang Ming and Chen Yuxin (1984, 63).

29. In the late 1930s and early 1940s, one hundred or so people belonged to the Shanghai teacher underground. Fewer than twenty were secondary school teachers; Liu Feng (1984, 54) and Ma Feihai (1997, 4).

30. In the early 1950s, the CCP defined unemployed intellectuals as jobless individuals who had completed junior high school or who had two years of such education plus "considerable" supplementary learning or work experience; U (2003, 109).

31. U (2004, 50–52).

32. Howe (1971, 97) and Lü (2000, 59–62).

33. SMA B127-1-78 (1956). SMA catalogue B127 consists of documents compiled by the post-1949 Shanghai Labor Bureau.

34. Li Dehong (197, 76).

35. After the revolution, the CCP widely deployed *tanbai* in the workplace as a tool of surveillance. During *tanbai*, individuals were required to disclose their social background, work history, political association, and personal beliefs to the authorities. Normally instructions were given. The authorities then checked the thoroughness of the confessions and pressured the individuals to fill in gaps or dig deeper to produce officially acceptable confessions, the definition of which varied locally as well as according to the individual under question and the political climate.

36. Taken during mid-1952, when the political climate was less oppressive

than in later periods, data such as these from *tanbai* probably understated the unemployed intellectuals' ties to the KMT regime and their other characteristics that the CCP considered undesirable. At this stage after the revolution, job seekers had a strong incentive to hide whatever might lessen their chance of a job assignment by the state; SMA B105-1-614 (1952–53).

37. U (2003, 104–8).

38. SMA B105-1-614 (1952–53, 5–9).

39. SMA B105-1-1191 (1954–55).

40. SMA B130-1-1 (1951–52, 22). SMA catalogue B130 is composed of documents related to the post-1949 Shanghai Committee for Handling Unemployed Intellectuals.

41. The label "key problem" applied to unemployed intellectuals indicated not especially heinous background but the need for special investigation. Many of the people with so-called key problems reported chronic unemployment, making their work histories hard to trace; others were suspected of falsely confessing to minor wrongdoing when they joined the teacher-training class to conceal the extent of their involvement in the KMT regime or other activities. Conversely, those unemployed intellectuals viewed as problematic by the SEB but not so labeled were not necessarily less politically objectionable than those with "key problems." Indeed, as the SEB discovered, they included former KMT and party officials, former "severely law-breaking" capitalists and "speculative merchants," and expellees from government, military, or industry. Some had long confessed their backgrounds to the authorities; others disclosed such information promptly when *Sufan* began. As long as the SEB found the unemployed intellectuals credible and free of outstanding charges, it would spare them further scrutiny and would regard their cases as "previously settled"; SMA B105-5-1705 (1956, 22–23).

42. SMA B105-5-1803 (1956, 25).

43. SMA B105-5-1705 (1956, 25) (my emphasis).

44. SMA B105-5-1538 (1955–58).

45. Ibid.

46. SMA B105-2-34 (1957).

47. During the Mao era, cadres included the political elite, most of the staff in the party and government, and state employees who were not manual laborers. All school principals, administrators, and teachers were cadres after the nationalization of education; Lee (1991, 4).

48. Harding (1981, 77).

49. SMA B105-1-882 (1954, 12–14).

50. Ibid., p. 10.

51. Ibid., p. 13.

52. SMA B105-5-1705 (1956, 1).

53. SMA B105-5-1358 (1955–58, 147).

54. Ibid., p. 148.

55. SMA B3-2-64 (1956, 45–46) and B105-5-1707 (1956, 16–17). SMA catalogue B3 consists of materials from the post-1949 Shanghai Office for Culture and Education.

56. SMA B3-2-64 (1956, 48).

57. Ibid., p. 53.
58. SMA B105-5-1707 (1956, 3–24).
59. SMA B105-2-946 (1960, 42).
60. SMA B105-2-92 (1959, 6).
61. Ibid., p. 24.
62. SMA B105-2-585 (1959).
63. Informant no. 16.
64. Informant no. 1.
65. Lü Xingwei (1994, 296).
66. Informant no. 7.
67. Ibid.
68. Informant no. 19.
69. Informant no. 14.
70. Taylor (1973, 15, 22).
71. SMA B105-1-1200 (1955, 19).
72. SMA B105-5-1704 (1956, 2).
73. Ibid., p. 16.
74. Ibid., p. 3.
75. SMA B105-2-271 (1957, 45).
76. SMA B105-2-37 (1956–57, 44).
77. SMA B105-2-406 (1961, 12).
78. SMA B105-2-393 (1961, 14).
79. SMA B105-1-1164 (1961).
80. SMA B105-2-654 (1963).
81. Informant no. 17.
82. SMA B105-1-1685 (1957, 5).
83. SMA B105-1-1685 (1957).
84. Ibid.
85. In 1947 28 percent of the faculty and staff in regular secondary schools were women; *Zhonghua minguo sanshiwu nian Shanghaishi jiaoyu tongji* (1947, 96–103). The proportion of women increased after the revolution. In 1964, 38 percent of the faculty and staff in regular schools and schools run by state-owned enterprises and collectives in the urban area were women; SMA B105-2-797 (1964–65, 16).
86. Informant no. 6.
87. Informant no. 31.
88. Informant no. 10.
89. Informant no. 9.
90. Informant no. 7.
91. Informant no. 19.

CHAPTER 3

1. Lenin ([1918] 1965, vol. 27, 246).
2. Ibid., p. 275.
3. In the 1950s the CCP leadership ruled that a party branch (*dangzhibu*), the

smallest form of a party cell, should be set up whenever an organization or its division had three or more regular party members on the staff.

4. SMA B105-1-514 (1952, 30).

5. SMA B105-1-1504 (1956, 1) and A94-1-633 (1956, 32). SMA catalogue A94 is composed of documents compiled by the post-1949 Department of Organization of the Shanghai Communist Party Committee.

6. SMA A23-2-582 (1960, 94). SMA catalogue A23 is composed of documents compiled by the Department of Education and Health of the Shanghai Communist Party Committee.

7. Shen Yiling and Yao Jinghua (1996, 22).

8. Where the original principals had fled or resigned, appointees who were seasoned educators became school principals. Where the principals remained on campus, the appointees became deputy principals. Those who had teaching experience but were not veteran teachers were appointed as heads of instruction.

9. Duan Lipei (1992, 62–73).

10. Yao Jing (1992, 185–87).

11. It is unclear how many CCP officials were assigned to the schools in the early 1950s. Data show that 96 arrived in the fall of 1952 and 33 arrived in June 1953. Based on the figures on school party membership, it is likely that 150 to 200 of such officials joined the profession between 1952 and 1954; SMA B105-1-462 (1952–53).

12. SMA B105-1-462 (1952–53).

13. SMA B105-5-752 (1953).

14. SMA B105-1-462 (1952–53, 7–8).

15. Ibid., pp. 22–26.

16. The estimate is based on a report that 213 soldiers who were party members were reassigned to the primary and secondary schools in Shanghai between 1949 and 1959; SMA B105-2-641 (1959, 9).

17. Lee (1991, 51) and Lü (2000, 77).

18. SMA A23-2-582 (1960, 37).

19. SMA B105-2-92 (1959, 6).

20. Pepper (1996, 175).

21. SMA A23-2-1123 (1965, 5).

22. Shirk (1982).

23. In the autumn of 1960, the SEB planned to deliver 861 four-year college graduates and 900 two-year college graduates to the schools. In the following year, the numbers were 936 and 1,207 respectively; SMA B105-2-257 (1960, 17–18) and SMA B105-2-407 (1961, 15–16).

24. SMA B105-1-268 (1951, 1).

25. Chen (1960) and Xiang Bolong (1996).

26. SMA B105-5-665 (1952, 27).

27. SMA B105-1-662 (1952) and B105-1-664 (1952).

28. Xiang Bolong (1996, 46).

29. SMA B105-1-684 (1952–53) and B105-1-694 (1953).

30. SMA A22-1-275 (1956, 55). SMA catalogue A22 is composed of docu-

244 Notes to Pages 72–84

ments compiled by the Department of Propaganda of the Shanghai Communist Party Committee.

31. SMA A23-2-429 (1959, 1).
32. SMA B105-2-781(1964, 7).
33. Walder (1986, 88–92, 147–53).
34. Lü (1994, 32).
35. SMA B105-1-5 (1949, 95).
36. Informant no. 10.
37. Xiang Bolong (1996, 46).
38. Informant no. 6.
39. SMA A23-2-582 (1960, 37).
40. Informant no. 17.
41. SMA A94-1-1041 (1961, 1–6).
42. In 1961 more than one-third of the college students in Shanghai were from worker or peasant families. Teachers colleges contained fewer such students, but their proportion was still significant compared to the proportion of such students in teachers colleges before 1949; SMA B243-1-214 (1961, 10).
43. SMA B105-1-8 (1949, 133).
44. SMA B105-1-5 (1949, 13).
45. SMA B105-1-8 (1949, 124–28) and B105-5-306 (1950–52).
46. Informant no. 6.
47. SMA B105-5-1352 (1955, 12–14).
48. Ibid., p. 12.
49. SMA B105-1-906 (1954, 4).
50. Ibid.
51. Ibid.
52. Bourdieu (1977, 189–91).
53. SMA B105-1-890 (1954, 39).
54. Bourdieu (1977, 190).
55. To a large extent, CCP cadres saw rightist errors as political wrongdoing, because some were stripped of their party membership and punished by labor reeducation during the Anti-Rightist Campaign. Leftist mistakes, however, were seen as issues in leadership style that carried lighter sanctions; Zweig (1989, 38).
56. SMA A23-2-234 (1957, 1–5, 42).
57. SMA A23-2-752 (1961, 3–25).
58. SMA A23-2-765 (1961, 66).
59. SMA A23-2-1703 (1960–62, 31–38).
60. The name of the school has been changed for reasons of confidentiality.
61. Informant no. 24.
62. Informant no. 6.
63. Informant no. 35.
64. SMA B105-1-890 (1954, 101–2).
65. SMA A23-2-1703 (1960–62, 32).
66. SMA B105-1-673 (1953, 55).
67. SMA B105-1-664 (1952).

68. SMA B105-5-1969 (1954–55, 54).
69. Ibid., p. 53.
70. SMA B105-5-1354 (1955, 34–35).
71. Ibid., p. 49.
72. Whyte (1974) is the best statement on the deployment of the small group in the workplace as a tool of political indoctrination and surveillance.
73. SMA B105-5-1354 (1955, 49–50).
74. SMA A94-1-771 (1957, 17).
75. SMA B105-2-392 (1961, 5).
76. SMA B105-2-1417 (1963, 3–4).
77. In 1962 a total of 235 out of 468 heads of instruction in the urban schools were party members; SMA B105-2-527 (1962, 7, 56).
78. Sponsored by the party, these meetings encouraged intellectuals in education and other sectors to critique the party's work in a manner of "mild wind and gentle breeze." They symbolized official efforts to improve the productivity of intellectuals because the Anti-Rightist Campaign and the Great Leap Forward had weakened their social status and increased their passive resistance. Local governments organized the meetings and promised that the party would not after anyone for speaking their mind. However, aired in front of party officials in the wake of the Anti-Rightist Campaign, the views of intellectuals could not but involve self-censorship.
79. SMA A23-2-568 (1960, 67).
80. SMA A23-2-737 (1961, 41).
81. SMA B105-5-1969 (1954–55).
82. SMA B105-2-1270 (1962, 23).
83. SMA A23-2-568 (1960, 71.)
84. Whyte (1989, 235–37).
85. Mao ([1960] 2002).
86. Schram (1989, 163).

CHAPTER 4

1. SMA B105-5-1415 (1955–56, 35).
2. Lenin ([1919] 1965, vol. 29, 114).
3. Vogel (1969, 41–90), Lieberthal (1980, 29–52, 78–96), Pepper (1996, 192–205), and U (2004).
4. Zhuan Qidong et al. (1986, 46).
5. In a small number of cases, the authorities cut salaries they considered unreasonably high. In other cases, they raised salaries to improve workers' livelihoods; Zhuan Qidong et al. (1986, 47).
6. Zhuan Qidong et al. (1986, 53–54).
7. SMA B3-2-66 (1956, 56).
8. SMA B105-5-738 (1953, 7).
9. SMA B105-5-1089 (1954, 14).
10. SMA B105-5-1537 (1955).
11. SMA B105-1-1296 (1955, 8).

12. SMA B3-2-66 (1956, 58).

13. SMA B127-1-941 (1954, 1).

14. SMA B105-5-1182 (1954, 34–35).

15. Ibid.

16. SMA B105-5-52 (1949–50, 9) and B105-5-1693 (1956).

17. SMA B105-5-78 (1949, 5) and B105-5-1693 (1956).

18. Informant no. 14.

19. Ibid.

20. SMA B105-5-1416 (1955).

21. Ibid.

22. SMA B3-2-66 (1956, 5–7).

23. SMA A11-2-15 (1958, 24). SMA catalogue A11 contains documents compiled by the post-1949 Committee of Wages and Salaries of the Shanghai Municipal Government and Shanghai Communist Party Committee.

24. SMA B105-5-1415 (1955–56, 35–36).

25. SMA B105-5-1812 (1956–57, 7–8).

26. Ibid., p. 7

27. SMA B105-5-1415 (1955–56, 35–36).

28. SMA B105-5-1816 (1957, 83).

29. Zhuan Qidong et al. (1986, 82–105).

30. SMA B105-2-660 (1963, 41).

31. SMA B3-2-221 (1963, 28).

32. SMA A23-2-911 (1963–64, 33) and B105-2-660 (1963, 42–44).

33. White (1981, 57).

34. SMA B105-2-1919 (1965, 3).

35. SMA B105-2-669 (1964, 10).

36. White (1981, 47–59) and Walder (1986, 28–68) discuss financial assistance in schools and factories.

37. Only by the 1970s did the housing stock in Shanghai slightly exceed the 1952 level; Howe (1968) and (1978, 173), and Walder (1986, 226).

38. Informant no. 13.

39. SMA catalogue number cannot be disclosed, for reasons of confidentiality.

40. Informant no. 12.

41. SMA B105-5-1816 (1957, 82).

42. SMA B105-5-1415 (1955–56, 35).

43. Ibid., p. 36.

44. Ibid., p. 35.

45. SMA B105-5-1816 (1957, 86).

46. SMA B105-5-1813 (1956, 41).

47. Ibid., p. 42.

48. SMA B105-5-1816 (1957, 87).

49. Ibid., p. 85.

50. Ibid., p. 88.

51. SMA A23-2-234 (1957, 3).

52. SMA B3-2-66 (1956, 64).

53. SMA B105-2-1133 (1961, 4).

54. SMA B105-5-1807 (1956, 95–96).
55. Ibid.
56. SMA B3-2-66 (1956, 66).
57. Zhuan Qidong et al.. (1986, 101) (my emphasis).
58. SMA B105-2-1418 (1963, 3).
59. SMA A23-2-911 (1963–64, 40).
60. SMA B105-2-1418 (1963, 1).
61. White (1989, 113).
62. Ibid.

CHAPTER 5

1. SMA B105-5-733 (1953, 1–25).
2. Chen (1960), Lifton (1963), Wu (1992), and Seymour and Anderson (1998).
3. Greenblatt (1977, 82).
4. Cohen (1968, 297–98).
5. Ibid., pp. 9–14.
6. Ibid., pp. 12, 18, 49.
7. Ibid., p. 13; and MacFarquhar (1974, 78–83).
8. Cohen (1968, 20).
9. Seymour and Anderson (1998, 19–20, 23) and Wu (1992).
10. SMA B105-5-1696 (1956).
11. Informant no. 35.
12. Cohen (1968, 277–79) and SMA A22-2-140 (1953).
13. SMA B105-5-729 (1953).
14. SMA B105-5-1793 (1956).
15. Seymour and Anderson (1998, 190–92).
16. Teiwes (1993, 28–32) and Whyte (1974, 87–88).
17. Chen (1960, 73–74).
18. Some faculty and staff were arrested during the Campaign to Suppress Counterrevolutionaries. Official statistics from July 1951 show that 99 people had been arrested in schools and colleges. Among 43 people who had been sentenced, 3 were given capital punishment; 20 imprisoned, 8 put under criminal control, 10 exiled, and 2 released; SMA A71-2-94 (1951). The impact of the campaign on secondary schools was twofold: it rid the campuses of some counterrevolutionaries, criminals, and lawbreakers, but others were permitted to stay. SMA catalogue A71 is composed of documents compiled by the post-1949 Committee on Rural Work of the Shanghai Communist Party Committee, the Rural Office of the Women's Federation of the Shanghai Municipal Government, and the Shanghai Committee on Rural Work of the Chinese Communist Youth League.
19. SMA B105-1-662 (1952–53, 36).
20. Strauss (2002, 89–92).
21. SMA B105-1-661 (1951–53).
22. SMA B105-1-662 (1952–53, 32–39).

23. Ibid., pp. 11–12.
24. SMA B105-1-661 (1951–53, 24).
25. Ibid., p. 15.
26. SMA B105-1-1423 (1955–64, 1).
27. Ibid.
28. Teiwes (1993, 130–66) and Vogel (1969, 137–38).
29. SMA B105-1-1428 (1955–57, 3–4).
30. Ibid., p. 31.
31. SMA B105-2-548 (1957–59, 2).
32. SMA B105-1-1428 (1955–57, 1–7).
33. Cohen (1968, 303–4).
34. Ibid.
35. SMA B105-2-548 (1957–59, 2).
36. SMA B105-2-46 (1954–57).
37. SMA B105-5-1393 (1954–57, 86–87).
38. SMA B105-2-548 (1957–59, 7).
39. SMA A23-2-1398 (n.d.).
40. Ibid.
41. SMA A23-1-156 (1958–59, 32).
42. Since these figures were taken more than a year after the Anti-Rightist Campaign had begun, the ranks and positions were probably the actual responsibilities the offenders held after sanctions.
43. SMA B105-2-1257 (1962, 28–30).
44. SMA A23-2-429 (1959, 2).
45. A few people received long prison sentences or the death penalty for being rightists as well as counterrevolutionaries, or what officials called "tigers with double layers of furs."
46. For instance, included in the arrests and removals was a former official in the puppet regime who had implemented the occupiers' demands in schools and newspapers as well as a former KMT special-service agent who had written reports on the CCP's Eighth Route army; SMA B105-2-329 (1957–58).
47. SMA B105-5-733 (1953).
48. SMA B105-2-1936 (1964–65).
49. Greenblatt (1977, 82).
50. SMA A23-2-65 (1961, 69).
51. SMA A23-2-911 (1963, 40).
52. SMA B105-2-1418 (1963, 2).
53. Vogel (1966, 419).
54. Informant no. 24.
55. Informant no. 6.
56. Yang (2005).

CHAPTER 6

1. Feng Jicai (1998, 355).
2. Bridgham (1971, 26) and Meisner (1986, 330–32).

3. Harding (1981, 293–95).

4. For example, Lee (1978), Unger (1982), Thurston (1987), Lü, Xiuyuan (1994), and Walder (2002).

5. For example, Yue and Wakeman (1985), Cheng (1987), Gao (1987), and Ke Ling (1998).

6. Pepper (1996, 368).

7. Meisner (1986, chapter 18) summarizes Mao's political thinking on the eve of the Cultural Revolution; also, Lü (2000, 118).

8. Nee (1969, 54–55).

9. Xiong Yuezhi (1999, vol. 14, 18).

10. SMA A23-2-1178 (1966).

11. Hunter (1969, 35–47).

12. SMA A23-2-1706 (1966).

13. Informant no. 6.

14. Thurston (1987, 94).

15. Bennett and Montaperto (1971, 39–42), Gao (1987, 39–60), and Diamant (2000, 285–301).

16. SMA A23-2-1706 (1966).

17. Liang and Shapiro (1983, 45).

18. Lee (1978, 36–41) and Harding (1981, 238–41).

19. SMA A23-2-1179 (1966).

20. SMA A23-2-1707 (1966, 21).

21. Ibid.

22. Hunter (1969, 70–71).

23. Harding (1993, 187).

24. The question of which faculty or staff members perished in the Cultural Revolution is a complicated one. It has to do with the victims' and the attackers' backgrounds and the dynamics of the local rebellion. A key factor that shaped the fate of campus officials was their leadership style. At Guoguang Secondary School, multiple interviewees described their party-member principal as a "good old chap" who had worked hard and had not targeted large numbers of faculty when student mobilization began. Instead, he tried to limit the number of individuals to be attacked. As a result, he "got away pretty easy," without being physically beaten by the rebels; also, Lü Xingwei (1994, 369–70).

25. SMA B105-4-58 (1967, 127).

26. SMA A23-2-1706 (1966).

27. SMA A23-2-1188 (1966, 2–8).

28. Informant no. 1

29. Pepper (1996, 357, 367).

30. SMA A23-2-1188 (1966, 138–39).

31. SMA A23-2-1712 (1966).

32. Lü Xingwei (1994, 351–54).

33. Cheng (1987, 71) (my emphasis).

34. SMA B105-4-7 (1966, 7).

35. Ibid., pp. 89–90.

36. Informants no. 6, 14, and 61.

37. Lee (1978, 110–14).
38. Pepper (1996, 362).
39. Informants no. 9, 15, and 21.
40. SMA B105-4-7 (1966, 81–82).
41. Nee (1969, 43–53).
42. Yue and Wakeman (1985, 197).
43. Lee (1978, 209).
44. In their research on the Cultural Revolution in Shanghai factories, Perry and Li (1997) note that among those workers who assumed leadership roles early on were quite a few who had been disciplined for embezzlement and other wrongdoing. In many cases, these people had "black marks" in their personal dossiers that had prevented them "from enjoying the raises and promotions" (p. 39). The deviant teachers in schools and colleges did not emerge as leaders of rebellion as quickly as these workers. Despite their poor records, the latter used their state-ascribed "good" class background as workers to legitimize their rebellion. Teachers were unable to do so, unless they had grown up in a worker or peasant family. Deviant teachers thus had to wait for the political tide to change before they could openly participate in the uprising.
45. Hinton (1972, 108–37).
46. Ibid., pp. 109–11.
47. Informants no. 6, 17, and 24.
48. Informant no. 35.
49. SMA B105-4-322 (1969, 104).
50. Informant no. 61.
51. SMA B105-4-64 (1966–67, 35).
52. SMA B105-4-58 (1967, 81).
53. SMA B105-4-64 (1967, 46).
54. SMA B105-4-58 (1967, 3).
55. Pepper (1996, 370).
56. Lü Xingwei (1994, 357) and Pepper (1996, 370).
57. SMA B105-3-61 (1968, 18–19).
58. SMA B1055-4-58 (1967, 2).
59. Informant no. 6.
60. SMA B105-4-64 (1966–67, 13).
61. SMA B105-4-58 (1967, 12).
62. Schoenhals (2005).
63. SMA B105-4-138 (1967–68, 7).
64. Ibid., p. 28.
65. Pepper (1996, 371).
66. Lü Xingwei (1994, 359).
67. SMA B105-3-64 (1968, 4–5).
68. SMA B105-4-158 (1968, 10).
69. SMA B105-4-58 (1968, 134–35).
70. Quoted in Lü Xingwei (1994, 376).
71. Ibid., pp. 377, 379.

72. SMA B105-4-320 (1968, 107–8).
73. Informants no. 6, 24, and 61.
74. Lü Xingwei (1994, 377).
75. Ibid., p. 379.
76. Lü Xingwei (1994, 383, 633).
77. Ibid., p. 374
78. *Zhonggong Shanghai dangzhi* (2001, 66) and SMA B244-3-961 (1969). SMA catalogue B244 is composed of documents compiled by the Office of Education and Health of the Shanghai Municipal Government.
79. Lü Xingwei (1994, 373).
80. Informant no. 6.
81. Lü Xingwei (1994, 374).
82. Ibid., p. 373.
83. *Jiading xianzhi* (1992, 811).
84. Pepper (1996, 403–13).
85. Lee (1978, 288).
86. SMA B105-4-156 (1968–69, 1).
87. Lü Xingwei (1994, 362).
88. Lee (1978, 291).
89. SMA A22-2-1447 (1966, 13).
90. SMA B227-1-1 (1967, 44). SMA catalogue B227 is composed of documents compiled by the Wage and Salary Division of the Shanghai Revolutionary Committee.
91. Ibid.
92. Ibid., p. 45
93. SMA B227-2-25 (1967–68, 1).
94. Pepper (1996, 391).
95. Lü Xingwei (1994, 546).
96. Informants no. 1, 6, 14, 24, and 61.

CHAPTER 7

1. Weber (1978a, 987).
2. Bourdieu (1977, 184).
3. Bailes (1978, 4), Fitzpatrick (1999, 70), and Kuromiya (1988, 287).
4. Lampert (1979, 14–15).
5. Bailes (1978, 45–50) and Ball (1987, 6).
6. Bailes (1978, 51).
7. Bailes (1978, 45–48) and Lampert (1979, 13–21).
8. Bailes (1978, 50–52, 59).
9. Kenez (1999, 45–46).
10. Ibid., pp. 44, 46.
11. Ibid., pp. 47–48, 59.
12. Bailes (1978, 64).
13. Kenez (1999, 61).
14. Bailes (1978, 63).

15. Ibid., pp. 65–66.
16. Ibid., p. 64.
17. Bailes (1978, 66) and Lampert (1979, 30, 34).
18. Ball (1987, 10–11).
19. Tucker (1990).
20. Kenez (1999, 82).
21. Fitzpatrick (1994, 132).
22. Lampert (1979, 92).
23. Bailes (1978, chapters 3 and 4) discusses two famous cases, the 1928 Shakty Affair and 1930 Industrial Party Affair, involving attacks on industrial personnel and Stalin's role in the matters.
24. Lampert (1979, 92–93).
25. Ibid., p. 94.
26. Ibid., p. 63.
27. Lampert (1979, 62) and Bailes (1978, 222).
28. Lampert (1979, 65, 69).
29. Kuromiya (1988, 213–14) and Fitzpatrick (1999, 6).
30. Kuromiya (1988, 215).
31. Kenez (1999, 94).
32. Tucker (1977, 90).
33. Fitzpatrick (1999, chapter 2) provides a succinct description of economic privation in the 1930s.
34. Bailes (1978, 269).
35. Ibid., p. 301.
36. Ibid., p. 305.
37. Ibid.
38. Bailes (1978, 305–9) and Fitzpatrick (1999, chapter 3).
39. Kuromiya (1988, 94) and Fitzpatrick (1999, chapter 2)
40. Kenez (1999, 108).
41. Cohen (1977) and Fitzpatrick (2000).
42. Kenez (1999, 109).
43. Harris (2000, 267).
44. Ibid., p. 279.
45. Bailes (1978, 288).
46. Davies (2000, 61–67) and Kotkin (1995, 343).
47. Wright (1980, 116).
48. Fitzpatrick (1999, 194–99).
49. Wright (1980, 117).
50. Ibid.
51. Kotkin (1995, 42).
52. For example, Barnett (1967), Vogel (1969), and Lieberthal (1980).
53. SMA A94-1-8 (1949, 2) and SMA A94-1-264 (1953, 17).
54. Kau (1971, 101).
55. Lee (1991, 50–51)
56. Kau (1969).
57. *Zhonggong Shanghai dangzhi* (2001, 306).

58. Ibid., pp. 308–10, 328–29.
59. Lee (1991, 66).
60. Joffe (1966, 45).
61. Ibid., pp. 52–55.
62. Oksenberg (1969).
63. Harding (1981, 72).
64. Kau (1971, 104).
65. Harding (1981, 74).
66. Chang (1997, 103).
67. Harding (1981, 72, 74).
68. Kau (1971) and Harding (1981).
69. Harding (1981, 92–93).
70. Kau (1971, 116–17).
71. *Zhonggong Shanghai dangzhi* (2001, 337).
72. SMA B127-1-100 (1957, 9–10).
73. Howe (1978, 180–84).
74. Teiwes and Sun (1999, 5) and Chan (2001, 4).
75. The original argument is most clearly stated in MacFarquhar (1974–97, vol. 2). Recent works include Teiwes and Sun (1999), Chan (2001), and Bernstein (2006).
76. Chan (2001, 17–37).
77. Ibid., pp. 39–40.
78. See MacFarquhar (1974–97, vol. 2, chapter 10) for the conflict between Mao and Peng Dehuai.
79. In Shanghai, 110,000 party members were subjected to the 1959 campaign, of which 4,600 were criticized or punished. One of the punishable offenses was "seriously lacking enthusiasm" (*yanzhong ganjing buzu*) in carrying out one's work; *Zhonggong Shanghai dangzhi* (2001, 257) and Bernstein (2006).
80. Production in Shanghai's textile and food industry declined by 20 and 12 percent respectively between 1959 and 1960, and cotton production in 1960 declined by 38 percent compared to two years before; *Zhonggong Shanghai dangzhi* (2001, 257–58).
81. Chan (2001, 58, 120).
82. Ibid., pp. 121, 125, 130.
83. Teiwes and Sun (1999, 5) and Chan (2001, 4).
84. MacFarquhar (1974) and Teiwes (1993). Zhu (1998) summarizes the complaints in different sectors.
85. Cf. White (1989).
86. Besides the discussion about the Cultural Revolution in schools and colleges in this book, see Wang (1995, 96–99) and Perry and Li (1997, 7–28).
87. Blecher and White (1979), Harding (1981), Wang (1995), and Perry and Li (1997).
88. Two months later, when the popular rebellion against the official authorities was validated by the Sixteen-Point Decision, Premier Zhou Enlai still emphasized that the movement should unite "ninety-five percent of the cadres" and refrain from the use of physical force; Harding (1993, 179).

89. *Zhonggong Shanghai dangzhi* (2001, 66).

90. Howe 1973b.

91. Harding (1981, 296–328).

92. Walder (1982, 220).

93. Howe (1973b, 251).

94. Walder (1982, 226) and (1986, 190–221).

95. Howe (1978) looks at the overall economic performance of the Chinese socialist economy.

96. According to Chinese economists, the last ten years of Mao's rule cost the country nearly 300 billion yuan; Schoenhals (2006, 19). Walder (1989) summarizes the unimpressive performance of the Chinese economy.

97. Walder (1989, 408).

98. As Ken Jowitt has noted, "the Soviet Union had created a German industry of the 1880s in the 1980s," quoted in Verdery (1996, 32).

CHAPTER 8

1. For example, Meyer (1970) and Hough (1977)

2. Hough (1977, 52).

3. Burns (1987), Lee (1991), and Manion (1993).

4. Other features that Pakulski named were patronage, rule bending and stretching, absence of clearly defined lines of authority and spheres of responsibilities, and lack of private and individual autonomy (Pakulski [1986a, 6–11]).

5. Zhou et al. (1996), Walder et al. (2000), Bian et al. (2001), and Walder (2004).

6. Quoted in Pakulski (1986a, 6).

7. Gold (1984).

8. Clark (1993) and Lubman (1999).

9. Pakulski (1986a, 7).

10. Yang (1994) and Lü (2000) provide the most insightful looks at the spread of personal relations and official corruption in China.

11. Jowitt (1992, 140).

12. Ibid., p. 63.

13. Ibid., p. 139.

14. Ibid., p. 78. Lü (2000) extends Jowitt's concept of "neotraditionalism" to contend that CCP "policies, institutions, and norms" before and during the Mao era were the primary factors causing widespread corruption afterward.

15. Jowitt (1992) argues that state violence and mass terror reinforced within the general population "a cultural disposition that was highly calculative toward the political realm" (pp. 70–71).

16. Pakulski (1993, 76).

17. The fact that both the Soviet Union and China saw economic growth but also economic problems after Stalin and after Mao raises further questions about the relation between counter-bureaucracy and economic growth in Soviet-type societies. Did the growth in these countries after the high tide of

counter-bureaucracy reflect the extent of organizational rationalization, however limited, that the ruling regimes pursued? In other words, did the growth confirm findings in development studies that even limited rationalization can go a long way in promoting growth? Alternatively, one may hypothesize that the growth had little to do with organizational rationalization, but reflected other changes such as market expansion or redistribution of investment. Longitudinal accounts of firm structure and firm performance in Soviet-type societies would seem necessary for explaining the relations between modern bureaucracy, counter-bureaucracy, and growth during those periods. Guthrie (1999) and Lin (2002) are useful in this regard with respect to China's growth after the Mao era.

18. Pakulski (1986b, 48).

19. Pakulski (1993, 82–83).

20. Burawoy and Lukács (1992), Yang (1994), and Pakulski (1993).

21. Pakulski (1993).

22. Various explanations for the decline of socialism can be found in *Theory and Society* 23, no. 2 (1994).

23. Lipset and Bence (1994).

24. Arendt (1951).

25. Baehr (2002, 813).

26. Weber (1978a, 225).

27. Brzezinski (1962, 27), Aron (1965, 235), and Friedrich and Brzezinski (1965, 205).

28. Friedrich and Brzezinski (1965, 213).

29. Hough (1977, 49–53).

30. Huntington (1968, 8).

31. Laird (1970, 108).

32. Pakulski (1993).

33. Gouldner (1979, 61) and Tellenback (1978).

34. Szelényi (1981, S304).

35. Konrád and Szelényi (1979, 148).

36. Ibid., pp. 204, 206.

37. Ibid., p. 247.

38. Grossman (1977), O'Hearn (1980), Ericson (1982), and Lomnitz (1988).

39. Quoted in Pakulski (1986a, 8).

40. For instance, Yang (1994) observes that the prevalence of a gift economy in post-Mao China "alters and weakens in a piecemeal fashion the structural principles and smooth operations of state power" (p. 189).

41. For example, Walder (1986) argues that the patron-client relations Chinese industrial workers mobilized to satisfy their own needs helped curtail workers' solidarity and produce within the working class "a stable pattern of tacit acceptance and active cooperation" toward the CCP regime (p. 249).

42. Bauman (1979, 185).

43. Fukuyama (1992).

44. Kornai (1992) best exemplifies such an argument.

45. Miliband (1994, 78).
46. Effort to rethink the viability of socialism has been patchy. Recent examples are Miliband (1994) and Burawoy (2003).
47. Weber ([1922] 1978b, 260).
48. Antonio (1986, 21).

References

Anderson, Kevin. 1995. *Lenin, Hegel, and Western Marxism*. Urbana, IL: University of Illinois Press.

Antonio, Roberto. 1979. "The Contradiction of Domination and Production in Bureaucracy: The Contribution of Organizational Efficiency to the Decline of the Roman Empire." *American Sociological Review* 44(6): 895–912.

———. 1984. "Weber vs. Parsons: Domination or Technocratic Models of Social Organization." In *Max Weber's Political Sociology*, edited by Ronald Glassman and Vatro Murvar. Westport, CT: Greenwood Press.

———. 1986. "Dialectics of Authoritarian Bureaucracy: Extraction and Patrimony in Ancient Rome." *Research in Political Sociology* 2: 19–47.

Arendt, Hannah. 1951. *The Origins of Totalitarianism*. New York: Harcourt, Brace.

Aron, Raymond. 1965. *Democracy and Totalitarianism*. London: Weidenfeld and Nicolson.

Bachman, David. 1991. *Bureaucracy, Economy, and Leadership in China*. Cambridge: Cambridge University Press.

Baehr, Peter. 2002. "Identifying the Unprecedented: Hannah Arendt, Totalitarianism, and the Critique of Sociology." *American Sociological Review* 67(6): 804–31.

Bailes, Kendall. 1978. *Technology and Society under Lenin and Stalin*. Princeton, NJ: Princeton University Press.

Ball, Alan. 1987. *Russia's Last Capitalists*. Berkeley: University of California Press.

Barnard, Chester. 1962. *The Functions of the Executive*. Cambridge, MA: Harvard University Press.

Barnett, A. Doak. 1967. *Cadres, Bureaucracy, and Political Power in Communist China*. New York: Columbia University Press.

Bauman, Zygmunt. 1979. "Comments on Eastern Europe." *Studies in Comparative Communism* 12(2, 3): 184–89.

Bendix, Reinhard. 1960. *Max Weber.* London: William Heinemann.

Bennett, Gordon, and Ronald Montaperto. 1971. *Red Guard: The Political Biography of Dai Hsiao-ai.* London: George Allen and Unwin.

Bernstein, Thomas. 2006. "Mao Zedong and the Famine of 1959–60: A Study in Willfulness." *China Quarterly* 186: 421–45.

Bian, Yanjie, Xiaoling Shu, and John R. Logan. 2001. "Communist Party Membership and Regime Dynamics in China." *Social Forces* 79(3): 805–841.

Blecher, Marc, and Gordon White. 1979. *Micropolitics in Contemporary China.* Armonk, NY: M. E. Sharpe.

Bourdieu, Pierre. 1977. *Outline of a Theory of Practice.* Cambridge: Cambridge University Press.

Bridgham, Philip. 1971. "Mao's 'Cultural Revolution': Origin and Development (Part One)." In *China in Ferment,* edited by Richard Baum with Louise Bennett. Englewood Cliffs, NJ: Prentice-Hall.

Brzezinski, Zbigniew. 1962. *Ideology and Power in Soviet Politics.* New York: Praeger.

Burawoy, Michael. 1979. *Manufacturing Consent.* Chicago: University of Chicago Press.

———. 2003. "For a Sociological Marxism: The Complementary Convergence of Antonio Gramsci and Karl Polanyi." *Politics and Society* 31(2): 193–261.

Burawoy, Michael, and János Lukács. 1994. *The Radiant Past.* Chicago: University of Chicago Press.

Burns, John. 1987. "Civil Service Reforms in Post-Mao China." *Australian Journal of Chinese Affairs* 18: 47–84.

Callaghy, Thomas. 1984. *The State-Society Struggle: Zaire in Comparative Perspective.* New York: Columbia University Press.

Chan, Alfred. 2001. *Mao's Crusade: Politics and Policy Implementation in China's Great Leap Forward.* Oxford: Oxford University Press.

Chan, Anita. 1985. *Children of Mao.* London: MacMillan.

Chang, Julian. 1997. "The Mechanics of State Propaganda: The People's Republic of China and the Soviet Union in the 1950s." In *New Perspectives on State Socialism in China,* edited by Timothy Cheek and Tony Saich. Armonk, NY: M. E. Sharpe.

Chen Jingshan, ed. 1984. *Shanghai jiaoshi yundong huiyilu* (Recollections on the teachers' movement in Shanghai). Shanghai: Shanghai jiaoyu chubanshe.

Chen Xuexun, ed. 1994. *Zhongguo jiaoyushi yanjiu: xiandai fenjuan* (History of Chinese education, the contemporary period). Shanghai: Huadong shifan daxue chubanshe.

Chen, Theodore. 1960. *Thought Reform of the Chinese Intellectuals.* Hong Kong: Hong Kong University Press.

Cheng, Nien. 1987. *Life and Death in Shanghai.* New York: Grove.

Clark, William. 1993. "Crime and Punishment in Soviet Officialdom 1965–90." *Europe-Asia Studies* 45(2): 259–279.

Cohen, Jerome. 1968. *The Criminal Process in the People's Republic of China.* Cambridge, MA: Harvard University Press.

Cohen, Stephen. 1977. "Bolshevism and Stalinism." In *Stalinism: Essays in Historical Interpretation*, edited by Robert Tucker. New York: W. W. Norton.

Dangshi wenji (Writings on the history of the CCP). 1996. Shanghai: Tongji daxue chubanshe.

Davies, Sarah. 2000. "Us Against Them": Social Identity in Soviet Russia, 1931–9." In *Stalinism: New Directions*, edited by Sheila Fitzpatrick. London: Routledge.

Deng Yuchang. 1989. "Zhonggong Yucai Zhongxue zhibu dixia douzheng huiyi" (Remembering the struggle of the communist underground at Yucai Secondary School). In *Zhonggong Shanghaishi jiaoyu weisheng tiyu xitong dangshi wenji* (Historical materials on Shanghai's education, health and sports). Shanghai: Tongji daxue chubanshe.

Diamant, Neil. 2000. *Revolutionizing the Family: Politics, Love, and Divorce in Urban and Rural China, 1949–1968*. Berkeley: University of California Press.

Djilas, Milovan. 1957. *The New Class: An Analysis of the Communist System*. New York: Holt, Reinhart, and Winston.

Douzheng (Struggle). 1949. Zhonggong zhongyang huadongju.

Duan Lipei. 1992. "Jiaohai chenfu huaganku" (My pains and travails in the teaching profession). In *Zai jiaoyu shiceshang* (On the annals of education). Shanghai: Shanghai jiaoyu chubanshe.

Ericson, Richard. 1982. "Inventory Stability and Resource Allocation Under Uncertainty in a Command Economy." *Econometrica* 50(2): 345–76.

Erlich, Alexander. 1960. *The Soviet Industrialization Debate, 1924–1928*. Cambridge, MA: Harvard University Press.

Evans, Peter. 1995. *Embedded Autonomy: States and Industrial Transformation*. Princeton, NJ: Princeton University Press.

Evans, Peter, and James Rauch. 1999. "Bureaucracy and Growth: A Cross-national Analysis of the Effects of 'Weberian' State Structures on Economic Growth." *American Sociological Review* 64(5): 748–65.

Fang Ming and Chen Yuxin. 1984. "Kangzhan shiqi dang lingdaoxia de Shanghai jiaoyu yundong" (The CCP-led resistance in Shanghai education against Japanese occupation). In *Shanghai jiaoshi yundong huiyilu* (Recollections on the teachers' movement in Shanghai). Shanghai: Shanghai renmin chubanshe.

Feng Jicai. 1998. "*Lao hongweibing de xinlu licheng*" (The psychological journey of an old red guard). In *Ershi shiji zhongguo jishi wenxue wenku 1966–1976: qiancheng yu miluan* (Twentieth-century China documentary literature series 1966–1976: Pious devotion and perplexing chaos). Shanghai: Wenhui chubanshe.

———. 1991. *Voices from the Whirlwind*. New York: Pantheon.

Fitzpatrick, Sheila. 1994. *The Russian Revolution*. Oxford: Oxford University Press.

———. 1999. *Everyday Stalinism*. Oxford: Oxford University Press.

———. 2000. "Varieties of Terror: Introduction to Part IV." In *Stalinism: New Directions*, edited by Sheila Fitzpatrick. London: Routledge.

Friedrich, Carl, and Zbigniew Brzezinski. 1965. *Totalitarian Dictatorship and Autocracy.* Cambridge, MA: Harvard University Press.

Fukuyama, Francis. 1992. *The End of History and the Last Man.* New York: Free Press.

Gao, Yang. 1987. *Born Red.* Stanford, CA: Stanford University Press.

Gold, Thomas. 1984. "Just in Time! China Battles Spiritual Revolution on the Eve of 1984." *Asian Survey* 24(9): 947–74.

———. 1986. *State and Society in the Taiwan Miracle.* Armonk, NY: M. E. Sharpe.

Gouldner, Alvin. 1954. *Patterns of Industrial Bureaucracy.* New York: Simon and Schuster.

———. 1979. *The Future of Intellectuals and the Rise of the New Class.* New York: Oxford University Press.

Greenblatt, Sidney. 1977. "Campaigns and the Manufacture of Deviance in Chinese Society." In *Deviance and Social Control in Chinese Society,* edited by Amy Wilson, Richard Wilson, and Sidney Greenblatt. New York: Praeger.

Grossman, Gregory. 1977. "The Second Economy in the USSR." *Problems of Communism* 16(5): 25–40.

Guthrie, Doug. 1999. *Dragon in a Three-piece Suit.* Princeton, NJ: Princeton University Press.

Harding, Harry. 1981. *Organizing China: The Problem of Bureaucracy, 1949–1976.* Stanford, CA: Stanford University Press.

———. 1993. "The Chinese State in Crisis." In *The Politics of China, 1949–1989,* edited by Roderick MacFarquhar. Cambridge: Cambridge University Press.

Harris, James. 2000. "The Purging of Local Cliques in the Urals Region 1936–7." In *Stalinism: New Directions,* edited by Sheila Fitzpatrick. London: Routledge.

Henriot, Christian. 1993. *Shanghai 1927–1937.* Berkeley: University of California Press.

Hinton, William. 1968. *Fanshen.* New York: Random House.

———. 1972. *Hundred Day War.* New York: Monthly Review Press.

Hochschild, Arlie. 1983. *The Managed Heart.* Berkeley: University of California Press.

Hodges, Donald. 1981. *The Bureaucratization of Socialism.* Amherst: University of Massachusetts Press.

Hollister, William. 1964. "Capital Formation in Communist China." In *Industrial Development in Communist China,* edited by Choh-Ming Li. New York: Praeger.

Hough, Jerry. 1977. *The Soviet Union and Social Science Theory.* Cambridge, MA: Harvard University Press.

Howe, Christopher. 1968. "The Supply and Administration of Urban Housing in Mainland China: The Case of Shanghai." *China Quarterly* 33: 73–97.

———. 1971. *Employment and Economic Growth in Urban China, 1949–1957.* Cambridge: Cambridge University Press.

———. 1973a. *Wage Patterns and Wage Policy in Modern China, 1919–1972.* Cambridge: Cambridge University Press.

―――. 1973b. "Labor Organization and Incentives in Industry, Before and After the Cultural Revolution." In *Authority Participation and Cultural Change in China*, edited by Stuart Schram. Cambridge: Cambridge University Press.

―――. 1978. *China's Economy*. New York: Basic Books.

―――. 1981. "Industrialization under Conditions of Long-Run Population Stability: Shanghai's Achievement and Prospect." In *Shanghai*, edited by Christopher Howe. Cambridge: Cambridge University Press.

Hu, Shi Ming, and Eli Seifman. 1976. *Toward a New World Outlook*. New York: AMS Press.

Hunter, Neale. 1969. *Shanghai Journal: An Eyewitness Account of the Cultural Revolution*. New York: Praeger.

Huntington, Samuel. 1968. *Political Order in Changing Societies*. New Haven: Yale University Press.

Jiading xianzhi (Jiading county gazette). 1992. Shanghai Jiading xianzhi bianzuan weiyuanhui. Shanghai: Shanghai renmin chubanshe.

Jing'an difangzhi (Jing'an district gazette). 1996. Shanghai: Shanghai shehui kexueyuan chubanshe.

Jing'an wenshi (History of Jing'an district). 1991–95. Shanghai: Zhonggong Shanghaishi Jing'an quwei weiyuanhui dangshi ziliao yanjiushi.

Jing'anqu wenshi ziliao xuanji (Historical materials on Jing'an district).1987–91. Zhonggong jing'an quwei dangshi zhengji weiyuanhui bangongshi.

Jinshan xianzhi (Jinshan County Gazette). 1985. Shanghai Jinshan xianzhi bianzuan weiyuanhui. Shanghai: Shanghai renmin chubanshe.

Joffe, Ellis. 1966. "The Conflict between Old and New in the Chinese Army." In *China under Mao: Politics Takes Command*, edited by Roderick MacFarquhar. Cambridge, MA: MIT Press.

Johnson, Chalmers. 1982. *MITI and the Japanese Miracle*. Stanford, CA: Stanford University Press.

Jowitt, Ken. 1992. *New World Disorder: The Leninist Distinction*. Berkeley: University of California Press.

Kahlberg, Stephen. 1985. "The Role of Ideal Interests in Max Weber's Comparative Historical Sociology." In *A Weber-Marx Dialogue*, edited by Robert Antonio and Ronald Glassman. Lawrence: University of Kansas Press.

Karabel, Jerome. 1976. "Revolutionary Contradictions: Antonio Gramsci and the Problems of Intellectuals." *Politics and Society* 6(1): 123–72.

―――. 1997. "Lenin and the Problem of the Intelligentsia." *Current Perspectives in Social Theory* 17: 261–312.

Kau, Ying-mao. 1969. "The Urban Bureaucratic Elite in Communist China: A Case Study of Wuhan 1949–1965." In *Chinese Communist Politics in Action*, edited by A. Doak Barnett. Seattle: University of Washington Press.

―――. 1971. "Patterns of Recruitment and Mobility of Urban Cadres." In *The City in Communist China*, edited by John Lewis. Stanford, CA: Stanford University Press.

Ke Ling, ed. 1998. *Ershi shiji zhongguo jishi wenxue wenku, 1966–1976*, (Twentieth-century China documentary literature series, 1966–1976, volumes 1–3). Shanghai: Wenhui chubanshe.

Kenez, Peter. 1999. *A History of the Soviet Union from the Beginning to the End.* Cambridge: Cambridge University Press.

Kirby, William. 1984. *Germany and Republican China.* Stanford, CA: Stanford University Press.

———. 2000. "Engineering China: Birth of the Development State 1928–1937." In *Becoming Chinese,* edited by Wen-hsin Yeh. Berkeley: University of California Press.

———. 2006. "China's Internationalization in the Early People's Republic: Dreams of a Socialist World Economy." *China Quarterly* 188: 870–90.;

Konrád, Gyorgy, and Iván Szelényi. 1979. *The Intellectuals on the Road to Class Power.* New York: Harcourt, Brace, Jovanovich.

Kornai, János. 1992. *The Socialist System: The Political Economy of Communism.* Princeton, NJ: Princeton University Press.

Kotkin, Stephen. 1995. *Magnetic Mountain: Stalinism as a Civilization.* Berkeley: University of California Press.

Kraus, Richard. 1981. *Class Conflict in Chinese Socialism.* New York: Columbia University Press.

Kuromiya, Hiroaki. 1988. *Stalin's Industrial Revolution.* Cambridge: Cambridge University Press.

———. 1979. *China Education in Transition.* Montreal: McGill-Queen's University Press.

———. 1988. *Cultural Revolution in China's Schools, May 1966–April 1969.* Stanford, CA: Hoover Institution Press.

Laird, Roy. 1970. *The Soviet Paradigm: An Experiment in Creating a Mono-hierarchical Polity.* New York: Free Press.

Lampert, Nicholas. 1979. *The Technical Intelligentsia and the Soviet State.* London: MacMillan.

Larson, Magali S. 1977. *The Rise of Professionalism.* Berkeley: University of California Press.

Lee, Hong Yung. 1978. *The Politics of the Cultural Revolution.* Berkeley: University of California Press.

———. 1991. *From Revolutionary Cadres to Party Technocrats in Socialist China.* Berkeley: University of California Press.

Lefort, Claude. 1986. *The Political Forms of Modern Society.* Cambridge: Polity Press.

Lenin, V. I. 1965. *Collected Works.* London: Lawrence and Wishart.

Leung, Edwin Pak-Wah, ed. 1992. *Historical Dictionary of Revolutionary China, 1839–1976.* New York: Greenwood.

Lewin, Moshe. 1969. *Lenin's Last Struggle.* New York: Random House.

Li Dehong, ed. 1997. *Shanghaishi zhongxue jiaoshi yundong shiliao xuan* (Teachers' movements in Shanghai). Shanghai: Shanghai jiaoyu chubanshe.

Li Huaxing, ed. 1997. *Minguo jiaoyushi* (History of education in the Republican Era). Shanghai: Shanghai jiaoyu chubanshe.

Liang, Heng, and Judith Shapiro. 1983. *Son of the Revolution.* New York: Random House.

Lieberthal, Kenneth. 1980. *Revolution and Tradition in Tientsin, 1949–1952.* Stanford, CA: Stanford University Press.

Lifton, Robert. 1963. *Thought Reform and the Psychology of Totalism.* New York: W. W. Norton.

Lin, Yi-min. 2002. *Between Politics and Market.* Cambridge: Cambridge University Press.

Lipset, Seymour M., and Gyorgy Bence. 1994. "Anticipations of the Failure of Communism." *Theory and Society* 23(2): 169–210.

Liu Feng. 1984. "Jiaolian zai Liangcai Buxi Xuexiao de huodong ji xuewei jiaowei jilue" (The activities of the teachers' association and the CCP student and teacher committees at Liangcai Supplementary School). In *Shanghai jiaoshi yundong huiyilu* (Teachers' movement in Shanghai). Shanghai: Shanghai jiaoyu chubanshe.

Lomnitz, Larissa. 1988. "Informal Exchange Networks in Formal Systems: A Theoretical Model." *American Anthropologists* 90(1): 42–55.

Lü, Xiuyuan. 1994. "A Step toward Understanding Popular Violence in China's Cultural Revolution." *Pacific Affairs* 67(4): 533–65.

Lü, Xiaobo. 1997. "Minor Public Economy: The Revolutionary Origins of the *Danwei*." In *Danwei: The Changing Chinese Workplace in Historical and Comparative Perspective,* edited by Xiaobo Lü and Elizabeth Perry. Armonk, NY: M. E. Sharpe.

———. 2000. *Cadres and Corruption: The Organizational Involution of the Chinese Communist Party.* Stanford, CA: Stanford University Press.

Lü Xingwei. 1994. *Shanghai putong jiaoyushi 1949–1989* (History of Shanghai education). Shanghai: Shanghai jiaoyu chubanshe.

Lubman, Stanley. 1999. *Bird in a Cage.* Stanford, CA: Stanford University Press.

Ma Feihai 1997. "xu'er" (Preface II). In *Shanghaishi zhongxue jiaoshi yundong shiliao xuan* (Teachers' movement in Shanghai). Shanghai: Shanghai jiaoyu chubanshe.

MacFarquhar, Roderick. 1974. *The Hundred Flowers Campaign and the Chinese Intellectuals.* New York: Octagon Books.

———. 1974–97. *The Origins of the Cultural Revolution,* volumes 1–3. New York: Columbia University Press.

Manion, Melanie. 1993. *Retirement of Revolutionaries in China.* Princeton, NJ: Princeton University Press.

Mao Zedong. (1950) 1977. *Mao Zedong xuanji,* volume 5 (Selected Works of Mao Zedong). Beijing: Renmin chubanshe.

———. (1960) 2002. "Zhongyang guanyu fandui guanliao zhuyi de zhishi" (Central Party instruction on opposing bureaucratism). In *Zhongguo wenhua de geming wenku* (The Chinese Cultural Revolution Library), CD version edited by Song Yongyi. Hong Kong: Chinese University of Hong Kong University Service Centre.

Mao Lirui, and Shen Guanqun. 1987. *Zhongguo jiaoyu tongshi, dewujuan* (History of Chinese education, volume 5). Shandong: Shandong jiaoyu chubanshe.

McNeal, Robert. 1959. "Lenin's Attack on Stalin: Review and Reappraisal." *American Slavic and East European Review* 18(3): 295–314.

Meisner, Maurice. 1986. *Mao's China and After*. New York: Free Press.

Meyer, Alfred. 1970. "The Comparative Study of Communist Political Systems." In *The Soviet Political System*, edited by Richard Cornell. Englewood Cliffs, NJ: Prentice-Hall Inc.

Miliband, Ralph. 1994. *Socialism for a Sceptical Age*. Cambridge: Polity Press.

Minguo renwu daicidian (Dictionary of notable characters in the Republican era). 1991. Hebei: Hebei renmin chubanshe.

Mommsen, Wolfgang. 1984. *Max Weber and German Politics, 1890–1920*, translated by Michael S. Steinberg. Chicago: University of Chicago Press.

———. 1985. "Capitalism and Socialism: Weber's Dialogue with Marx." In *A Weber-Marx Dialogue*, edited by Robert Antonio and Ronald Glassman. Lawrence: University of Kansas Press.

Moore, Barrington, Jr. 1954. *Terror and Progress USSR*. Cambridge, MA: Harvard University Press.

Nee, Victor. 1969. *The Cultural Revolution at Peking University*. New York: Monthly Review.

O'Hearn, Dennis. 1980. "The Consumer Second Economy: Size and Effects." *Soviet Studies* 32(2): 218–34.

Oksenberg, Michel. 1969. "Local Leaders in Rural China 1962–65: Individual Attributes, Bureaucratic Positions, and Political Recruitment." In *Chinese Communist Politics in Action*, edited by A. Doak Barnett. Seattle: University of Washington Press.

Pakulski, Jan. 1986a. "Bureaucracy and the Soviet System." *Studies in Comparative Communism* 19(1): 3–24.

———. 1986b. "Legitimacy and Mass Compliance: Reflections on Max Weber and Soviet-type Societies." *British Journal of Political Science* 16(4): 35–56.

———. 1993. "East European Revolutions and 'Legitimacy Crisis.'" In *From a One-Party State to Democracy*, edited by Janina Frentzel-Zagorksa. Amsterdam: Rodopi.

Parkin, Frank. 1982. *Max Weber*. New York: Tavistock Publications.

Pasqualini, Jean, and Rudolph Chelminski. 1973. *Prisoner of Mao*. New York: Coward, McCann and Geoghegan.

Pei, Minxin. 1994. *From Reform to Revolution: The Demise of Communism in China and the Soviet Union*. Cambridge, MA: Harvard University Press.

Pepper, Suzanne. 1996. *Radicalism and Education Reform in Twentieth Century China*. Cambridge: Cambridge University Press.

Perrow, Charles. 1993. *Complex Organizations*. New York: McGraw-Hill.

Perry, Elizabeth, and Li Xun. 1997. *Proletarian Power: Shanghai in the Cultural Revolution*. Boulder, CO: Westview.

Polan, A. J. 1984. *Lenin and the Ends of Politics*. London: Methuen and Co.

Priestley, K. E. 1971. "Education in the People's Republic of China: Beginnings." In *Education and Communism in China*, edited by Stewart Fraser. London: Pall Mall Press.

Rosen, Stanley. 1982. *Red Guard Factionalism and the Cultural Revolution in Guangzhou*. Boulder, CO: Westview.

Schneider, Ben. 1991. *Politics within the State*. Pittsburgh: University of Pittsburgh Press.

Schoenhals, Michael. 2005. "'Why Don't We Arm the Left?' Mao's Culpability for the Cultural Revolution's 'Great Chaos' of 1967." *China Quarterly* 182: 277–300.

————. 2006. "The Global War on Terrorism as Meta-Narrative: An Alternative Reading of Recent Chinese History (unpublished manuscript).

Schram, Stuart. 1989. *The Thought of Mao Tse-tung*. Cambridge: Cambridge University Press.

Schurmann, Franz. 1968. *Ideology and Organization in Communist China*. Berkeley: University of California Press.

Seymour, James, and Richard Anderson. 1998. *New Ghosts, Old Ghosts: Prison and Labor Reform Camps in China*. Armonk, NY: M. E. Sharpe.

Shanghai Municipal Archives. Documents A11-2-15 (1958), A22-2-140 (1953), A22-1-275 (1956), A22-2-1447 (1966), A23-1-156 (1958–59), A23-2-65 (1961), A23-2-234 (1957), A23-2-429 (1959), A23-2-568 (1960), A23-2-582 (1960), A23-2-737 (1961), A23-2-752 (1961), A23-2-765 (1961), A23-2-911 (1963–64), A23-2-1123 (1965), A23-2-1178 (1966), A23-2-1179 (1966), A23-2-1398 (n.d.), A23-2-1703 (1960–62), A23-2-1706 (1966). A23-2-1707 (1966), A23-2-1712 (1966), A71-2-94 (1951), A94-1-8, (1949), A94-1-264 (1953), A94-1-633 (1956), A94-1-771 (1957), A94-1-1041 (1961), B3-2-64 (1956), B3-2-66 (1956), B3-2-221 (1963), B105-1-5 (1949), B105-1-8 (1949), B105-1-268 (1951), B105-1-462 (1952–53), B105-1-514 (1952), B105-1-614 (1952–53), B105-1-661 (1951–53), B105-1-662 (1952-53), B105-1-664 (1952), B105-1-673 (1953), B105-1-684 (1952–53), B105-1-694 (1953), B105-1-882 (1954), B105-1-890 (1954), B105-1-906 (1954), B105-1-1164 (1961), B105-1-1191 (1954–55), B105-1-1200 (1955), B105-1-1296 (1955), B105-1-1423 (1955–64), B105-1-1428 (1955–57), B105-1-1504 (1956), B105-1-1685 (1957), B105-2-34 (1957), B105-2-37 (1956–57), B105-2-46 (1954–57), B105-2-92 (1959), B105-2-257 (1960), B105-2-271 (1957), B105-2-329 (1957–58), B105-2-392 (1961), B105-2-393 (1961), B105-2-406 (1961), B105-2-407 (1961), B105-2-527 (1962), B105-2-548 (1957–59), B105-2-585 (1959), B105-2-641 (1959), B105-2-654 (1963), B105-2-660 (1963), B105-2-669 (1964), B105-2-781(1964), B105-2-797 (1964–65), B105-2-946 (1960), B105-2-1133 (1961), B105-2-1270 (1962), B105-2-1417 (1963), B105-2-1418 (1963), B105-2-1257 (1962), B105-2-1919 (1965), B105-2-1936 (1964–65), B105-3-61 (1968), B105-3-64 (1968), B105-4-7 (1966), B105-4-58 (1967), B105-4-64 (1966–67), B105-4-138 (1967–68), B105-4-156 (1968–69), B105-4-158 (1968), B105-4-320 (1968), B105-4-322 (1969), B105-5-52 (1949–50), B105-5-78 (1949), B105-5-306 (1950–52), B105-5-665 (1952), B105-5-729 (1953), B105-5-733 (1953), B105-5-738 (1953), B105-5-752 (1953), B105-5-1089 (1954), B105-5-1182 (1954), B105-5-1352 (1955), B105-5-1354 (1955), B105-5-1358 (1955–58), B105-5-1393 (1954–57), B105-5-1415 (1955–56), B105-5-1416 (1955), B105-5-1537 (1955), B105-5-1538 (1955–58), B105-5-1693 (1956), B105-5-1693/2 (1956), B105-5-1696 (1956), B105-5-1704 (1956), B105-5-1705 (1956), B105-5-1707 (1956), B105-5-1793 (1956), B105-5-1969 (1954–55), B105-5-1803 (1956), B105-5-1807 (1956), B105-5-1812 (1956–57), B105-5-1813 (1956), B105-5-1816 (1957), B127-1-78 (1956), B127-1-100 (1957), B127-1-941 (1954), B130-1-1 (1951–52), B227-1-1 (1967, 44), B227-2-25 (1967–68), B244-3-961 (1969), Q1-18-250 (1947), Q235-2-597 (1948), Q235-2-621 (1948),

Shanghai wenshi ziliao xuanji: tongzhan gongzuo shiliao zhuanji (Historical materials on Shanghai: Special volumes on propaganda work). 1987–91.Zhongguo renmin zhengzhi xieshang huiyi Shanghaishi weiyuanhui wenshi ziliao weiyuanhui.

Shanghai ziben zhuyi gongshangye de shehui zhuyi gaizao (The socialist transformation of Shanghai's capitalist industries and commerce). 1980. Shanghai: Shanghai renmin chubanshe.

Shanghaishi dang'anguan zhinan (Guide to the Shanghai Municipal Archives). 1999. Beijing: Zhongguo dang'an chubanshe.

Shanghaishi jiaoyuju yewu baogao (Business report from the Shanghai Education Bureau). 1930. Shanghai: Shanghaishi jiaoyuju.

Shanghaishi jing'anqu jiaoyu xitong geming douzheng shiliao (Historical materials on revolutionary struggles in the educational system in Jing'an district). 1989. Zhonggong Shanghaishi jing'an quwei dangshi ziliao zhengji weiyuanhui bangongshi.

Shanghaishi renmin zhengfu gejuchu yijiuwulingnian gongzuo baogao (Shanghai municipal government's 1950 report on the work of bureaus and divisions). 1951. Shanghai renmin zhengfu bangongshi.

Shanghaishi zhongdeng jiaoyu gaikuang (Overview of Shanghai secondary education). 1948. Shanghai: Shanghaishi jiaoyuju.

Shen Yiling, and Yao Jinghua. 1996. "Jiefang chuqi Shanghai pujiao xitong de jieguan zhengdun he gaizao" (The takeover and reconstruction of primary and secondary education in Shanghai). In *Zhonggong Shanghaishi jiaoyu weisheng tiyu xitong dangshi wenji*. Shanghai: Tongji daxue chubanshe.

Shirk, Susan. 1982. *Competitive Comrades: Career Incentives and Student Strategies*. Berkeley: University of California Press.

Solomon, Richard. 1971. *Mao's Revolution and the Chinese Political Culture*. Berkeley: University of California Press.

Strauss, Julia. 1998. *Strong Institutions in Weak Polities: State Building in Republican China, 1929–1940*. Oxford: Clarendon Press.

———. 2002. "Paternalist Terror: The Campaign to Suppress Counterrevolutionaries and Regime Consolidation in the People's Republic of China, 1950–1953." *Comparative Studies in Society and History* 44: 80–105.

Szelényi, Iván. 1981. "The Intelligentsia in the Class Structure of State-Socialist Societies." *American Journal of Sociology* 88(supplement): 287–326.

Taylor, Robert. 1973. *Education and University Enrollment Policies in China, 1949–1971*. Canberra: Australian National University Press.

———. 1981. *China's Intellectual Dilemma*. Vancouver: University of British Columbia Press.

Teiwes, Frederick. 1993. *Politics and Purges in China: Rectification and the Decline of Party Norms, 1950–1965*. Armonk, NY: M. E. Sharpe.

Teiwes, Frederick, and Warren Sun. 1999. *China's Road to Disaster*. Armonk, NY: M. E. Sharpe.

Tellenback, Sten. 1978. "The Logic of Development in Socialist Poland." *Social Forces* 57: 436–56.

Thurston, Anne. 1987. *Enemies of the People*. Cambridge, MA: Harvard University Press.

————. 1990. "Urban Violence During the Cultural Revolution: Who Is to Blame?" In *Violence in China,* edited by Jonathan Lipman and Steven Harrell. Albany: State University of New York.

Trotsky, Leon. (1937) 1967. *The Revolution Betrayed.* Garden City, NY: Doubleday.

Tucker, Robert. 1977. "Stalinism as Revolution from Above." In *Stalinism,* edited by Robert Tucker. New York: W. W. Norton.

————. 1990. *Stalin in Power.* New York: W. W. Norton.

Tucker, Robert, ed. 1975. *The Lenin Anthology.* New York: W. W. Norton.

Turk, Austin. 1989. "Political Deviance and Popular Justice in China: Lessons for the West." In *Social Control in the People's Republic of China,* edited by Ronald J. Troyer, John Clark, and Dean G. Rojek. New York: Praeger.

U, Eddy. 2003. "The Making of *Zhishifenzi:* The Critical Impact of the Registration of Unemployed Intellectuals in the Early PRC." *China Quarterly* 173: 100–121.

————. 2004. "The Hiring of Rejects: Teacher Recruitment and the Crises of Socialism in the Early PRC Years." *Modern China* 30(1): 46–80.

Unger, Jonathan. 1982. *Education under Mao.* New York: Columbia University Press.

Verdery, Katherine. 1996. *What Was Socialism and What Comes Next?* Princeton, NJ: Princeton University Press.

Vogel, Ezra. 1966. "From Friendship to Comradeship: The Change in Personal Relations in Communist China." In *China under Mao,* edited by Roderick MacFarquhar. Cambridge, MA: MIT Press.

————. 1969. *Canton under Communism.* Cambridge, MA: Harvard University Press.

Wakeman, Frederic, ed. 1996. *Shanghai Badlands.* Cambridge: Cambridge University Press.

————. 1995. *Policing Shanghai, 1927–1937.* Berkeley: University of California Press.

————. 2000. "*Hanjian* (Traitor)! Collaboration and Retribution in Wartime Shanghai." In *Becoming Chinese,* edited by Wen-hsin Yeh. Berkeley: University of California Press.

Walder, Andrew. 1982. "Some Ironies of the Maoist Legacy in Industry." In *The Transition to Socialism in China,* edited by Mark Selden and Victor Lippit. Armonk, NY: M. E. Sharpe.

————. 1986. *Communist Neo-Traditionalism: Work and Authority in Chinese Industry.* Berkeley: University of California Press.

————. 1989. "Social Change in Post-Revolution China." *Annual Review of Sociology* 15: 405–24.

————. 1996. "The Chinese Cultural Revolution in the Factories: Party-State Structures and Patterns of Conflicts." In *Putting Class in Its Place,* edited by Elizabeth Perry. Berkeley: Institute of East Asian Studies, University of California at Berkeley.

————. 2002. "Beijing Red Guard Factionalism: Social Interpretations Reconsidered." *Journal of Asian Studies* 61(2): 437–72.

————. 2004. "The Party Elite and China's Trajectory of Change." *China: An International Journal* 2(2): 189–209.

Walder, Andrew, Bobai Li, and Donald J. Treiman. 2000. "Politics and Life Chances in a State Socialist Regime: Dual Career Paths into the Urban Chinese Elite 1949–1996." *American Sociological Review* 65(2): 191–209.

Wang Bingzhao. 1997. *Zhongguo gudai sixue yu jindai sili xuexiao yanjiu* (China's private schools from the ancient to the contemporary period). Jinan: Shandong jiaoyu chubanshe.

Wang, Shaoguang. 1995. *Failure of Charisma*. New York: Oxford University Press.

Wasserstrom, Jeffrey. 1991. *Student Protests in Twentieth-Century China*. Stanford, CA: Stanford University Press.

Weber, Max. ([1904–11) 1978a. *Economy and Society: An Outline of Interpretative Sociology*, edited by Guenter Roth and Claus Wittch. Berkeley: University of California Press.

————. 1978b. *Selections in Translation*, translated by W. G. Runciman, edited by E. Matthews. Cambridge: Cambridge University Press.

Weiss, Johannes. 1985. "On the Marxist Reception and Critique of Max Weber in Eastern Europe." In *A Weber-Marx Dialogue*, edited by Robert Antonio and Ronald Glassman. Lawrence: University of Kansas Press.

White, Gordon. 1981. *Party and Professionals: The Political Role of Teachers in Contemporary China*. Armonk, NY: M. E. Sharpe.

White, Lynn. 1978. *Careers in Shanghai*. Berkeley: University of California Press.

————. 1984. "Bourgeois Radicalism in the 'New Class' of Shanghai 1949–1969." In *Class and Social Stratification in Post-Revolution China*, edited by James Watson. Cambridge: Cambridge University Press.

————. 1989. *Policies of Chaos: The Organizational Causes of Violence in China's Cultural Revolution*. Princeton, NJ: Princeton University Press.

Whyte, Martin. 1973. "Bureaucracy and Organization in China: The Maoist Critique. *American Sociological Review* 38(2): 149–63.

————. 1974. *Small Groups and Political Rituals in China*. Berkeley: University of California Press.

————. 1989. "Who Hates Bureaucracy? A Chinese Puzzle." In *Remaking the Economic Institutions of Socialism*, edited by Victor Nee, David Stark, and Mark Selden. Stanford, CA: Stanford University Press.

Whyte, Martin, and William Parish. 1984. *Urban Life in Contemporary China*. Chicago: University of Chicago Press.

Wright, Arthur. 1980. "Soviet Economic Planning and Performance." In *The Soviet Union since Stalin*, edited by Stephen Cohen, Alexander Rabinowitch, and Robert Sharlet. Bloomington: Indiana University Press.

Wright, Erik. 1974. "To Control or to Smash the Bureaucracy: Weber and Lenin on Politics, the State and Bureaucracy." *Berkeley Journal of Sociology* 19: 69–108.

Wu, Harry. 1992. *Laogai: The Chinese Gulag*. Boulder, CO: Westview.

Wu Li. 1994. "Jianguo chuqi dang guanyu jiuye wenti de zhengce" (The CCP policies on employment in the first years of nation building). In *Zhonggong dangshi ziliao 52* (Materials on the history of the CCP). Beijing: Zhonggong dangshi chubanshe.

Xiang Bolong. 1996. "Huiyi jiefang chuqi Shanghaishi zhongdeng xuexiao jiao-zhiyuan de sixiang gaizao yundong" (Remembering thought reform of the faculty and staff in Shanghai secondary schools). In *Zhonggong Shanghaishi jiaoyu weisheng tiyu xitong dangshi wenji*. Shanghai: Tongji daxue chubanshe.

Xing Ping. 1996. *Cong Shanghai faxian lishi* (Discovering history through Shanghai). Shanghai: renmin chubanshe.

Xiong Yuezhi, ed. 1999. *Shanghai tongshi* (A general history of Shanghai). Shanghai: Shanghai renmin chubanshe.

Xiong Yuezhi, ed. 1997. *Lao Shanghai mingren mingshi mingwu daguan* (Overview of notable people, events, places, and things in old Shanghai). Shanghai: Shanghai chubanshe.

Xu Zhong'an. 1991. *Shanghai mingxiao banxue tese* (Notable organizational features of Shanghai's top schools). Shanghai: Guangming ribao chubanshe.

Xu, Xiaoqun. 2001. *Chinese Professionals and the Republican State*. Cambridge: Cambridge University Press.

Yang Fengcheng. 2005. *Zhongguo gongchandang de zhishifenzi lilun yu zhengce yanjiu* (The CCP's Theory of and Policies on Intellectuals). Beijing: Zhonggong dangshi chubansh.

Yang, Mayfair. 1994. *Gifts, Favors, and Banquets: The Art of Social Relationships in China*. Ithaca, NY: Cornell University Press.

Yao Jing. 1992. "Wo ai jiangtai; wo ai xuesheng" (I love teaching; I love my students). In *Zai jiaoyu shiceshang*. Shanghai: Shanghai jiaoyu chubanshe.

Yao Zhuangxing and Yuan Cai. 1992. *Zai jiaoyu shiceshang*. Shanghai: Shanghai jiaoyu chubanshe.

Ye, Weili. 2001. *Seeking Modernity in China's Name*. Stanford, CA: Stanford University Press.

Yeh, Wen-hsin. 1990. *The Alienated Academy*. Berkeley: University of California Press.

———. 1996. *Provincial Passages: Culture, Space, and the Origins of Chinese Communism*. Berkeley: University of California Press.

Yue, Daiyun, and Carolyn Wakeman. 1985. *To the Storm*. Berkeley: University of California Press.

Zhonggong dangshi ziliao 52 (Materials on the history of the CCP). 1994. Beijing: Zhonggong dangshi chubanshe.

Zhonggong Shanghai dangzhi (Gazette of the CCP in Shanghai). 2001. Shanghai: Shanghai shehui kexueyuan chubanshe.

Zhongguo gongchandang zai Shanghai 1921–1991 (The Chinese CCP in Shanghai). 1991. Shanghai: Shanghai renmin chubanshe.

Zhongguo zhengdang cidian (Dictionary of China's political parties). 1988. Jilin: Jilin wenshi chubanshe.

Zhongguo ziben zhuyi gongshangye de shehui zhuyi gaizao: Shanghaijuan, xia (The socialist transformation of China's capitalist industries and commerce—Shanghai, volume 2). 1993. Beijing: Zhonggong dangshi chubanshe.

Zhonghua minguo sanshiwu nian Shanghaishi jiaoyu tongji (Shanghai's education statistics in the thirty-fifth year of the Republic of China). 1947. Shanghai: Shanghaishi jiaoyuju.

Zhonghua renmin gongheguo jingji dang'an ziliao xuanbian–laodong gongzi he zhigong fuli juan 1949–1952 (Economic documents of the People's Republic of China—volume on wages and welfare). 1994. Beijing: Zhongguo shehui kexue yuan.

Zhou, Xueguang. 2001. "Political Dynamics and Bureaucratic Career Patterns in the People's Republic of China 1949–1994." *Comparative Politics Studies* 34(9): 1036–62.

Zhou, Xueguang, Nancy B. Tuma, and Phyllis Moen. 1996. "Stratification Dynamics under State Socialism: The Case of Urban China 1949–1993." *Social Forces* 74(3): 759–96.

Zhu Zheng. 1998. *1957 nian de xiaji* (The summer of 1957). Zhengzhou: Henan renmin chubanshe.

Zhuan Qidong, Yuan Lunqu, and Li Jianli. 1986. *Xinzhongguo gongzi shigao* (Wages and salaries in New China). Beijing: Zhongguo caizheng jingji chubanshe.

Zweig, David. 1989. *Agrarian Radicalism in China, 1968–1981*. Cambridge, MA: Harvard University Press.

Index

In this index an "f" after a number indicates a separate reference on the next page, and an "ff" indicates separate references on the next two pages. A continuous discussion over two or more pages is indicated by a span of page numbers, e.g., "57–59." *Passim* is used for a cluster of references in close but not consecutive sequence.

Activists, 73, 85, 142, 181f, 202ff. *See also* Student activists; Teacher activists

Actually existing socialism, xif, 1–3 *passim*, 10, 14, 178, 192, 207, 211, 218, 227, 229; and modern bureaucracy, 4–9; research on, 5–9, 218–26; and counter-bureaucracy, 20–26. *See also* Soviet-type societies

Administrative sanction, 122–26 *passim*, 132

Anti-rightist Campaign, 47f, 75, 82–83, 86–87, 115, 151, 195, 201, 203, 212, 245n78; and faculty punishment, 133–36, 139, 244n55, 248n42

Arendt, Hannah, 219

Authority, 10–11, 121–24; in counter-bureaucracy, 18–24, 210, 176, 226, 254n4; relations in Shanghai schools, 27–28, 32, 58, 61–84, 90; and remuneration in Shanghai schools, 93–95, 102–3, 110, 117–18, 174; relations in schools because of Cultural Revolution, 159, 161–64, 177. *See also* Patriarchal authority

Bailes, Kendall, 187, 190

Bauman, Zygmunt, 224f

Bi'le Secondary School, 155, 165

Bolshevik revolution, x, 2, 14ff. *See also* October Revolution

Bourdieu, Pierre, 79f, 179

Bourgeois and petty-bourgeois intellectuals, 95, 117, 198; Lenin's view on, 17, 92, 147; Chinese schoolteachers as, 75, 83, 107, 156, 165. *See also* Bourgeois experts; Bourgeois specialists

Bourgeois experts, 17–20 *passim*, 61; and remuneration, 18, 22, 28, 92–95 *passim*, 117. *See also* Bourgeois and petty-bourgeois intellectuals; Bourgeois specialists

Bourgeois specialists, 181–87. *See also* Bourgeois and petty-bourgeois intellectuals; Bourgeois experts

Bourgeoisie, x, 14–18 *passim*, 60, 96, 228f

Brezhnev, Leonid, 212

"Bureaucratic" models of socialism, 3–9, 219–22

Bureaucratic technocrats, 212

Bureaucratism, 4, 89f

Bureaucratization, 5–8, 13–15, 31–36, 219–21, 237n15

C.C. Clique, 35, 240n25

Campaign Against Spiritual Pollution, 214

Campaign to Suppress Hidden Counter-revolutionaries (*Zhenfan*), 125f, 247n18

Campaign to Wipe Out Counterrevolutionaries, *see Sufan*